THE INTERNATIONAL DESIGN YEARBOOK 2000

THE INTERNATIONAL DESIGN YEARBOOK 2000

Published 2000 by Laurence King Publishing
an imprint of Calmann & King Ltd

71 Great Russell Street
London WC1B 3BN
Tel: +44 20 7831 6351
Fax: +44 20 7831 8356
Email: enquiries @ calmann-king.co.uk
www.laurence-king.com

EDITOR: **INGO MAURER**
GENERAL EDITOR: **SUSAN ANDREW**
ASSISTANT EDITOR: **JENNIFER HUDSON**
DESIGN: **STATE**

A catalogue record for this book is available from
the British Library.

ISBN 1 85669 180 2

Based on an original idea by Stuart Durant

Printed in Hong Kong

 LAURENCE KING

CONTENTS

INTRODUCTION

BY SUSAN ANDREW

Fifteen years ago the first edition of *The International Design Yearbook* was published – an annual review of domestic design chosen by a leading figure in the design world. It was 1985, midway through a decade of design excess and decadence, of Memphis and Alessi, a decade when household objects became design icons, a time when the Apple Macintosh and the CD had just been born. Then, it was impossible to find a definition of 'internet' in the dictionary and possible to publish a book on twentieth-century design without mentioning Philippe Starck. Fifteen years on, more than 100 million people use the internet, and Starck is widely recognized as the most famous designer of the late twentieth century.

Since that first edition, thirteen different guest editors have made their selections for the *Yearbook*. Initially, many found the task of reducing the mountain of slides overwhelming and some were frustrated that the selection can only represent a minority of the vast quantity of manufactured products around the world. To celebrate the first edition in the new century, this year's guest editor, Ingo Maurer, invited the previous incumbents to comment on how design has changed over the last decade and a half, welcoming strong, uncensored and individual statements on what they think of design today: their contributions have been inserted throughout the book.

The following 240 pages feature over 400 designed objects which inhabit an increasingly fast-changing domestic landscape. Architect Robert A.M. Stern, the first editor of *The International Design Yearbook* and one of the leading exponents of post-modern architecture, considers design in post-post-modern 1999, 'very serious, with everyday objects no longer conceived as playthings ... the emphasis turned to straightforward solutions which are often best found in generic objects, thereby eliminating the "designer" from the process'. Oscar Tusquets Blanca (editor 1989/90) describes the nineties as '...reasonable, circumspect, strict and moral', but fears that 'these years have in reality been conservative, non-risk-taking and simply obsessed with commercialism'. While Philippe Starck (editor 1987/8 and 1997) writes that 'with the increasing speed with which fashions have changed, quality and creativity have been decreasing in reverse proportions', and Borek Sipek (editor i1993) decides: 'Speed! This one word probably epitomizes the essential change in design over the last fifteen years.'

The ideal home at the end of the nineties is often presented by the media as a place of refuge and comfort, a retreat from a confusing, end-of-century, angst-ridden world of cloning, Millennium Bugs, genetically modified foods and health scares. Spaces which suggest we have control over our environment, where we can create our own fantasies and experiences. Multifunctional loft-style living which adapts to the needs of families comprising parents and children of previous marriages, growing numbers of single-person households, and the blurring boundaries between home and work. Andrée Putman (editor 1992) hopes '...that people will relax, and stop being so tense about what is "in" and what is "out" – let's avoid being design victims (fashion victims seem to have disappeared)!'

With an overwhelming amount of possibilities, choice and information, what is the design of the near-future domestic world? Perhaps there will be fewer products with more functions, products that are complex on the inside and simple on the outside. More than a few researchers predict a future in which domestic appliances will interact with each other using technology such as Wireless Application Protocol (WAP), and devices which enable us to 'communicate' with our domestic appliances (for example, programme the video recorder and turn on the microwave) via a mobile phone are just a few years away. A situation in which mainframe computers operate all the equipment in the home is further off, but companies such as Philips are conducting research to find out what kind of intelligence we want objects to have. They suggest the new appliance might be intelligent but also 'caring', that hi-fi systems will come in the shape of ceramic pots, and television remote controls will be housed within the arms of sofas. Then there are 'wearable' products (examples on page 208) which combine features such as keyboards and electronic navigation aids.

Fewer products? It may be a slow mutation. As Rem Koolhaas, Professor of Architecture at Harvard, and his students discovered in a new research project investigating the current state of shopping, more than one third of all new construction in the world is for shopping: 'there is no activity which is not intertwined with shopping, from hospitals and museums to religious buildings and naval bases. Shopping is working hard to entrench itself in any programme' (*Blueprint*, September 1999). The internet, too, is changing the *way* we shop – along with the way we learn and find information. It is estimated that in the UK website shopping will rise to £6 billion by 2003, as consumers are delivered everything from groceries and clothes to books and holidays.

And what happens when we grow tired of all these domestic appliances and products – the car, the computer or vacuum cleaner we bought just a couple of years ago? According to research by the Eternally Yours Foundation, a Dutch product think-tank, 25 per cent of vacuum cleaners, 60 per cent of stereos and 90 per cent of computers still have life in them when they are thrown away. One option is to return our purchases to the manufacturer for recycling. Europe has decreed that by 2001, car manufacturers will produce cars that are 95 per cent recyclable and they will also be responsible for taking back each one they have produced. It may not be long before this is a requirement for the makers of computers, televisions, hairdryers, cameras, etc., encouraging companies to develop greener products and perhaps to lease products to consumers instead of selling them.

The end of the throw-away society and a linear approach to product lifecycles would require a rejection of short-term thinking when designing and producing objects. As Umberto Eco, novelist and Professor of Semiotics, points out in a recent book *Conversations About the End of Time:* 'The engineers who produced the computers which cannot work beyond the year 2000 indeed thought of their invention as belonging to the short term, like all late-twentieth-century inventions ... It would be so easy to decide to produce [for example] tape recorders that last twenty or more years! ... Petrol-driven cars, for example! It is obvious that they are killing us (not only killing the earth, but also ourselves). Such a realization would require us to move on to electric cars without delay ... But that's still science fiction. No one is ready to negotiate ... Let's get all of us together around a table, engineers, manufacturers and consumers, and engage in intelligent negotiations to find a solution which everyone will be forced to respect.'

Will consumerism and environmentalism go hand in hand in the twenty-first century? Will there be a shift towards more socially responsible design? Can we be encouraged to become more attached to the objects that surround us, so fewer materials are used and less space is required in landfills and incinerators? Richard Sapper (editor 1998) thinks beauty is a key: 'the desire for beauty is something innate in us, something elementary, but also indefinable with rationale, productivity, cost effectiveness, numbers or profits. It comes from somewhere else, a reflection of eternity.' Jean Nouvel (editor 1995) believes 'in the search for the essence: for a demanding design, with no concession to indulgence or the picturesque ... More than ever I believe that poetry is not incompatible with this attitude ...': while the Italian architect Gaetano Pesce in a recent interview stated: 'the beauty of the future is imperfection. It is about giving people the capacity to think that the future will be a fantastic time' (*Blueprint*, September 1999).

Perhaps more personalized products will prevent us falling out of love with objects? The customization of everyday things would provide an alternative to the globalized sameness of many products mass produced in their millions. Consumers would become what US futurologist Alvin Toffler has labelled 'prosumers' (**pro**ducers + con**sumers**). Computer technology has given designers the ability to create almost any form, and now the consumer can join in. Already, buyers in one Levi's store in the United States can have their body measurements machine-scanned and sent off and a pair of bespoke jeans returned: there are cars with adjustable panels that enable the owner to change the colour of the bodywork, and a recent project called Yoo, involving Philippe Starck and the Manhattan Loft Corporation, allows buyers to select from a catalogue all the components of their new house, the number of bedrooms, bathrooms and balconies, as well as the style and decor.

Alessandro Mendini (editor 1996) writes: '...the only objects that can be justifiably admitted to the next millennium are those that have been designed to have soul, that are capable of relating to human beings in a deep and broad manner.' For the Sony Corporation (it is twenty-one years since it launched the first Walkman) the 'soul' is digital. Toshitada Doi, President of Sony's new Digital Creatures Laboratory, explains, 'The 1980s was the age of the PC and the 1990s was the age of the internet. I think the next decade, the 2000s, will be the age of the entertainment robot. Human beings relate better to digital creatures than to PCs.' Following six years of development, Sony has produced AIBO (Artificial Intelligence roBOt), the digital dog. Derived from Playstation technology, the battery-powered computer-controlled companion can experience six emotions with accompanying physical actions: dislike, fear, sadness, joy, surprise and anger. With a body full of sensors and motors, AIBO communicates via a series of musical tones, body language and wagging tail, and with additional kit it is possible to create your own custom moves and sounds on a PC. AIBO may be just the next in a line of virtual pets, following the Tamagotchi of a couple of years ago: it is certainly a more expensive one at $2,500. In Japan 90 per cent of the 'early adopters' who snapped up the first 3,000 AIBOs in 20 minutes were male, and nearly half of them were in their thirties.

Perhaps it's not such a leap to Ray Kurzweil's vision of life in 2019. In his recent book *The Age of Spiritual Machines* Kurzweil, a world expert on artificial intelligence, suggests, 'The vast majority of transactions include a simulated person. Household robots for performing cleaning and other chores are now ubiquitous and reliable ... People are beginning to have relationships with automated personalities ... and use them as companions, teachers, caretakers and lovers ... Computers are now largely invisible and are embedded everywhere – in walls, tables, chairs, desks, clothing, jewellery and bodies ... Keyboards are rare and most interaction with computing is through gestures and natural-language spoken communication ... Paper books or documents are rarely used...' The evidence of the past makes it all too clear that predicting the future is hazardous. It's just over fifty years since the first computer was built and Professor John von Neumann of the Institute for Advanced Study at Princeton said, 'It would appear that we have reached the limits of what is possible to achieve with computer technology...' (*The Guardian*, 16 January 1999).

However, for British product designer Richard Seymour the consequence of designers not imagining the future is that 'it may fall to more malign forces (do you really want another technically led blooper, like the fact that you still can't programme your video recorder after twenty years in the marketplace?).' Emilio Ambasz (editor 1986/7) challenges designers to make the shift from 'further polishing already perfect spheres' and 'concentrate on inventing images of diverse *futures*, so as to guide our actions ethically in the present. It is a daunting task, no doubt, but one that cannot be relinquished.'

It seems no coincidence that Ingo Maurer is guest editor for the first edition of *The International Design Yearbook* in the new century. Ron Arad (editor 1994), commenting on Maurer's Birds Birds Birds light, described him as 'probably the only designer who can get away with attaching bird wings to light bulbs, touch dimmers to tin foil. The mass-manufactured industrial light looks as if it was just assembled *ad hoc* by an artist, and with that it is the light itself that matters not the fitting.' Words such as poetic, conceptual, humorous, exquisite and passionate are frequently used to describe Maurer's distinctive lighting. As the text accompanying a recent exhibition of his work at the Museum of Modern Art, New York stated: 'Be it about joy or rage, playfulness or meditation, future or past, Maurer's lamps have the ability to speak directly to everybody's soul.'

As Ingo Maurer said in a fax following the invitation to be this year's editor:
'Let's work hard, but have fun too!'

Lucellino
1992

Bulb
1966

Wo bist Du, Edisson...?
1997

Subway Station Munich Westfriedhof
1998

INTRODUCTION

BY INGO MAURER

There are some situations that can drive almost anyone to despair – choosing the works to be featured in *The International Design Yearbook* must surely be one of them. Imagine being stuck in a basement opposite the British Museum in London. There is a big table, with a light-box at one end. You sit in front of it on a tubular steel chair with a seat that is far too low. The space is cluttered with lever-arch files and mounds of slides, black and white photos and CD-Roms, all waiting to be inspected.

At this point I felt like the loneliest person in the world. Who am I to decide whether something is good or bad? Why did they choose me as their guest editor? Me, an untrained designer whose main business is making lamps? What on earth have I got myself into? I can see I'm going to end up making myself unpopular. There's nothing wrong with having one or two decent enemies – but hundreds?

Shortly before I started, I met Jasper Morrison. I confessed to feeling nervous. 'Don't worry,' he said, 'Jennifer will be a great help.' And indeed she was. *The International Design Yearbook* without Jennifer Hudson – inconceivable. Her knowledge of design and her memory for detail are astonishing, and her preparation of the entries was meticulously organized – a formidable task, since most of the material arrives in a state of total disarray.

And a book is only as good as the available material. In a visual age, good pictures are essential for a good result. Over 4,000 entries had to be seen and assessed in the space of three days. I sat in the low chair – a Bauhaus icon – with my chin slightly above the surface of the light-box. The first slide was put in front of me. Silence to the left and right, the tension mounting. 'It's a no', I said. Sighs of relief all round the table. And so the day continued, with remarkably little chat (except for information purposes), just endless hours of staring at transparencies, punctuated only by litres of tea and a short break for lunch. I must admit I found myself hankering for the long lunch breaks in Italy.

I included a good deal of trash design and kitsch. Some of the things I chose were downright ugly, but they all conveyed a sense of vitality and freedom that struck a chord with me.

At the Milan Fair (which is still the Mecca of design) in April 1999, I went round the stands with Jennifer and Susan. The general impression was one of great effort, with endless expensive and boastful presentations, and an awful lot of 'good' taste. All those carefully styled and well-chosen fabrics, sofas, chairs, tables and so forth: aesthetically sound, but all so calculated, studiously avoiding any kind of risk. The results were boring, devoid of energy and commitment, lacking the vital spark of real creativity.

As far as I could see, nothing had remained of the radical spirit of the 1960s and early 1970s, when Italy began to dominate the design world. Instead, what I call the '*Borghese* feeling' had taken over. Where, I asked myself, was the boldness and vigour of Gaetano Pesce, Ron Arad or Marc Newson?

But perhaps, I thought, I had failed to see the wood for the trees. It was in Milan that I decided to base my selection for the *Yearbook* on the opposition between creativity and 'good' taste. A further theme I wanted to explore was the need to sharpen our perceptions, to the point where we can see beauty even in ugliness.

I am keenly aware that, to many readers, this publication is a source of inspiration and encouragement – which we all need from time to time. I have abandoned the conventional *Yearbook* approach, featuring beautiful products designed by well-known colleagues, and I hope they will understand the point I am trying to make. It was difficult for me not to include some of their work, but I trust they will understand my preference for the unknown designers/creators, the risk-takers, the mavericks and rebels. We should not be disdainful of newcomers, self-taught designers and others who are not 'real' professionals. The raw power of an idea or a vision is what counts and what drives design forward. Why exclude ugliness or kitsch if it is genuinely powerful?

While wandering through Milan, I suddenly remembered an exhibition I had seen years ago at the Centre Georges Pompidou. It was a show about the 1950s, curated by Jean Nouvel, whose strategy was to heap all manner of products from the period together, mixing rubbish with famous, exemplary designs. I wondered what such an exhibition of today's design would look like in the year 2050. Would one be able to speak of a period, a style, as strong as the 1950s? I doubt it. At present, I can't see any general trend, except the preference for an anaemic form of 'good' taste.

I was asked to separate the good from the bad. But that's something I don't really like doing because I respect the individual's creative impulse. And objectivity is a fiction. Everything is political.

Since this is the first edition of the *Yearbook* in the new millennium, I decided to ask all the former guest editors for a statement summarizing their feelings and thoughts about design at the moment. I am very grateful for their contributions.

What impressed me most was work from The Netherlands – not only that of Droog, but also the individual Dutch designers producing intelligent solutions and results that reflect the way people – at least north of the Alps – think and live today. Bob Copray

Porca Miseria!
1994

Zettel'z
1997

Mozzkito
1996

Ya Ya Ho
1984

Hot Achille
1994

El Ee Dee
1999

and Stefan Scholten are very powerful and convincing: their Units are refreshingly free of 'designer' mannerisms. Back to basics! (page 16). Jurgen Bey, who works for Droog Design, shows his exceptional strengths as a creator (pages 61, 64, 65).

One of the few really interesting things I saw in Milan was a shelving system by the German designer Lorenz Wiegand (page 25). The system, entitled Italic, is an example of minimalism at its best, without a hint of pretension – unlike Claudio Silvestrin's bathtub, which I see as an example of minimalism with pretensions (pages 218–19). Wiegand's result is genuine, instead of being intellectually constructed, and he deserves whole-hearted congratulation. Then there is Maarten Van Severen, from Belgium, whose chairs are brilliant (page 33). I like the thinking behind these and, again, the lack of affectation.

In my own field, lighting, I noticed that people are thinking more about the quality of light than the shape of the lamp. An outstanding example of real imaginative flair is to be found in the work of two Czech designers, Radim Babàk and Jan Tucek (page 103). Lacking access to sophisticated technology, they have nevertheless managed to transform an ordinary, almost vulgar material into a poetic expression.

Design is beginning to flourish in other parts of eastern Europe, too. I have also included a piece by an Estonian designer called Priit Verlin (page 49). In a way it looks hideous, but it embodies a special kind of energy, coupled with a keen urge to become part of the European design scene. Welcome, and keep up the good work! The piece featured here has an emotional quality that I like very much.

There was some wonderful feedback from my own hologram lamp Wo bist Du, Edison...? in the shape of lamps – though without holograms – by Jurgen Bey (page 99), Radi Designers from France and Carlo Tamborini from Italy (page 98). These pieces I found interesting and, obviously, rather flattering.

Uwe Fischer, from Germany, has a technically brilliant solution for a standing lamp (page 97), and Sottsass Associati from Italy has done a wonderful job for Zumtobel (page 113). Georg Baldele, from Austria, the creator of the Caveman standard lamp, is a promising young talent (page 106).

I'm always impressed by textiles, although I don't know much about the subject. Some remarkable designs were submitted. Artistically as well as technically, Japan still leads the field. Here I have to say that one depends heavily on photographs. There is no direct contact with the material, with its specific feel and colour.

I certainly musn't forget to mention the 'Home Alone' project for Post Design, the new Memphis trademark, which commissioned work from a group of students at the Royal College of Art in London. This presentation was perhaps the most stimulating event in Milan. The remote-controlled table Abstract Animal 2 by Karl Pircher (page 21), the mirror by Pascal Anson which puts stars in the viewer's eyes (page 203), and a number of further entries show enthusiasm, intelligence and poetry.

In my private life I don't spend too much time obsessing over tableware, but I do appreciate good and functional solutions or objects that have a certain emotional impact. The most impressive piece in this field is Ron Arad's champagne glass (page 131), proving once again that he has a remarkable talent for reconciling form with function, although this is not always apparent from a superficial glance at his work. I like the work of the young Frenchman Ronan Bouroullec (pages 138, 139), and Konstantin Grcic is already a classic designer who continues to produce excellent things (page 126).

Nina Tolstrup from Denmark has created a Cutlery tool, combining the functions of spoon, fork and knife in a single utensil (page 162). It is a beautiful object, although if I used it at the dinner table I'm afraid I might still be hungry after the meal.

Having seen over 4,000 slides, I notice that most of the entries are classified as 'prototype' or 'limited batch production'. Only a minority of the items are produced in any substantial quantity. This reflects my firm belief that the spontaneous idea is only 5–10 per cent of a design; the rest is a matter of technical imagination. As a manufacturer, I know what I'm talking about. To carry an idea through, from the initial flash of inspiration to the marketing of a finished product, demands a specific combination of willpower, stubbornness and sensitivity. However, I think prototypes and limited editions are very important, particularly in this book, which I see, as I said earlier, as a source of creative inspiration rather than a design bible or a sourcebook of commercial classics.

I am sure that some of my choices will be controversial, but perhaps they may encourage some readers to take a different view of ugliness and kitsch. Without the willingness to take risks, to engage with things that don't quite match our established notions of beauty, our ideas will grow stale and the aesthetic quality of our work will gradually deteriorate. And that we must avoid at all costs. To paraphrase, yet again, a certain well-worn maxim – sometimes, less taste is more taste.

FURNITURE

The *Salone del Mobile* has made furniture as important as fashion in Milan. In April 1999 the fair was in its 38th year: *Salone Satellite*, introduced for the first time in 1998, featured some of the most interesting work from over a hundred young designers, individual designers and nine design schools from around the world. Milan's 13th Eurocucina, the biennial exhibition of kitchen furniture, also took place. In New York, the 1999 International Contemporary Furniture Fair (ICFF) was the biggest and best to date, involving 500 exhibitors from 17 countries and, in the tradition of Milan, a growing number of events outside the main show.

Many of the furniture collections of the Italian manufacturers featured low, boxy shapes, often with metal frameworks and textured upholstery – much of it grey, though space-age white was also a popular choice (white leather upholstery and white hi-gloss lacquer on furniture). Jasper Morrison's day-glow orange, pink and yellow low-level Plan sideboards for Cappellini were notable exceptions. White was also a popular colour for kitchen furniture, and the low sideboard-inspired, free-standing cupboards, with hobs and sinks sunk into tables or worktops, showed kitchens becoming less like work spaces and more like spaces for living.

Mutant furniture – portable, flexible and folding, suitable for single-space loft-inspired living and designed to move on with its owner – included Jan Dranger's Stunsig armchair for IKEA, and Copray & Scholten's five stand-alone units for sleeping, cooking, washing, working and relaxing. The latter stood out as Ingo Maurer's favourite design in Milan – 'for its honest simplicity and sense of proportion and for presenting a way of living which has nothing to do with good taste'. Lorenz Wiegand's Italic shelving system was also singled out by Maurer who described it as 'a beautiful idea, ultra simple, very graphic, very functional'. Maurer's sense of playfulness and humour is reflected in his selection of Falt Design's Mito d'Europa 'love chair' and Priit Verlin's Allegro.

Perhaps prompted by the new millennium, numerous manufacturers have chosen to look back into their past and reissue some design classics. This is not a new phenomenon, however. In the first edition of the *Yearbook* (1985/6) a whole chapter entitled 'Revivals' was devoted to re-productions of designs from the work of Rietveld, Le Corbusier, Jeanneret, Perriand, Mackintosh and Eileen Gray. Two of the re-issues that attracted Ingo Maurer's attention were Vitra's Panton Chair by Verner Panton, a designer known for his daring and experimentation who died in 1998, and Zanotta's Primate stool by Achille Castiglioni. Now aged 81, Castiglioni's curiosity and his rethinking of design functions and forms is still apparent in the 40/80 chair for Moroso, designed in collaboration with Ferruccio Laviani, forty years his junior.

Bob Copray and Stefan Scholten
Range of furniture, Unit
Wood, leather, Corian, concrete moulding plate, plastic
Sleeping unit: h. 55cm (21⅝ in) w. 61cm (24in) l. 225cm (88⅝ in)
Cooking unit: h. 160cm (63in) w. 180cm (70⅞ in) d. 65cm (25½ in)
Washing unit: h. 200cm (78⅝ in) w. 175cm (68⅞ in) d. 80cm (31½ in)
Working unit: h. 76cm (29⅞ in) w. 75cm (29½ in) l. 220cm (86⅝ in)
Relaxing unit (stool/chair/bench): h. 25/57cm (9⅞ /22⅜ in) l. 90/180cm (35⅜ /70⅞ in) d. 90cm (35⅜ in)
Copray & Scholten, The Netherlands

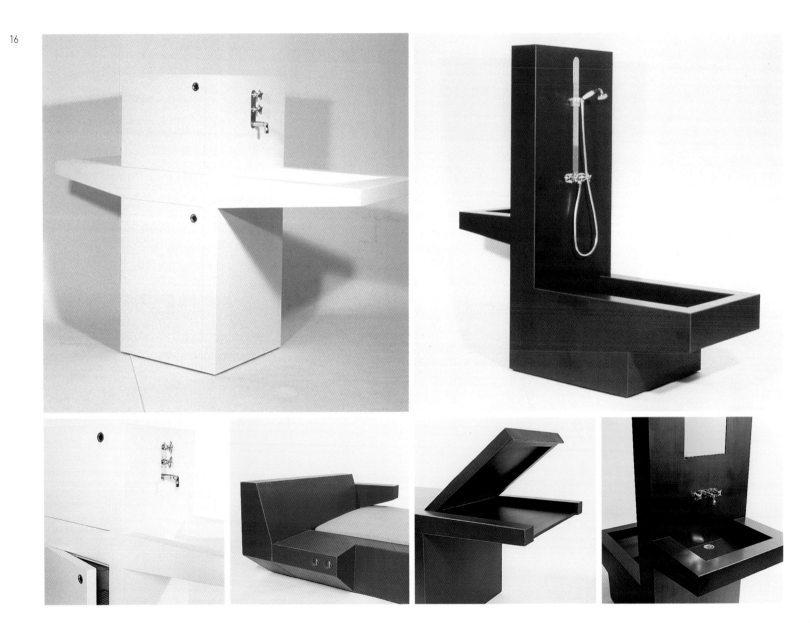

Copray & Scholten

Bob Copray and Stefan Scholten started working together after leaving college in 1996. Two years later they formed Dutch Individuals (DI) with a number of other young Dutch designers who wanted to exhibit in Milan. The group mounted its first show at the 1998 Furniture Fair in Milan, receiving enormous interest and publicity. Keen to be seen as a collection of individuals, rather than a permanent group, DI now comes together purely for international exhibitions. Up to now Copray & Scholten have mostly designed furniture and usually manufacture their own designs. Unit, their mobile domestic environment, started out as an open-ended research project to make a basic compact and movable environment independent of the surrounding architecture.

Maarten Van Severen
Sofa, Blue Bench
Polyurethane
h. 40cm (15¾ in) l. 200cm (78⅝ in)
d. 110cm (43¼ in)
Edra, Italy

Massimo Morozzi
Sofa, Cubista
Polyurethane foam, Dacron
h. 72cm (28⅜ in) w. 108cm (42½ in)
l. 180–216cm (70⅞ –85in)
Edra, Italy

Ludovica and Roberto Palomba
Benches, Rhino
Oak
h. 16cm (6¼ in)
l. 60/90/120cm (23⅝ / 35⅜ / 47⅛ in)
d. 42cm (16½ in)
Lema, Italy

Francesco Mancini
Bench, Crux
Fir, expanded polyurethane, stainless steel, velvet
h. 60cm (23⅝ in) w. 110cm (43¼ in)
l. 210cm (82⅝ in)
Partner & Co., Italy

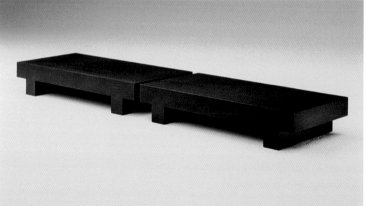

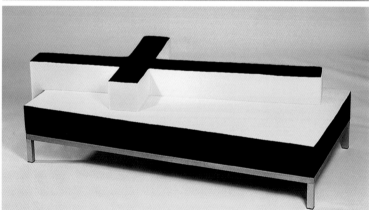

Andrea Anastasio
Chest of drawers, Alba
Metal, wood, methacrylate
h. 121cm (47⅝ in) w. 126cm (49½ in)
d. 50cm (19⅝ in)
Design Gallery Milan, Italy
Limited batch production

Roberto Guzman
Felix the Bench
MDF, lacquer
h. 35.5cm (14in) w. 129.5cm (51in) d. 35.5cm (14in)
Comma, USA
Prototype

Marc de Groot
Coffee table, Tempter 2
MDF, aluminium
h. 33cm (13in) w. 80cm (31½ in) l. 128cm (50⅜ in)
SDB Industries, The Netherlands

Dante Donegani and Giovanni Lauda
Chaise longue, Passepartout
Soft polyurethane, steel
h. 190cm (74¾ in) w. 56cm (22in)
l. 190cm (74¾ in)
Edra, Italy

Tim Power
Couch/bed, Floppy
Steel, polyurethane
h. 33/80cm (13/31½ in) l. 200cm (78⅝ in)
d. 47/160cm (18½ /63in)
BRF, Italy

Karim Rashid
Chair, Arp
Injection urethane foam, wool
h. 90cm (35⅜ in) w. 75cm (29½ in)
d. 80cm (31½ in)
Idee, Japan

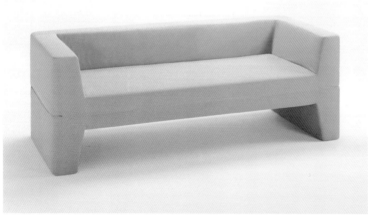

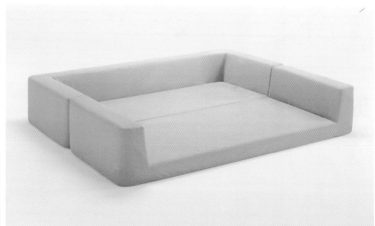

Karl Pircher
Moving table, Abstract Animal 2
Painted wood, steel legs, electronics
h. 50cm (19⅝ in) w. 40cm (15¾ in)
d. 40cm (15¾ in)
Post Design for Memphis, Italy

Daniel Charny
Stool, Red Russian
Wood
h. 52cm (20½ in) w. 46cm (18⅛ in)
d. 14cm (5½ in)
Post Design for Memphis, Italy

Daniel Charny and Eddy Mundy
Television/video stand, TV Foam
Foam
h. 42cm (16½ in) w. 66cm (25⅞ in)
d. 42cm (16½ in)
Post Design for Memphis, Italy

Ulrika Liffner
Table, Marry Me
Wood, painted tiles
h. 40cm (15¾ in) w. 98.5cm (38¾ in)
d. 98.5cm (38¾ in)
Post Design for Memphis, Italy

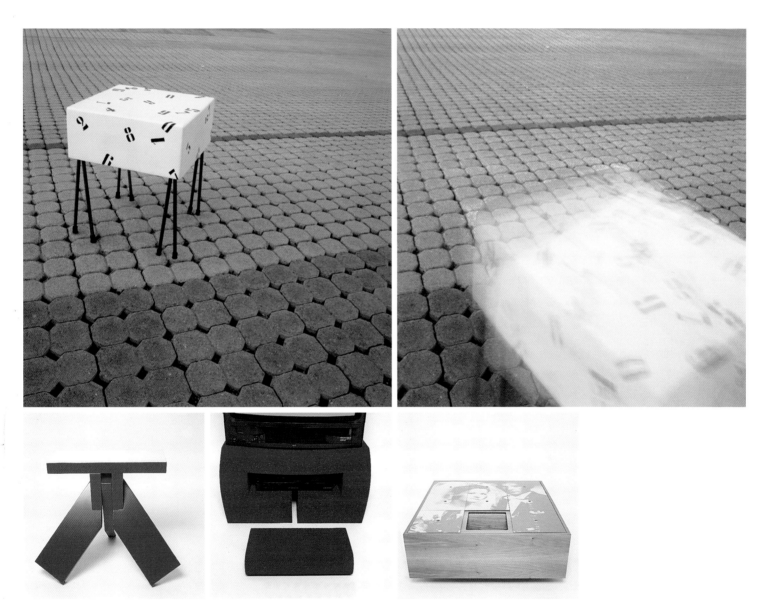

'Home Alone', RCA Furniture Design students and Post Design for Memphis

The idea of the 'Home Alone' project was that Post Design, the new Memphis trademark, would commission designs from students on the Royal College of Art Industrial Design and Furniture course in London run by Ron Arad. The results of the project were then exhibited in Milan and the exhibition catalogue states: '"Home Alone" is about the tensions of contemporary art and contemporary design, about living in London with its complexity, its vastness and density.' The project directed students to look first at themselves and at people's behaviour, as a 'way of revitalizing the connection between life and design'. Daniel Charny and Eddy Mundy's high-density foam TV Foam is a refreshing and simple solution for a television and video stand; Karl Pircher's amusing Abstract Animal 2 table can 'walk' with the aid of a remote control unit.

David Khouri
Screen, Your
High-pressure laminate by Wilsonart
International, plywood
h. 183cm (72in) w. 156cm (61½in) d. 2cm (¾in)
i.d. W/wilsonart, USA

David Khouri
Table, Agenda
High-pressure laminate by Wilsonart International,
plywood
h. 136cm (53½in) w. 232.4cm (91½in)
d. 136cm (53½in)
i.d. W/wilsonart, USA

Jan Eisermann
Container system, Stapelware
Plywood, aluminium
One box: h. 16.2cm (6⅜in) w. 32.5cm (12¾in)
l. 32.5cm (12¾in)
Kraut Royal, Germany
Prototype

22

Jasper Morrison
Cabinets, Plan
Lacquered oak, stainless steel
Various sizes
Cappellini, Italy

Nick Dine
Low book cart, Joan Deere
Powder-coated steel
h. 15.2cm (6in) w. 45.7cm (18in) l. 61cm (24in)
Pure Design, Canada

Richard Clack
Hat and shoe rack, Jakt
Polypropylene, steel
h. 20cm (7 ⅞ in) l. 66cm (25 ⅞ in) d. 30cm (11 ¾ in)
IKEA, Sweden

Knut and Marianne Hagberg
Drawer unit, Nero
Polypropylene
h. 64cm (25 ⅛ in) w. 35cm (13 ¾ in) d. 33cm (13in)
IKEA, Sweden

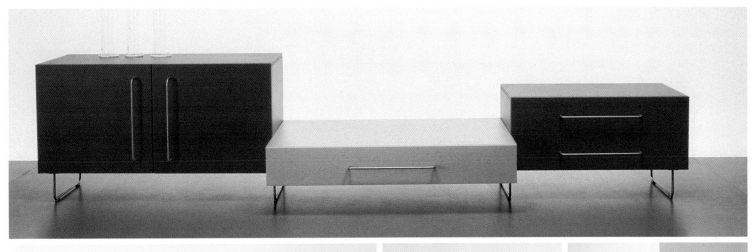

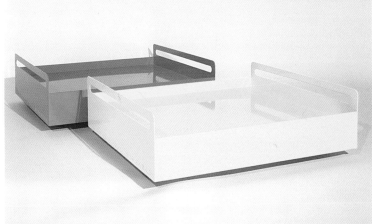

Achim Heine
Furniture system, Syntax
Aluminium
h. 200cm (78 ¾ in) w. 200cm (78 ⅝ in)
d. 35cm (13 ¾ in)
Vieler International, Germany

Lorenz Wiegand
Shelving system, Italic
Bent steel dipped into natural liquid gum, wood
h. 120cm (47⅛ in) w. 40cm (15¾ in)
l. 190cm (74¾ in)
Prototype

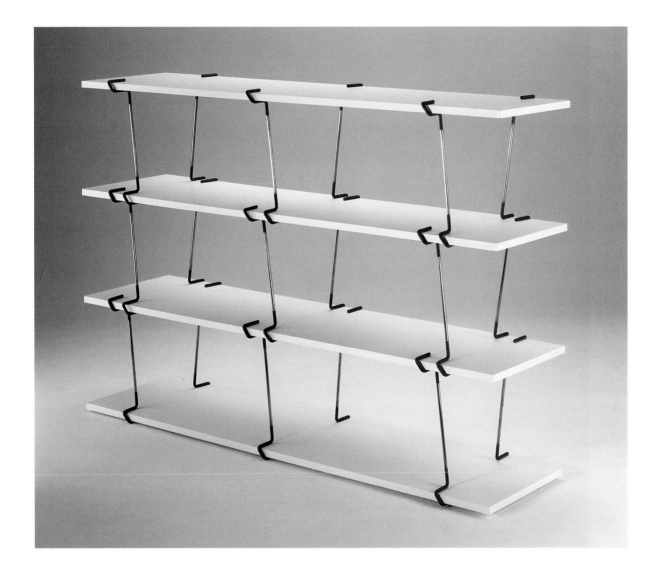

Stephen Burks
Display shelving
Mild steel, stainless steel
h. 91.4cm (36in) w. 35.5cm (14in) l. 213cm (84in)
Readymade, USA
Limited batch production

François Duris
Shelving system, Treillis
Injected plastic, steel
Module: h., w. & d. 20cm (7 ⅞ in)
Configuration shown: h. 120cm (47⅛ in)
w. 220cm (86⅝ in)
Prototype

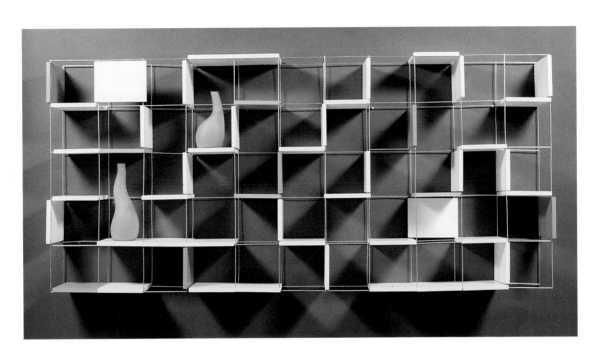

ROBERT A. M. STERN

EDITOR, THE INTERNATIONAL DESIGN YEARBOOK 1985/6

28

In the 1980s, when I was the first guest editor of *The International Design Yearbook*, the post-modernist devolution many different strands of artistic enquiry, from the cartoon-like simplicity of the Memphis movement to the coc also less playful. In fact design seems very serious, with everyday objects no longer conceived as playthings, an generic objects, thereby eliminating the 'designer' from the process. It is only one step from buying Philipp anonymous paring knife on the shelves of a big-box retailer, say Home Depot. Is this victory or defeat?

s at its zenith, with designers at last liberated to explore, without prejudice, terity and high sheen of high-tech. **Today, the situation seems less open, and emphasis turned to straightforward solutions which are often best found in** rck's line of kitchen tools to looking for a time-honoured, well-designed,

Philippe Starck
Armchair, Toy
Polypropylene
h. 78cm (30⅝ in) w. 61.5cm (24¼ in)
Driade, Italy

Mario Bellini
Table/stool, Tavollini
Fibreglass and polypropylene composite
h. 46.5cm (18¼ in) di. 40cm (15¾ in)
Heller, USA

Philippe Starck
Chair, Slick Slick
Polypropylene
h. 80cm (31½ in) w. 44cm (17⅜ in)
d. 52cm (20½ in)
XO, France

Matthew Hilton
Chair, Wait
Polypropylene
h. 77.5cm (30½ in) w. 47.5cm (18¾ in)
d. 51cm (20⅛ in)
Authentics, Germany

Wait chair, Matthew Hilton, Authentics
The German manufacturer Authentics has added a chair to its range of translucent plastic products. Armless and stackable, this low-cost injection-moulded plastic chair is available in a choice of seven solid and translucent colours and is suitable for interior or exterior use.

Jasper Morrison
Chairs and stools, Hi-Pad
Plywood, polyurethane foam, stainless steel, fabric or leather
Chair: h. 75cm (29½ in) w. 45cm (17¾ in) d. 40cm (15¾ in)
Stool: h. 70/80cm (27½ /31½ in) w. 44cm (17⅜ in) d. 35cm (13¾ in)
Cappellini, Italy

Frank Gehry
Chair, Fog
Anodized aluminium, stainless steel
h. 80.7cm (31¾ in) w. 47.5/63cm (18¾/24¾ in)
d. 43.8cm (17¼ in)
Knoll International, UK

Maarten Van Severen
Chair, 03
Polyurethane, aluminium, tubular steel
h. 79cm (31⅛ in) w. 44cm (17⅜ in)
d. 52cm (20½ in)
Vitra, Switzerland

FOG chair, Frank Gehry, Knoll International

FOG – which derives its name from the initials of Frank O. Gehry – is a stackable chair intended for outdoor use. Gehry's brief from Knoll was for a chair with a low production cost, so the design needed to be simple, and to use an uncomplicated manufacturing process and high-volume tooling. In order to arrive at the most comfortable angle for the seat, Gehry made models in silver paper and stainless steel. The creased, moulded aluminium seat is supported by stainless steel tube legs which become the armrests.

03 Chair, Van Severen, Vitra

The 03 chair for Vitra is the first time the Belgian designer Maarten Van Severen, best-known for handbuilt pieces, has collaborated with a manufacturer on the development of a new product. The polyurethane integral foam shell is designed to 'give' when you lean back and return when you sit up, making it an extremely comfortable chair. It is also available with armrests.

Denis Santachiara
Folding chair, Santachair
Polypropylene, aluminium
h. 80cm (31½ in) w. 52.5cm (20¾ in)
d. 49cm (19⅜ in)
Vitra, Switzerland

34

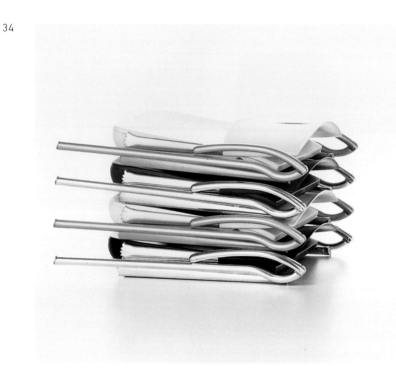

Santachair, Denis Santachiara, Vitra

Although Santachiara and Vitra have collaborated since 1987, the aluminium and polypropylene Santachair is the first project they have worked on together that is scheduled to go into full production. The chair folds completely flat and can be stacked on top of or alongside others, occupying a minimal amount of space.

Charles and Ray Eames
Plastic Chair
Polypropylene
h. 80cm (31½ in) w. 42/56cm (16½ /22in)
d. 40/48cm (15¾ /18⅞ in)
Vitra, Switzerland

Verner Panton
Panton Chair
Polypropylene
h. 84cm (33in) w. 49.5cm (19½ in)
d. 58cm (22⅞ in)
Vitra, Switzerland

Vitra - reissued designs

As a new century begins, Vitra chooses to reproduce the Plastic Chair by Charles and Ray Eames, one of the most influential furniture design partnerships of the twentieth century, and the Panton Chair by Verner Panton, a designer way ahead of his time who combined the futuristic and space-age with a fascination for new technologies and materials. Sometimes called the Fibreglass Chair, the Plastic Chair was first produced in fibreglass-reinforced polyester, a new material which the designers came across while developing their experimental metal shell chair for the 1948 'International Competition for Low-Cost Furniture Design' at the Museum of Modern Art, New York. The stackable Plastic Chair was in production until a few years ago when Vitra discontinued it due to the costly manufacturing process and the ecological problems of the non-recyclable fibreglass-reinforced polyester. The new version is polypropylene with the Eiffel Tower base and comes with or without linking mechanism.

Like its designer, the 1967 Panton Chair was ahead of its time: it was the first chair to be moulded from a single piece of plastic. Vitra feel that 'only now is it possible to manufacture this chair in the way that Panton wished and anticipated'. The designer first showed a model of his chair to Vitra in 1960 and after many attempts it finally went into production seven years later. In 1970 production stopped due to technical problems, however, at Panton's instigation the Plastic Chair was re-launched in the 1980s, this time made from polyurethane. It has been rolling off the production line ever since. For the new chair, which probably looks most like the injection-moulded models of the 1960s, extruded polypropylene is used which makes it more affordable. Panton designed many firsts: the first inflatable stool, prototypes for the first ever spherical television, the Pantower – a furniture environment in which several people could sit or lounge at the same time – and a restaurant with walls, floor and ceiling covered in geometric-patterned fabric which he had also designed. He will be remembered for his passion for colour: as he said, 'Most people spend their lives dwelling in dreary, grey-beige conformity, mortally afraid of using colours... I try to find ways to encourage people to use their fantasy and make their surroundings more exciting.'

Hans Sandgren Jakobsen
Stool, Gallery
Moulded veneer in cherrywood, beech or maple
h. 48cm (18⅞ in) w. 52cm (20½ in)
d. 36cm (14⅛ in)
Fredericia Stolefabrik, Denmark

Pernille Vea
Chair, Felt Chair
Felt, natural plank fibre
h. 88cm (34⅝ in) w. 60cm (23⅝ in)
d. 88cm (34⅝ in)
Prototype

Peter Karpf
Lounge chair, XUS
Laminated beech
h. 104cm (40⅞ in) w. 65cm (25½ in)
d. 90cm (35⅜ in)
Iform, Sweden

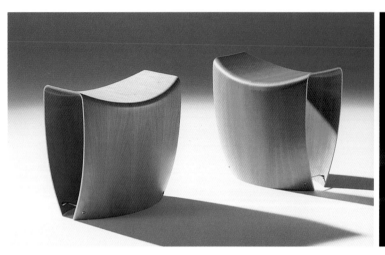

Ron Arad
Chair, Tom Vac
Corrugated polypropylene, tubular steel
h. 76cm (29 ⅞ in) w. 62cm (24 ⅜ in)
d. 63cm (24 ¾ in)
Vitra, Switzerland

Ron Arad/Inflate Design Studio
Inflatable chair, Memo
PVC, styrene
di. 95cm (37 ⅜ in)
Inflate, UK

Ron Arad
Chair, New Orleans
Glass fibre, polyester
h. 96.5cm (38in) w. 132cm (52in) d. 61cm (24in)
The Gallery Mourmans, The Netherlands

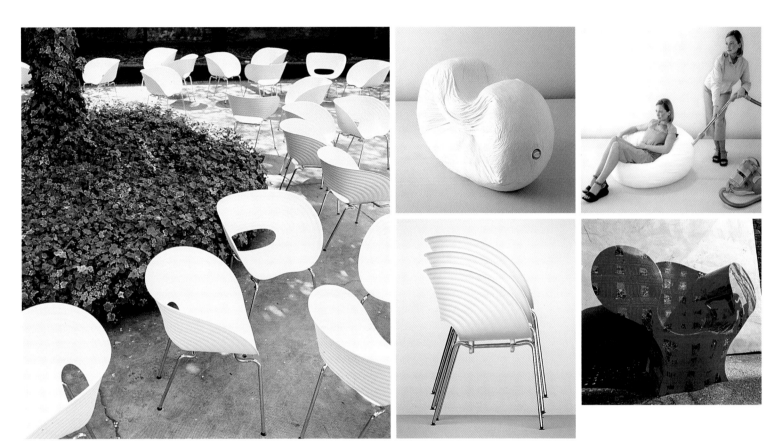

Ron Arad

Arad's work demands attention: as he has commented, 'It is not the kind of work that fades into the background'. Born in Tel Aviv, he has lived in London for over twenty-five years and first made his name in 1981 with the Rover chair, a car seat supported on Kee Klamp scaffolding. Arad's career is going from strength to strength, and his one-off and limited-edition pieces are already highly collectable, selling for art-world prices. In 1994 he started designing more commercial, mass-market products including the Bookworm shelving which is one of Kartell's most popular items with over 1,000 kilometres sold a year. Arad's Tom Vac chair, designed in 1997, has now been launched in a plastic version. His New Orleans chair, a new version of the Big Easy he designed in 1988, is constructed from hand-cast layers of coloured resin. Made in a limited edition of nine, each piece is unique and bears a different inscription, such as 'I must go and see the Pollock show'. Another new seat based on an Arad design of fifteen years ago is Memo, created in collaboration with design group Inflate. Once the chair is inflated and occupied, a vacuum cleaner is used to suck the air out of it, leaving a seat moulded to the shape of the sitter. It is based on Arad's Transformer chair, about which he has said, 'I thought it was going to make us rich, but the world wasn't ready, we weren't ready'.

Maya Lin
Tables / seats, Stones
Spray-moulded fibreglass reinforced cement
Coffee table: h. 28cm (11in) w. 107cm (42⅛ in) d. 75cm (29½ in)
Adult seat: h. 38cm (15in) w. 69cm (27⅛ in) d. 48cm (18⅞ in)
Child seat: h. 25cm (10in) w. 41cm (16⅛ in) d. 30cm (11¾ in)
Knoll International, UK

Antonio Cagianelli
Sofa, Aria
Elastic fabric
h. 70cm (27½ in) w. 50cm (19⅝ in)
l. 120cm (47⅛ in)
Edizioni Galleria Colombari, Italy
Prototype

Jaime Bouzaglo
Ottoman, UFO
Maple, foam, Dacron
h. 43cm (17in) di. 117cm (46in)
Brueton Studio, USA

Hugo Eccles
Chair, Globe
Moulded polyethylene, steel
h. 72.5cm (28½ in) w. 89cm (35in)
d. 62.5cm (24⅝ in)
Mesh Co., UK

Michael Koenig
Chair, Häng Rum
Recycled inner tube, synthetic fur fabric
h. 45cm (17¾ in) di. 140cm (55⅛ in)
Cotelletto, Germany

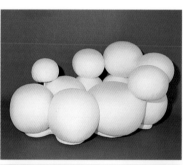

Stones, Maya Lin, Knoll International
The American architect Maya Lin describes these reinforced concrete seats – based upon pre-Columbian millstones and part of a new collection for Knoll – as being 'as much about pure sculptural form as about furniture'. Lin's previous projects include the design of the Vietnam Veterans' Memorial in Washington and a barn conversion for the American Children's Defense Fund Library. 'The Earth is (Not) Flat' collection, of which the Stones are a part, is Knoll's most extensive collaboration with an architect since it produced Frank Gehry's bentwood range in 1992.

Achille Castiglioni
Kneeling stool, Primate
Polyurethane, polystyrene, stainless steel
h. 47cm (18½ in) w. 50cm (19⅝ in)
d. 80cm (31½ in)
Zanotta, Italy

De Pas, D'Urbino, Lomazzi and Scolari
Armchair, Blow
PVC
h. 83cm (32⅝ in) w. 110cm (43¼ in)
d. 102cm (40⅛ in)
Zanotta, Italy

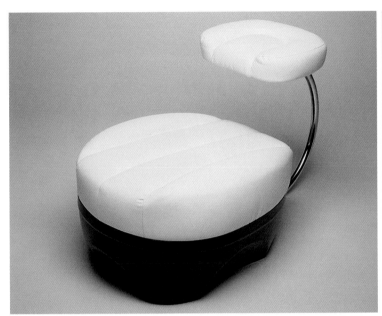

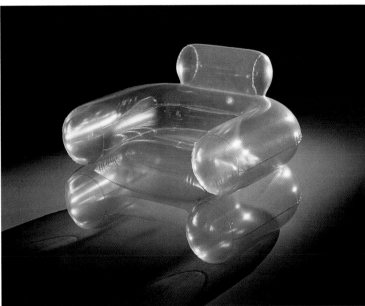

Primate, Achille Castiglioni, Zanotta and Blow, De Pas, D'Urbino, Lomazzi, Scolari, Zanotta

Zanotta is another furniture manufacturer that has chosen to re-issue designs from its past. The Blow chair was pioneering because prior to 1969 an armchair had never been produced with only air as the frame. At its launch the designers recall the Blow receiving a lot of criticism for being too cumbersome and simply too different. However, it was extremely popular with consumers: easy to move – just deflate and take it away – and suitable for indoor or outdoor use, it is a design that has aged well. Castiglioni's Primate was first launched in 1970, when seats like this were rare: in fact the designer believes that Primate is the earliest of its type. He designed it with children in mind, who often cannot reach the table when sitting on normal chairs and kneel on them instead.

Max Shepherd
Armchair, WHY
Welded, bronzed and stove-enamelled steel wire
h. 60cm (23⅝ in) di. 90cm (35⅜ in)
Limited batch production

Shin and Tomoko Azumi
Wire Frame Bench
Steel rod, nickel-plated or coated wire mesh
h. 40cm (15¾ in) w. 170cm (66⅞ in)
d. 40cm (15¾ in)
Azumi, UK
Limited batch production

Shin and Tomoko Azumi
Stacking stool/shelving unit, Wire Frame
Stool=Shelf
Steel rod, wire mesh
h. 38cm (15in) w. 35cm (13¾ in) d. 25cm (9⅞ in)
Azumi, UK
Limited batch production

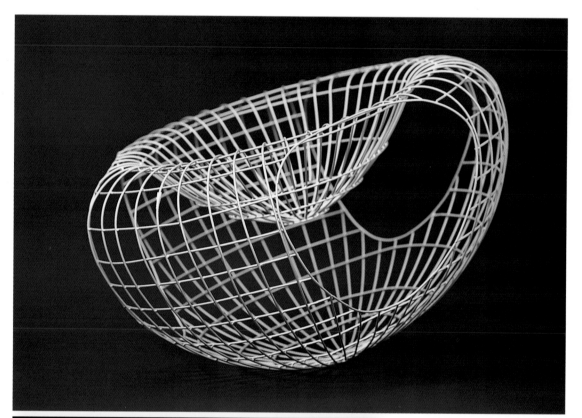

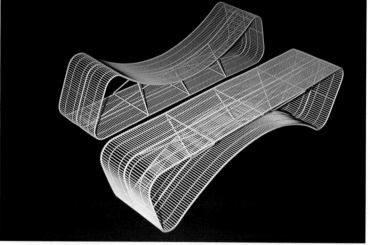

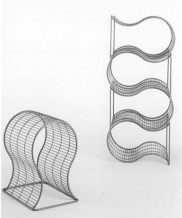

Pierre Bouguennec
Lounge chair, Colombo
Plexiglass, PVC
h. 76.2cm (30in) w. 61cm (24in) l. 122cm (48in)
Boum Design, USA
Limited batch production

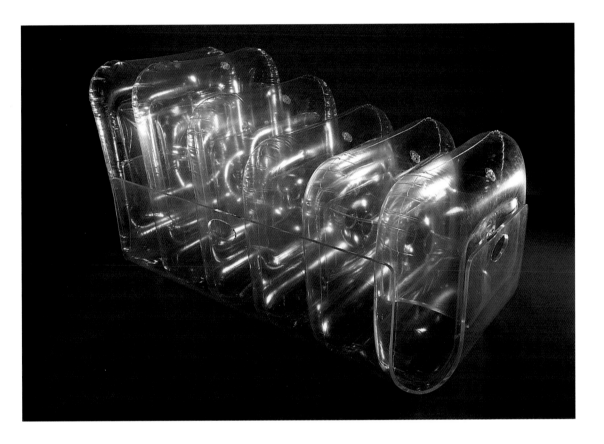

EMILIO AMBASZ

EDITOR, THE INTERNATIONAL DESIGN YEARBOOK 1986/7

In 1972, as the Curator of the Department of Architecture and Design at the Museum of Modern Art in New Yo
and specially commissioned environments illustrated the remarkable vitality of Italian design. The exhibition

The 1972 show clearly marked the high point of Italian design as a free-wheeling creative process. Since the
heroic mission of changing the way we were to live, concentrating instead upon improving the quality of lo
gracefully juxtaposed and skilfully combined; how component elements can be well built and better joined; how
the tale *design* tells whole.

Today, as we examine Italian design as a micromodel of the worldwide design condition, we observe that it
Italian colleagues, these designers have grown fonder of, and increasingly dextrous with, colours, curves, patte

No longer the unbending seekers of eternal truths after their Bauhausian ancestor, the Italian designers
the ephemeral.

**Design, once perceived as yet another method for redemption through sensory deprivation, has in the last dec
a new type of designer, one who takes joy in the exercise of his or her stylistic gifts, has emerged.**

Many products since 1972 have travelled from the museum to the marketplace. Once fancied harbingers
society. But, if they have not fulfilled their Utopian promises of '68, they have nevertheless enriched and impro
given pleasure, performed faithfully; they have tickled our fancy and flattered our pride. We have bought th
they still touch our minds and alert our senses. Many may rightly ask: what greater badge of 'Honourable Serv
unwilling to leave it at that may seek the reasons for the present day's paucity of substantial innovation in a lar

One possible answer may be that today's designer finds justification in relinquishing what his elders conside
public willing to accompany him in exploring new modes of life.

At the same time, today's designer is amply rewarded for his collaboration in spreading the notion that the *pres
irritants, even if stasis may be the price to pay later.

Should design, as a long-established forerunner of cultural consciousness, seek, in St Francis fashion, to bleed

**Perhaps, rather than haemorrhaging rhetoric, or further polishing already perfect spheres, designers of
guide our actions ethically in the *present*.**

It is a daunting task, no doubt, but one that cannot be relinquished.

cted and installed 'Italy: the New Domestic Landscape'. This collection of objects
ave a deep and pervasive imprint upon the perception of design in the USA.

siderable portion of day-to-day Italian design activity has given up its original
iblished ideas, with much given, for example, to how different materials can be
lity of colours, patterns and textures can be subtly enhanced. *Details* have become

wned a number of gifted American, European and Japanese offspring. Like their
textures.

icular, and the world's designers in general, have learned to make peace with

un to open up its tightly closed fist to embrace fashion and caress ornament. Thus

oming social change, these objects have today become integral elements of
quality of our daily existence. The designs of the last two and a half decades have
ducts gleefully and used them with delight. If they fail today to move our hearts,
be bestowed upon an object and the design culture that created it? Those
text.

r ethical duty – to propose Alternative Futures – for he feels bereft of a supporting

he *best of all possible worlds*. There are ample comforts in the absence of vital

nanity's sin of global acquiescence to the doctrine of *consume ergo sum*?

iominations should concentrate on inventing images of diverse *futures*, so as to

Ross Lovegrove
Office chair, Spin
Polypropylene, steel, die-cast aluminium
h. 77–90cm (30 ⅜ – 35 ⅜ in) w. 68cm (26 ¾ in)
d. 45cm (17 ¾ in)
Driade, Italy

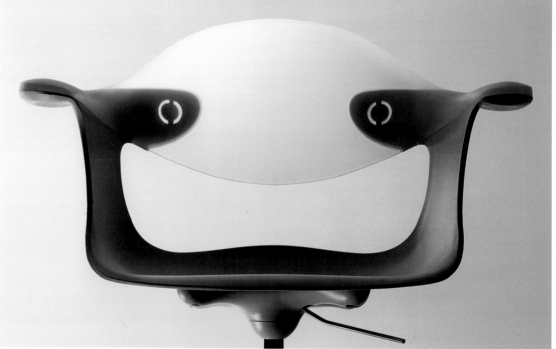

Fernando and Humberto Campana
Chair, Cone
Polycarbonate, steel
h. 77cm (30⅜ in) w. 97cm (38⅛ in)
d. 85cm (33½ in)
Edra, Italy

Achille Castiglioni and Ferruccio Laviani
Armchair, 40/80
Inox tube, plastic, fabric
h. 100cm (39⅜ in) w. 96cm (37¾ in)
d. 76cm (29⅞ in)
Moroso, Italy

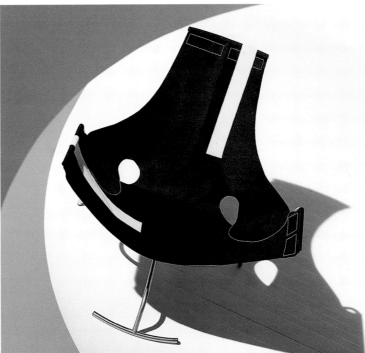

40/80 chair, Castiglioni/Laviani, Moroso
The 40/80 chair's name is a reference to the ages of Achille Castiglioni and the designer
Ferruccio Laviani, his collaborator on the project. Castiglioni says the main inspiration for
40/80 came from the hammock and the deckchair: 'It is just two pieces of fabric hung
between three points. There is no upholstery.'

Ayala Sperling Serfaty
Chair, TUT
Leather, suede, brass
h. 68cm (26 ¾ in) w. 49cm (19 ⅜ in) d. 50cm (19 ⅝ in)
Aqua Creations, Israel
Limited batch production

Werner Aisslinger
Easy chair, Soft Cell™
Polyurethane-derived gel-pads by Levagel,
fibreglass, steel tube
h. 75cm (29 ½ in) w. 47cm (18 ½ in)
l. 60cm (23 ⅝ in)
Soft Cell™, Germany
Limited batch production

Soft-Cell™ Chair, Werner Aisslinger

Gel is a new material which up to now has been used for medical applications, keyboard units, elbow rests and bicycle saddles. For his Soft Cell™ furniture Werner Aisslinger uses transparent yellow, green and blue Levagel® gel-pads which, unlike ordinary water-based or silicone-based gels, retain their elastic and mechanical properties.

Jan Dranger
Armchair from the IKEA a.i.r series, Stunsig
Polyurethane, polyester
h. 72cm (28⅜ in) w. 75cm (29½ in)
d. 80cm (31½ in)
News Design DFE, Sweden

Albert Heer
Low table, Consus
Chromium-plated steel, crystal glass plate or
varnished MDF
h. 46/64cm (18⅛ /25⅛ in) w. 110cm (43¼ in)
d. 46cm (18⅛ in)
ClassiCon, Germany

Fernando and Humberto Campana
Bubble-wrap chair
Chromium-plated iron, bubble wrap
h. 110cm (43¼ in) w. 70cm (27½ in)
d. 60cm (23⅝ in)
Campana Objetos, Brazil
Limited batch production

Rane Vaskivuori and Timo Vierros (Valvomo)
Chair, Dress
Steel, upholstery
h. 82cm (32¼ in) w. 63cm (24¾ in)
d. 75cm (29½ in)
Valvomo Design, Finland

Philippe Starck
Stool, Gnomes
Polypropylene, wood
h. 73/80/97cm (28⅝ /34¼ /38⅛ in)
w. 48cm (18⅞ in) d. 48cm (18⅞ in)
Kartell, Italy

Philippe Starck, Gnomes

'A rebellion against minimalism and bland interior design' is how Starck describes the inspiration for this range of occasional tables and stools for Kartell. The Gnomes were specified for the first Starck-designed hotel in London, St Martin's Lane.

Julia Büttelmann
Double chair, Red Star
Paper, pasteboard, leather
h. 90cm (35⅜ in) w. 90cm (35⅜ in)
d. 34cm (13⅜ in)
Prototype

Emmanuel Fenasse
Stool, Flip-Flop
Polyethylene
h. 30cm (11¾ in) di. 31.5cm (12⅜ in)
3 Designers, France

Priit Verlin
Chair, Allegro
Plywood, wood, metal, precious metal, fabric
h. 180cm (70⅞ in) w. 30cm (11¾ in)
d. 60cm (23⅝ in)
Class X Furniture, Estonia
One-off

Sophie Larger
Armchair, Ioio
Steel, foam, Lycra
h. 90cm (35⅜ in) w. 80cm (31½ in)
d. 80cm (31½ in)
Prototype

Wayne Hudson
Bench, Twisted Love II
Cast iron, steel, leather
h. 45cm (17¾ in) w. 50cm (19⅝ in)
l. 180cm (70⅞ in)
One-off

Borek Sipek
Chair, Filzka
Felt, metal
h. 93cm (36½ in) w. 50cm (19⅝ in) d. 43cm (17in)
Studio Sipek, Czech Republic

Fabiaan Van Severen
Low chair, Crossed Legs
Steel, cow hide, canvas
h. 85cm (33½ in) w. 52cm (20½ in)
d. 72cm (28⅜ in)
Fabiaan Van Severen, Belgium

Philippe Starck
Shelves, OS
Ceramic, wood
h. 180cm (70⅞ in) w. 28cm (11in) l. 180cm (70⅞ in)
XO, France

Mary Little and Peter Wheeler (Bius)
Armchair, Binita
Steel, upholstery, silk
h. 83cm (32⅝ in) w. 84cm (33in)
d. 72cm (28⅜ in)
Bius, UK
One-off

Chiara Cantono
Armchair/chaise longue, Smile
Steel tube, polyurethane
h. 87–114cm (34¼ –44⅞ in) w. 61cm (24in)
l. 100–155cm (39⅜ –61in)
Brunati Italia, Italy

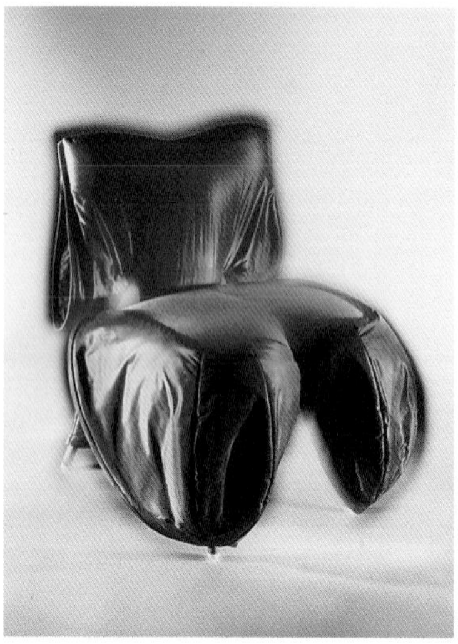

Gitta Gschwendtner
Chair, Ball
Polyurethane foam, fibreglass
h. 80cm (31½ in) di. 60cm (23⅝ in)
One-off

Gitta Gschwendtner
Chair, Ball
Polyurethane foam, fibreglass
h. 80cm (31½ in) di. 60cm (23⅝ in)
One-off

Ashley Hall
Lounge chair, Moby
Glass-reinforced polyester
h. 65cm (25½ in) w. 53cm (20⅞ in)
l. 72cm (28⅜ in)
Ashley Hall Design, UK
Limited batch production

52

Toshiyuki Kita
Armchair, Dodo
Steel, polyurethane, polyester
h. 106cm (41⅝ in) w. 78cm (30⅝ in)
d. 90cm (35⅜ in)
Adele C, Italy

Falt Design
Chaise longue, Mito d'Europa
Lacquered fibreglass, PVC-covered polyurethane
h. 136cm (53½ in) w. 86cm (33⅞ in)
l. 180cm (70⅞ in)
Kundalini, Italy

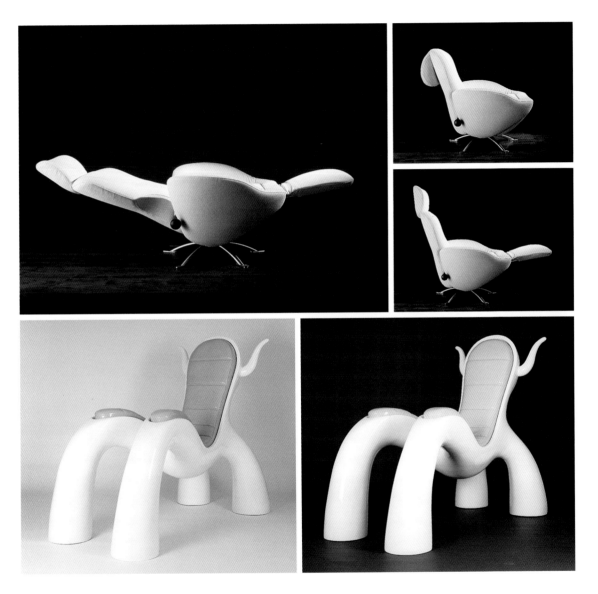

Nigel Coates
Chair, OXO
Beech, foam, wool, laminated plywood
O: h. 75cm (29½ in) l. 73.5cm (29in) d. 73.5cm (29in)
X: h. 75cm (29½ in) l. 79.5cm (31⅜ in) d. 80cm (31½ in)
Hitch Mylius, UK

54   FURNITURE

Nigel Coates

Nigel Coates is a partner in Branson Coates, the London-based architectural practice he set up with Doug Branson in 1984. The team has completed over twenty projects in Japan, three of which are new buildings. However, it was only in 1999 that their first new building project in the UK was completed – the National Centre for Popular Music in Sheffield. Professor of Architectural Design at the Royal College of Art since 1996, one of his current projects is the half man, half woman installation for the Body Zone of the Millennium Dome in London. The new OXO chair also features the human form: the effect is achieved using a process, pioneered by Noss & Lucas, of transferring photographs on to fabric.

Nigel Coates
Daybed
Rattan
h. 47cm (18½ in) l. 185cm (72¾ in)
Lloyd Loom of Spalding, UK
Limited batch production

Nigel Coates
Chair, Oyster
Rattan
h. 75cm (29½ in) w. 49cm (19⅜ in) d. 47cm (18½ in)
Lloyd Loom of Spalding, UK

Ross Menuez
Folding screen, JB Screen
Felt, aluminium, Bakelite
h. 198cm (78in) w. 1.3cm (½ in)
l. (flat) 198cm (78in)
Limited batch production

Piero Lissoni
Sofa, Nest
Chrome-plated or lacquered steel, polyurethane
foam, polyester, fabric or leather
h. 78cm (30⅝ in) l. 220/320cm (86⅝ /126in)
d. 96cm (37¾ in)
Cassina, Italy

Harry Allen
Chair, Chuck Too
Tubular steel, plywood, polyurethane foam, fabric
h. 86.5cm (34in) w. 117–183cm (46–72in)
d. 61–122cm (24–48in)
Prototype

Michael Young
Chair, MY 72 Love Chair
Polyurethane, stretch fabric
h. 78cm (30⅝ in) w. 102cm (40⅛ in)
d. 78cm (30⅝ in)
Sawaya & Moroni, Italy

Andrea Mehlhose, Martin Wellner
Stool, sf-uno
Steel, plastic
h. 46cm (18⅛ in) w. 39cm (15⅜ in)
l. 96cm (37¾ in)
Limited batch production

Matthew Hilton
Armchair, Glide
Beech, nickel-plated steel
h. 80cm (31½ in) w. 80cm (31½ in)
d. 104cm (40⅞ in)
SCP, UK

Glide armchair, Matthew Hilton, SCP
Matthew Hilton chose Tiree, a bouclé fabric manufactured by the Scottish company Bute, to cover this streamlined armchair.

PHILIPPE STARCK

EDITOR, THE INTERNATIONAL DESIGN YEARBOOK 1987/8/99

My friend Ingo Maurer, whom I love and respect, has asked me to write about design. My problem is that
somewhere in Germany where I was, as usual, violently depressed, I talked to him and he really listened to me

So let us take our courage into both hands.

Once upon a time, there was crystal made out of clay; that doesn't sound like much but it teaches us that at both
Then there was a great storm and a bit of electricity in our clay transformed us into a kind of bacteria; then
becoming monkeys and then the super monkeys we are, voyagers in an endlessly poetic mutant odyssey.

In the last few years, our two frightened primates, one out of love, the other out of a desire for the elsewhere
man. To build that progress which promised a better life, they started by breaking flint and inventing tools. Th

But before talking about today, we have to recall two interesting groups which have lasted for ages: work design
dominators, (advertising design such as the throne and the chalice). Graphics would make a notable comeback
coherent artistic direction with Albert Speer and his companion Adolf, the best A.D. of his generation but, alas

It's worth noting that design is essentially fascist, since it seeks the best of all possible worlds which we know to

So, on to the American colonial occupation troops, to American style, which must have been of Italian origin, wh
International Style, whose sole interest is that it's really industrial and really popular (mass-market in English).
Germanic industrial design was their good intentions.

Then, the worst and best happened. The best with the inspirational Italian design whose popularity was guarant
succeeded one another. An ecological design movement that is sufficiently backward-looking to, under cove
that followed, the 'I take', which thanks to poor translation turned into 'high tech', and the switch over from

As fashions have changed with increasing speed, quality and creativity have decreased in reverse proportion. W
talented elderly gentlemen and followed by a cohort of simpletons. But I will quote an umpteenth baroque cycle
able to be created and produced by just about any good do-it-yourselfer, not requiring culture, discipline
destruct, leaving room for more interesting things based on ecomony and politics.

A new generation is appearing at last. Some will scour the subject to get something subversive out of it, others
twenty years of narcissistic formalism. In Holland, France and Spain, they are our future.

These new trends are in fact boosting a production that is more moral, more iconoclastic, more legitimate
an awareness of our status as mutants, the hastening of our mutation and an acceptance of the fact that
biogenetics. That is where design should fit in today.

I know this has come to an abrupt end but writing isn't my profession; my profession is mainly to please, especi

[Translated from French by Carmona UK Ltd]

ind schedule but I'd really like to please Ingo, especially as recently,

are historically as close to a goblet of champagne as to my neighbour's pig.
ed into fish and then batrachians. I'll pass over several weird stages to our

otherwise, invented the amusing idea of progress – the first joke invented by
en things started to go wrong and design came into the picture.

dominated (for example, the cowherd's stool and the milk pail) and for the
cross, and then with the swastika, brilliantly supported by the debut of
somewhat misguided in his paranoid politics.

e remote from our paltry human needs.

spect of having been of Scandinavian origin. So here we are, the so-called
st remember that the only popular thing about the movements of pre-war

nks to its communist origins. After that, only passing and cyclical fashions
d intentions, kill more trees, cows and sheep. Then, in the amusing mistakes
ng office furniture to the unlikely high technology we are still seeking.

s over certain Italian formalist movements developed by cultured and
created to relax the atmosphere. The baroque has the advantage of being
estment, just a few good books. The destiny of baroque cycles is to self-

the humour for political gain. Those are on the right track and relieve us of

re human, capable of shaping the next developments of our species. That is,
tation can no longer be natural and entails fusion with 'bionics' and mastered

o.

Ralph Ball
Table, Archaeology of Style
Glass, reproduction legs in assorted styles
h. 45cm (17¾ in) w. 90cm (35⅜ in)
l. 90cm (35⅜ in)
One-off

Jurgen Bey
Furniture, Kokon
PVC coating, existing furniture
Various sizes
Droog Design, The Netherlands
Limited batch production

William Sawaya
Seat, Darwish
Cast aluminium
h. 75cm (29½ in) di. 140cm (55⅛ in)
Sawaya & Moroni, Italy

Mathias Bengtsson
Stacking chair
Aluminium
h. 75cm (29½ in) w. 80cm (31½ in)
d. 60cm (23⅝ in)
Prototype

Henk Vos
Armchair, 6400F Blow
Upholstery, steel, birchwood
h. 73cm (28⅝ in) w. 106cm (41⅝ in)
d. 59cm (23¼ in)
GelderLand, The Netherlands
Limited batch production

Tom Dixon
Crocodile series, Metal, crocodile skin
Chair: h. 100cm (39⅜ in) w. 52cm (20½ in)
d. 42cm (16½ in)
Chaise longue: h. 30/47/72cm (11¾ /18½ /28⅜ in)
w. 70cm (27½ in) l. 135cm (53⅛ in)
Box: h. 43cm (17in) w. 43cm (17in) d. 14.5cm (5¾ in)
Cappellini, Italy

Noa Hanyu
Table, Shutaku 53
Wood
h. 27cm (10⅝ in) w. 52cm (20½ in)
l. 140cm (55⅛ in)
One-off

Pawel Grunert
Chair, Eye-lash
Beech, wicker
h. 220cm (86⅝ in) w. 50cm (19¾ in)
d. 50cm (19¾ in)
Limited batch production

Pawel Grunert
Sofa/chair, The Draught
Wicker, steel
h. 70cm (27½ in) w. 70cm (27½ in) l. 300cm (118in)
Edizioni Galleria Colombari, Italy
Limited batch production

Natanel Gluska
Armchair
Oak
h. 77cm (30⅜ in) w. 59cm (23¼ in)
d. 57cm (22⅜ in)
One-off

Pawel Grunert
Chair, Stick
Beech, steel, wicker
h. 125cm (49¼ in) w. 50cm (19⅝ in)
l. 70cm (27½ in)
Edizioni Galleria Colombari, Italy
Limited batch production

Jurgen Bey
Tree trunk bench
Tree trunk, bronze seat backs
h. 75cm (29½ in) l. 400cm (157⅜ in)
d. 75cm (29½ in)
Droog Design, The Netherlands for Oranienbaum
Prototype

Jurgen Bey
Gardening bench
Hay, leaves, crushed wood
h. 75cm (29½ in) l. 200cm (78⅝ in)
d. 75cm (29½ in)
Droog Design, The Netherlands for Oranienbaum
Prototype

Jurgen Bey, benches, Droog Design

These pieces are part of the Droog Design project 'Couleur Locale' for the German town of Oranienbaum, located in the depressed former East German region of Dessau-Wörlitz. Once a coal-producing area, its mines closed down in 1990. The design collective became involved in the project when the Dutch government allocated money to restore Oranienbaum's seventeenth-century castle, originally commissioned by a Dutch princess. The town decided to devote some of the money to commission Droog to create a series of objects inspired by the region in an attempt to regenerate the local culture and encourage tourism. With a motto of 'Act global, think local', Droog's aim was to design products, 'inspired by the region but not provincial' so that they could be sold internationally. Reflecting elements of the castle's park, Jurgen Bey has designed two non-durable benches made from recycled and extruded hay, bark and hedges. 'It's up to nature to decide when it's reclamation time,' the designer says. The untreated tree trunk with gilded chair backs is a reference to the grandeur of Oranienbaum's past and its local abundance of wood.

John Gabbertas
Dining table and benches, F90
Douglas fir, beech
h. 74cm (29⅛ in) w. 75cm (29½ in)
l. 300cm (118in)
Prototype

Maarten Van Severen
Table, Schraag ('Trestle')
Oiled bamboo, aluminium
h. 73cm (28⅝ in) w. 300cm (118in)
d. 90cm (35⅜ in)
Bulo, Belgium

Evelyne Merkx
Desk, Spine
Multiplex massive tulip wood
h. 75cm (29½ in) w. 90cm (35⅜ in)
l. 309cm (121⅝ in)
Bulo, Belgium
Limited batch production

Fabiaan Van Severen
Cabinet, Annex, Fold & Profile
Stainless steel, maple
h. 66cm (25⅞ in) l. 40cm (15¾ in)
d. 80cm (31½ /in)
Fabiaan Van Severen, Belgium

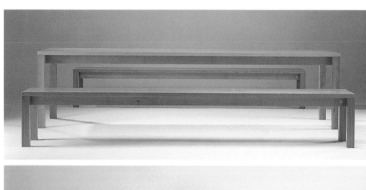

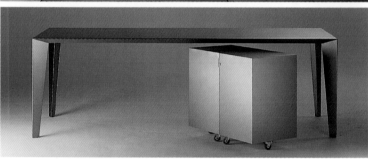

El Ultimo Grito
Coffee table and magazine rack, Mind the Gap
Rubber, steel
h. 31cm (12⅛ in) w. 50cm (19⅝ in) l. 70cm (27½ in)
El Ultimo Grito, UK
Batch production

Mind the Gap coffee table and magazine rack, El Ultimo Grito
This rubber-topped coffee table with built-in magazine rack was created by the award-winning London-based Spanish design trio
El Ultimo Grito – which translates into English as 'the last word' or into French as 'le dernier cri'.

N2
Bench/daybed, Wegtauchen
Polypropylene, birch plywood, aluminium
h. 35cm (13¾ in) l. 190cm (74¾ in)
d. 75cm (29½ in)
Prototype

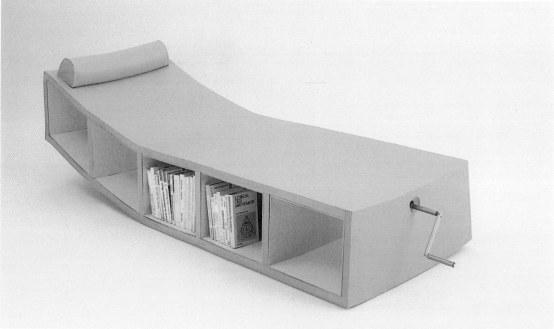

Cecilie Manz
Bench, Surface
Birch, steel, wool felt
h. 44cm (17⅜ in) w. 66cm (25⅞ in)
l. 190cm (74¾ in)
Prototype

Matthias Rexforth
Wardrobe, XE
Plywood, steel, plastic, cotton
h. 210cm (82⅝ in) l. 200–300cm (78⅝ –118in)
d. 50cm (19⅝ in)
One-off

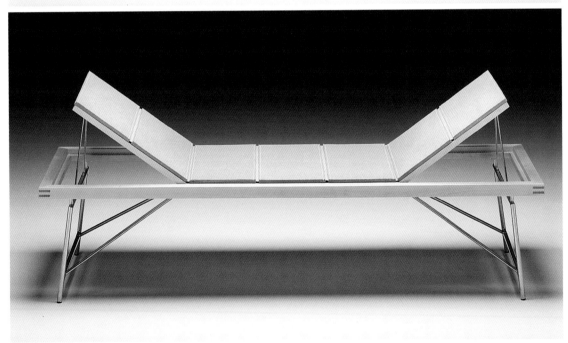

RE (Nicole Hüttner, Nina Nicolaisen and
Silke Warchold)
Modular shelving system
Reclaimed furniture / wood
Various sizes
Limited batch production

Cecilie Manz
Stackable storage units and base, Blackbox
Anodized aluminium, lacquered maple
h. 70cm (27½ in) w. 44cm (17⅜ in)
l. 120cm (47⅛ in)
Prototype

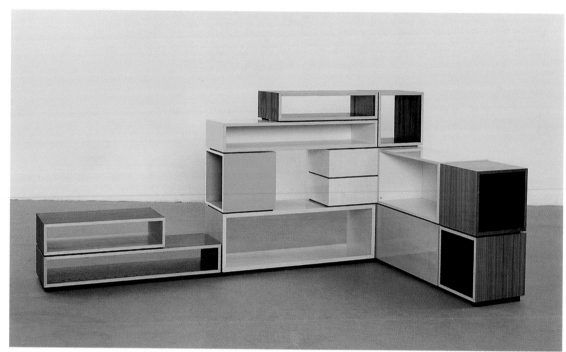

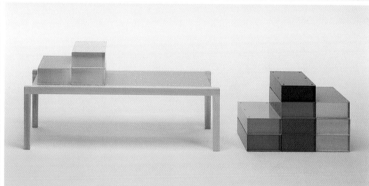

Dieter Rams
Container system, 980
Cherrywood, aluminium
h. 75cm (29½ in) w. 42.5cm (16¾ in)
d. 43.5cm (17⅛ in)
Sdr+, Germany

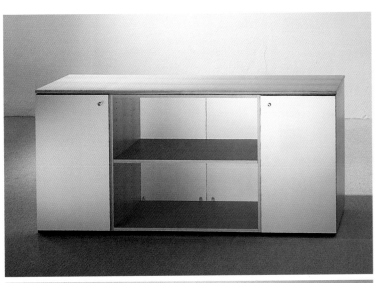

Jonas Lindvall
Wall-mounted cupboard, Speyside
Fibreboard with oak veneer
h. 37cm (14⅝ in) w. 37cm (14⅝ in) l. 163.5–270cm
or 120–224cm (64⅜–106¼ in or 47⅛–88⅛ in)
Kockums/David Design, Sweden

Anja and Stefan Böwer
Wall-container, Lulu
MDF, steel, aluminium, glass
Various sizes
Böwer, Germany
Limited batch production

72

Christian Heimberger
Sliding bookcase, Quantim
Cherrywood, maple or oak
h. 300cm (118in) w. various
d. (back shelf) 20/30cm (7⅞/11¾in)
d. (sliding shelf) 17cm (6⅝in)
Paschen & Companie, Germany

ARATA ISOZAKI

EDITOR, THE INTERNATIONAL DESIGN YEARBOOK 1988/9

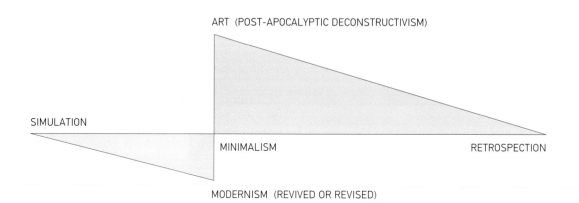

I proposed the diagram above to epitomize the design of the years 1988/9 when I was guest editor of
year, the pattern will probably look very different – a destiny surely to be shared by this *Yearbook*.' More than

At that time I expected that the diagram would be destroyed and renewed by the next year, at least. I was wrd
in the 1990s is that the information network has overlaid all visual production. This is characterized less by
existed. The look has become multifarious and heterogeneous, with no change in the basic structure.
would be represented by shortening the axis of retrospection while elongating that of simulation to the extreme

The main concepts of early twentieth-century design had all appeared by the 1920s, and mass production follow
had all appeared by the 1980s, and what has followed since, with tremendous speed, has been a manipulatio

Thus what can be read in the fifteenth volume of the *Yearbook* is this contrast: the concepts of the 1920s versus
media manipulation that is ongoing today.

[Translated from Japanese by Sabu Kohso]

rnational Design Yearbook. And in conclusion I wrote that 'this time, next

rs have now passed.

the structure of axes remains the same even now. **What has happened**

ation of anything new than by the detailed manipulation of what has already

racteristic of what is called 'simulation'. In the above diagram, this shift

ed upon these concepts. The main ideas of late twentieth-century design

se ideas by computer technology.

as of the 1980s, the mass production that followed the former versus the

Christof Burtscher and Patrizia Bertolini
Clothes stand, Twist
Beech
h. 165cm (65in) di. 65cm (25½in)
Horm, Italy

Ubald Klug
Coat stand, Spiga
Birch aviation plywood
h. 175cm (68⅞in) di. 52cm (20½in)
Röthlisberger Kollektion, Switzerland

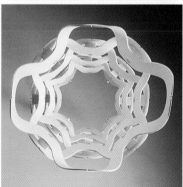

Kurt Thut
Clothes stand
Natural beech
h. 131cm (51⅝ in) w. 68cm (26¾ in)
d. 35cm (13¾ in)
Walter Thut, Switzerland

Konstantin Grcic
Shelves, ES
Beech, beech plywood
h. 145cm (57in) w. 40cm (15¾ in) l. 60cm (23⅝ in)
Moormann Möbel, Germany

ES shelves, Konstantin Grcic, Moormann Möbel
These shelves challenge the rules – they are designed to wobble gently when touched.
ES is manufactured by the experimental German company Moormann Möbel,
with whom the Munich-based Grcic has collaborated since 1995. Grcic is interested
in the aesthetic of everyday materials and products, and describes the shelves as an
alternative to 'very engineered, very rational' design; 'furniture needs to have some
element of humanity, even humour'.

Michele de Lucchi and Gerhardt Reichert
Table and container, Eccofatto
Steel, wood
h. 72cm (28⅜ in) w. 80cm (31½ in)
l. 120cm (47⅛ in)
Mauser Office, Germany

Antonio Citterio
Chair, Minni
Aluminium, various wood finishes, polypropylene
h. 67.5/80cm (26⅝/31½ in)
w. 47/52.5cm (18½/20¾ in) d. 50.5cm (19¾ in)
Halifax by Tisettanta, Italy

Michele de Lucchi and Gerhardt Reichert
Office chair, Attivo
Aluminium, polypropylene, fabric
h. 100–120cm (39⅜–47⅛ in) w. 60cm (23⅝ in)
l. 58cm (22⅞ in)
Mauser Office, Germany

Maurizio Peregalli
Computer table, Felix Work Station
Expanded metal, steel, linoleum, painted epoxy
h. 80cm (31½ in) w. 51cm (20⅛ in)
l. 140cm (55⅛ in)
Zeus, Italy

Hella Jongerius
Chair, Kasese (Sheep and Foam)
Glass fibre, carbon, organza silk and wool felt by
Claudy Jongsma or foam
h. 55cm (21⅝ in) w. 38cm (15in)
Cappellini, Italy

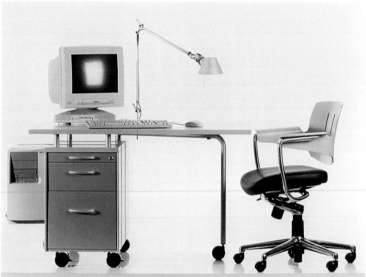

Pierpaolo Lenoci
PC table, Mouse
Lacquered MDF, aluminium
h. 74cm (29⅛ in) w. 78cm (30⅝ in)
l. 88cm (34⅝ in)
Costantino by Ardes, Italy

Dirk Wynants
Garden table, Gargantua
Timber, galvanized metal, stainless steel
Position 1: h. 75cm (29½ in) di. 200cm (78⅝ in)
Position 2: h. 45/60cm (17¾/23⅝ in)
di. 146/230cm (57½/90½ in)
Extremis, Belgium

Vico Magistretti
Chair, Cirene
Wood, steel
h. 75cm (29½ in) w. 57cm (22⅜ in)
d. 52cm (20½ in)
De Padova, Italy

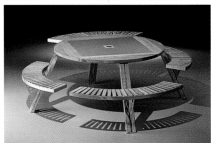

Gunilla Allard
Trolley, Cargo
Steel tube, leather, glass, laminate
h. 71.5cm (28⅛ in) w. 36cm (14⅛ in)
l. 81cm (31⅞ in)
Lammhults Möbel, Sweden

Donato D'Urbino and Paolo Lomazzi
Cabinet, Shine
Glass, silver-plated brass
h. 162cm (63¾ in) w. 40/80cm (15¾ / 31½ in)
d. 31cm (12⅛ in)
Tonelli, Italy

Konstantin Grcic
Trolley, Go
Polypropylene, chrome
h. 69cm (27⅛ in) w. 45cm (17¾ in)
l. 53cm (20¾ in)
Authentics, Germany

80

Christoph Böninger
Adjustable table, Sax
Chromium-plated steel, glass
h. 60–74cm (23⅝–29⅛ in) w. 60cm (23⅝ in)
d. 60cm (23⅝ in)
ClassiCon, Germany

Ehlén Johansson
Computer desk, IKEA/PS
Lacquered steel, laminated birch plywood
h. 102cm (40⅛ in) w. 67cm (26⅜ in)
d. 56cm (22in)
IKEA, Sweden

Teppo Asikainen and Ilkka Terho (Valvomo)
Desk-top computer table
Glass, steel, polystyrene, PC components
h. 72cm (28⅜ in) w. 180cm (70⅞ in)
d. 80cm (31½ in)
Snowcrash, Sweden

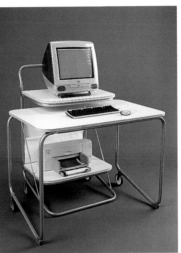

Desk Top computer table, Asikainen/Terho, Snowcrash
Snowcrash has produced a computer table which is particularly suitable for the home office as the working surface is kept free, allowing it to function as a dining table as well as a desk. The laminated glass top is a soft blue colour, except above the screen where it is transparent. The flat computer screen can be adjusted to different viewing angles.

Alan Chadwick
Folding table
Die-cast and pressed aluminium
h. 70cm (27½ in) w. 80cm (31½ in) l. 170cm (67in)
Baleri Italia, Italy

Alan Chadwick
Folding chair, Et-Voilà
Die-cast and pressed aluminium
h. 80–92cm (31½ – 36⅛ in) l. 49.5cm (19½ in)
d. 49.5cm (19½ in)
Baleri Italia, Italy

82

Michele de Lucchi and Silvia Suardi
Table system, Artu
Wood, leather
h. 72cm (28⅜ in) w. 110cm (43¼ in)
l. 230cm (90½ in)
Poltrona Frau, Italy

Vico Magistretti
Armchair, Samarcanda
Polyester, steel
h. 84cm (33in) w. 105cm (41⅜ in)
d. 88cm (34⅝ in)
Campeggi, Italy

LIGHTING

For this year's guest editor a single lightbulb is 'the perfect meeting between poetry, industry and design'. Regularly featured in successive editions of *The International Design Yearbook*, Ingo Maurer has been involved with lighting for over three decades, as a designer, manufacturer and distributor. In his selection Maurer focused on the light each piece creates, rather than the shape of the light itself, and is passionate in claiming that lighting, rather than dictating to the user, must leave space for their imagination.

Humour and wit run through this selection, illustrated by the inclusion of the Water Can Chandelier by F. Th. Gärtner Industrial Design, Ralph Ball's Red Sky at Night, Hand (to Hold) by Anette Hermann, and Rainer Spehl's Television Light, the hidden television screen creating a flickering, multicoloured glow.

The choice of Jan Broekstra's glass and porcelain disposable suspension light, Ralph Ball's Power Tower of lighting flex, sockets and bulbs, and Aleksej Iskos' chandelier made with water-filled plastic bags are a reminder that found objects have long been a source of inspiration and experimentation for Maurer. He loved the spontaneity of Gregory Prade's Little Moon reading light with its ingenious light switch, and the play of light created by DesignHospital's Blackout 2000 (incorporating a candle set behind a disconnected lightbulb). He enjoyed Richard Hutten's Table-lamp for its simplicity – feeling this combination could be taken even further – and applauded Tunnel designers Babàk and Tucek for showing 'enormous ability and vision in the transformation of a banal material (plastic foam) into a poetic expression' with their D1 light. Jurgen Bey's Lightshade-shade he described as 'very smart', perhaps remembering the process he went through to create his own Wo bist Du, Edison...? (Where Are You Edison?) with its hologram of a lightbulb.

As a manufacturer, Maurer's attention was drawn to the Galhāo floor lamp by Reno Bonzon, Ligia Miguez and Lincoln Lucchi, for its thoughtful alternative to the lamp base, the folding legs allowing for easy packing and shipping. Finally, to show 'how light can be a celebration, a feast, a chaotic thing with enormous expression', he included Sigi Bussinger's cast resin light fountain Li Wasku for 'its combination of the technical and spiritual'.

Ricardo Bello Dias
Self-illuminating lamp, Tramonto
Polypropylene, acrylic (Perspex)
h. 70cm (27½ in) di. 20cm (7⅞ in)
Codice 31, Italy

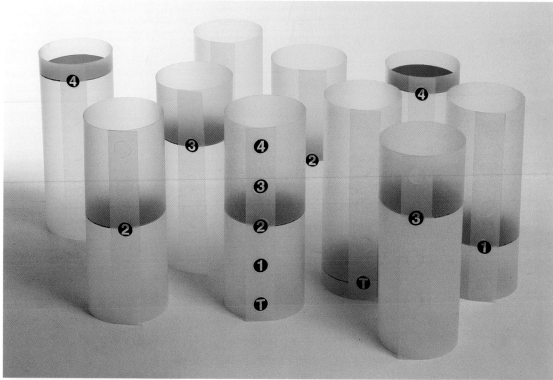

Maxine Naylor
Suspension light, Theo
PVC, aluminium
60w bulb
h. 50cm (19 ⅝ in) w. 50cm (19 ⅝ in) d. 20cm (7 ⅞ in)
Prototype

Stefanie Klein
Table lamp, Alva: Lan
Polypropylene
Max. 60w bulb
h. 46cm (18 ⅛ in) w. 29cm (11 ⅜ in) d. 24.5cm (9 ¾ in)
Starfish, UK
Limited batch production

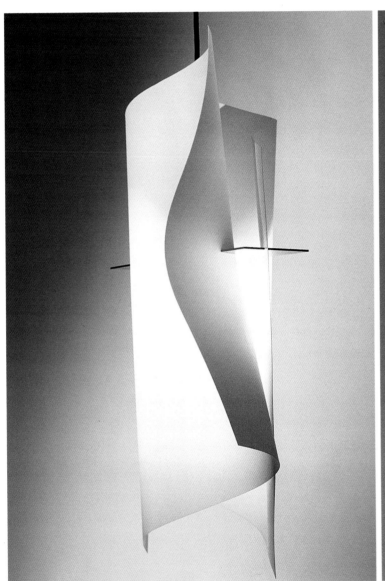
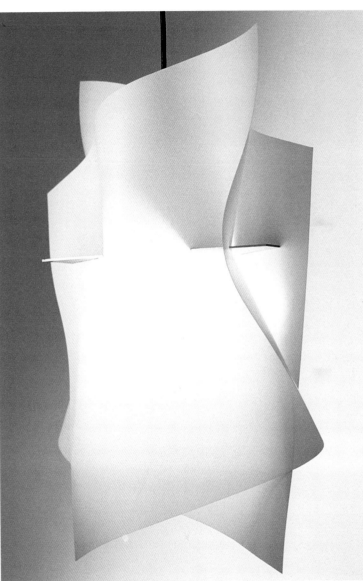

Andrea de Benedetto
Wooden Candle
h. 5cm (2in) w. 29cm (11⅜ in) d. 20cm (7⅞ in)
Post Design for Memphis, Italy
Prototype

Maria Pessoa and Vera Lopes
Candle, Piramidal
Steel, paraffin
h. 25cm (9⅞ in) l. 22/33/40cm (8¾ /13/15¾ in)
d. 25cm (9⅞ in)
Ferro e Fogo, Brazil
Limited batch production

Sebastian Bergne
Table lamp, Candloop
Chrome, aluminium
h. 11cm (4⅜ in) w. 47cm (18½ in) d. 4.5cm (1¾ in)
Wireworks, UK

Renaud Thiry
Candle, Minuit
Wax
h. 23.4cm (9¼ in) di. 8.5cm (3⅜ in)
Habitat, UK

Ronan Bouroullec
Oil lamp, Brand
Ceramic
h. 25.5cm (10in) l. 11cm (4⅜ in) di. 5.5cm (2⅛ in)
Gilles Peyroulet & Cie, France

Carl Clerkin
Table lamp, Corkscrew Lamp
Cast bronze
40w bulb
h. 50cm (19⅝ in) l. 12cm (4¾ in) d. 12cm (4¾ in)
Limited batch production

Gregory Prade
Reading light, Little Moon
Quartz crystal, stainless steel, woven glass
20w halogen reflector bulb
h. 10cm (3⅞ in) di. 8cm (3⅛ in)
Studio Gregory Prade, Germany

Isabel Hamm
Table lamp, Switch
Glass, porcelain
9w halogen reflector bulb
h. 30cm (11¾ in) d. 11cm (4⅜ in)
Prototype

Monica Förster
Table or floor lamp, Silikon
Silicone rubber
Low-energy bulb
h. 10cm (3 ⅞ in) di. 25cm (9 ⅞ in)
David Design, Sweden

Ernesto Gismondi
Indoor/outdoor light, Felsina Reflex
Phosphated, chrome-plated, die-cast aluminium
and polished anodized aluminium
150w CDM-T bulb
h. 57.5cm (22½in) w. 13.6cm (5⅜in)
Artemide, Italy

DesignHospital
(Rolf Bürger/Stiletto collaboration)
Energy-saving light, Blackout 2000
Stainless steel, frosted bulb, candle
h. 10.5cm (4⅛in) w. 7cm (2¾in)
d. 10.5cm (4⅛in)
Stiletto, Germany

Ernesto Gismondi
Ceiling light, Menelao Plafoniera
Painted aluminium, blown glass
Max. 3 x 60w incandescent opal and max. 1 x 100w
incandescent reflector bulbs
w. 37cm (14⅝in) di. 24cm (9½in)
Artemide, Italy

Lionel Dean
Wall light, Lampis
Polycarbonate plastic
20w bulb
h. 21.5cm (8½in) w. 13.5cm (5¼in)
IKEA, Sweden

Ernesto Gismondi
Ceiling or wall light, Niki
Stainless steel, polycarbonate
2 x 18w or 1 x 75w bulbs
h. 9.8cm (3⅞in) d. 31.2cm (12⅜in)
Artemide, Italy

Jan Broekstra
Disposable suspension light, Brand
Glass, porcelain, 5/25w bulb (glass/porcelain)
h. 250cm (98⅜in) l. 250cm (98⅜in)
d. 190cm (74¾in)
JKN Arnhem, The Netherlands
One-off

Toshiyuki Kita
Table lamp, Sol Quoque
Blown and etched glass, technopolymer
1 x max. 100w bulb or 1 x max.
20w fluorescent bulb
h. 72cm (28⅜in) di. 40cm (15¾in)
Gloria, Italy

Michele de Lucchi
Table lamp, Aria
Blown Murano glass
60w bulb
h. 28cm (11in) di. 23cm (9in)
Architetto Michele de Lucchi
(Produzione Privata), Italy
Limited batch production

Rainer Spehl
Television Light
h. 80cm (31½in) di. 60cm (23⅝in)
Post Design for Memphis, Italy
Prototype

Antoni Arola
Ceiling light, Sandy 1
Stainless steel, ostrich egg
50w bulb
h. 80cm (31½ in) l. 120cm (47⅛ in)
Metalarte, Spain

Mark Lee
Floor lamp, Zen Water Bowl
Rice paper
60w bulb
h. 50.8cm (20in) w. 50.8cm (20in) d. 30.5cm (12in)
Mark Lee Lighting, USA

Chiara Cantono
Water/light holder, JAR
Polypropylene, polyethylene
60–100w bulb
h. 35–42cm (13¾–16½ in)
d. 16–21cm (6¼–8¼ in)
Chiara Cantono, Italy
Limited batch production

Roberto and Ludovica Palomba
Table lamp, Simple
Murano glass
60w bulb
Large: h. 30cm (11¾ in) di. 30cm (11¾ in)
Medium: h. 40cm (15¾ in) di. 15cm (5⅞ in)
Small: h. 23cm (9in) di. 22cm (8¾ in)
Allglass, Italy

Moonlight
Outdoor lighting
Moulded polyethylene
5/15/23w bulb
di. 25/35/55/75cm (9⅞/13¾/21⅝/29½in)
Moonlight Aussenleuchten, Germany

Julie Nelson
Table lamp, Ellipse
Ceramic
60w bulb
h. 30cm (11¾ in) w. 42cm (16½ in)
d. 21cm (8¼ in)
Limited batch production

Marre Moerel
Table lamp, Soft Box
(MS4, LS2, LH2, SS2, MS2 shown)
Earthenware, porcelain
75w incandescent bulb
h. 25–40.6cm (9 ⅞ –16in)
w. 14.6–18.5cm (5 ¾ –7 ¼ in)
d. 11.5–14.6cm (4 ½ –5 ¾ in)
Prototype

Richard Hutten
Table and lamp, Table-lamp
Oak, steel, fabric
60w bulb
h. 110cm (43¼ in) w. 50cm (19⅝ in)
l. 50cm (19⅝ in)
REEEL, The Netherlands
Limited batch production

Reno Bonzon, Ligia Miguez and Lincoln Lucchi
Floor lamp, Galhão
Sand-cast aluminium, fabric, papyrus paper
110 or 220v incandescent bulb
h. 150cm (59in) w. 40cm (15¾ in) d. 40cm (15¾ in)
Limited batch production

Enrico Baleri
Floor lamp, Talis Amor
Steel, polycarbonate
Max. 150w halogen or 25w fluorescent bulb
h. 166–181cm (65¼ –71¼ in) d. 42cm (16½ in)
Gloria, Italy

96

Uwe Fischer
Floor lamp, Jones
Aluminium, glass fibre
250w bulb
h. 154–172cm (60 ⅝ – 67 ⅝ in) d. 34cm (13 ⅜ in)
Serien Raumleuchten, Germany

'Jones' floor lamp, Uwe Fischer

Fischer has developed a floor lamp combining a variety of lighting tasks using one halogen lamp. A mechanism designed on the pulley block principle enables the height of the lamp to be adjusted within the glass shade. The light passes through the shade at different heights, producing a glow suitable for reading, moving into a diffuse ambient light and then a ceiling flood. The height of the floor lamp can also be adjusted by extending or retracting the telescopic tubular stand, while a dimmer with sensor button allows further flexibility.

Radi Designers
Floor lamp, Fabulation
Two-way mirror, epoxy-coated steel
32w Osram lumilux circline bulb
h. 179.5cm (70⅝ in) d. 47.6cm (18¾ in)
Kreo, France
Limited batch production

Carlo Tamborini
Suspension light, Duplex
Acrylic (Perspex)
2 halogen bulbs
h. 20cm (7⅞ in) w. 10cm (3⅞ in) l. 20cm (7⅞ in)
Fontana Arte, Italy

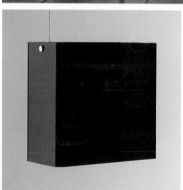

Jurgen Bey
Lightshade-shade
Polyester foil, one-way mirror foil, steel
15–60w bulb
h. 75cm (29½ in) d. 36cm (14⅛ in)
Droog Design, The Netherlands

Davide Groppi
Table lamp, Tropical
Chrome-plated steel, polypropylene
Max. 20w bulb
h. 31cm (12⅛ in) d. 13.5cm (5¼ in)
Davide Groppi, Italy

Sigi Bussinger
Light fountain, Li Wasku
Transparent cast resin
6 x 50w halogen reflectors
h. 155cm (61in) w. 85cm (33½ in) l. 85cm (33½ in)
One-off

100

Jan Bremermann
Suspension light, Ecco
Aluminium, polycarbonate (Lexan)
10 x 15w bulbs
h. 24cm (9½ in) w. 5cm (2in) l. 140cm (55⅛ in)
Lucefer-Licht, Germany

Fernando and Humberto Campana
Floor, table or wall light, Pillow Lamp
Polycarbonate, glass wool, plastic fabric
25w fluorescent bulb
h. 15.5cm (6⅛ in) w. 40cm (15¾ in)
l. 40cm (15¾ in)
Campana Objetos, Brazil
Prototype

Radim Babák and Jan Tucek
Suspension light, D1
Plastic foam
Eco-light bulbs
Shade: h. 40cm (15¾ in) w. 50cm (19⅝ in)
d. 40cm (15¾ in)
Tunnel, Czech Republic

Radim Babák and Jan Tucek
Floor lamps, A7
Steel, plastic foam
Eco-light bulbs
h. 130cm (51⅝ in)
Tunnel, Czech Republic

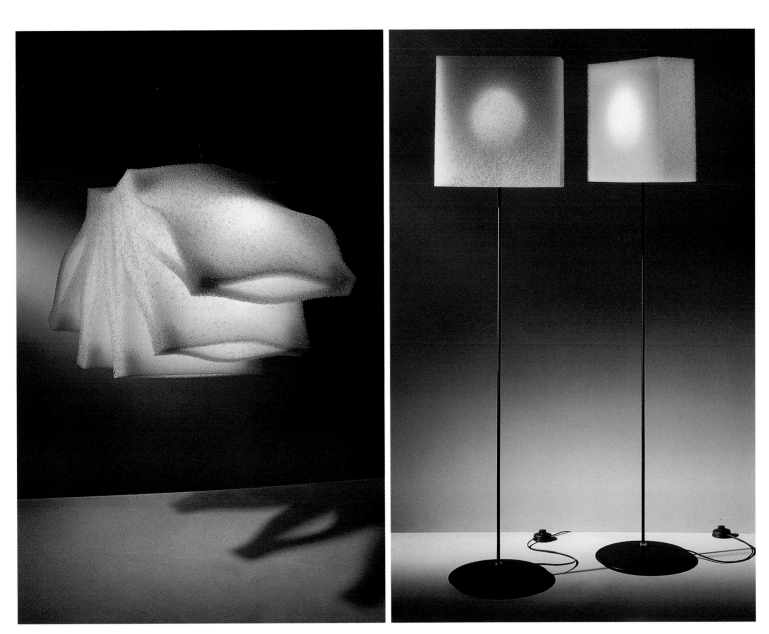

Tunnel

Tunnel is a team of designers who came together in 1998 with the aim of making a connection between Czech designers, architects and manufacturers. Radim Babák and Jan Tucek are two of Tunnel's youngest members.

Gaetano Pesce
10 Feet Lamp
Resin
10 x 12v bulbs
h. 5cm (2in) l. 100cm (39⅜ in) d. 3cm (1⅛ in)
Pesce Limited, USA

Jeremy Lord
Wall light, Microchrome mc32
Polycarbonate, polished aluminium
128 coloured 10mm wedge bulbs
h. 27cm (10⅝ in) l. 48cm (18⅞ in) d. 95cm (37⅜ in)
The Colour Light Company, UK
Limited batch production

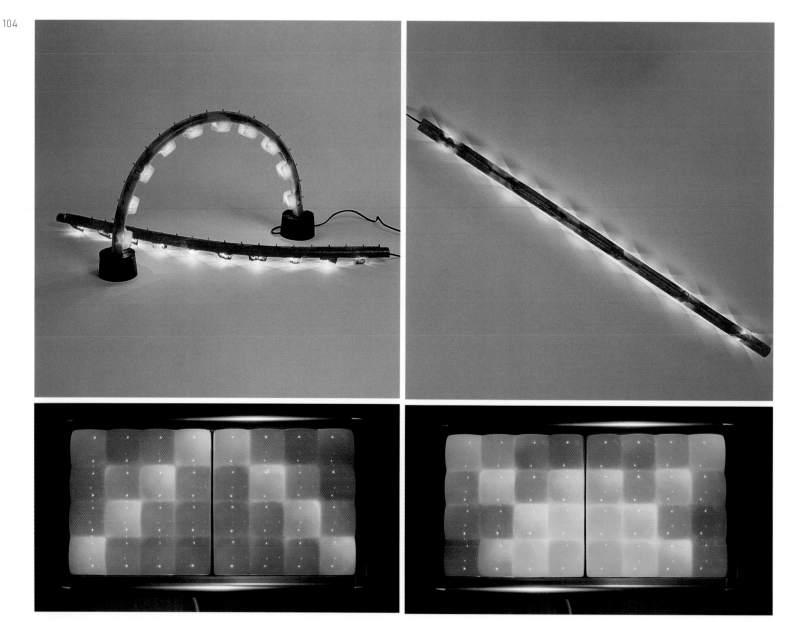

Microchrome

A contemporary light which walks the fine line between a work of art and a light source, Microchrome is an electronically controlled colour-changing light mosaic. Jeremy Lord, who formed The Colour Light Company in 1994 and has worked on lighting installations with designers such as Tom Dixon and Michael Young, says his lights 'are designed to attract attention, but they are not demanding intellectually − a bit like watching the rain or a fire'.

Anette Hermann
Table lamp, Hand (to Hold)
Latex
4w bulb
h. 25cm (9 ⅞ in) w. 12cm (4 ¾ in) d. 8cm (3 ⅛ in)
Frandsen Lyskilde, Denmark

Ralph Ball
Wall light, Red Sky at Night
Fibreglass
2 x 60w bulbs
h. 20cm (7 ⅞ in) w. 56cm (22in)
Post Design for Memphis, Italy
Prototype

F. Th. Gärtner Industrial Design
Water Can Chandelier
Steel, polyethylene
42 x 55w bulbs
h. 35cm (13 ¾ in) di. 120cm (47 ⅛ in)
F. Th. Gärtner Industrial Design, Germany

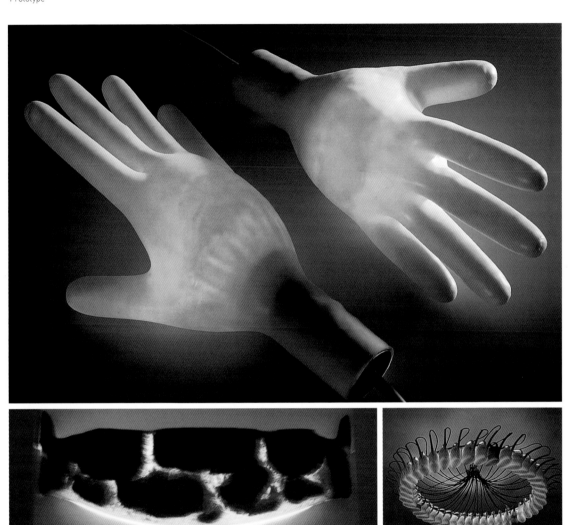

Georg Baldele
Floor lamp, Caveman
Nomex
35w bulb
h. 160cm (63in) d. 45cm (17¾in)
Artificial Nürnber, Germany

Georg Baldele
The work of the young designer Georg Baldele is refreshingly inventive and incorporates an element of chance. The Caveman series of paper lanterns are made from coiled rolls of heat-resistant paper and lit from within.

Peter Christian
Wall/ceiling light, Icon Long
Aluminium, polycarbonate
18/36/58/70w linear fluorescent bulb
h. 188cm (74⅛ in) w. 20cm (7⅞ in) d. 11cm (4⅜ in)
Aktiva, UK
Limited batch production

Ichiro Iwasaki
Table lamp, Ponder
Bronze
0.2mm fluorescent sheet
h. 16.5cm (6½ in) w. 10cm (3⅞ in) d. 4cm (1½ in)
Iwasaki Design Studio, Japan
Limited batch production

f. maurer
Floor lamp, Colour Column
Acrylic
2 x 120w bulbs
h. 205cm (80⅝ in) w. 13cm (5⅛ in) d. 21cm (8¼ in)
Iris Licht, Brüder Veverka, Austria
Limited batch production

Matijs Korpershoek (Droog Design)
Candle, Changing Candlelight
Glass
h. 28.5cm (11¼ in) d. 9.6cm (3¾ in)
Salviati, Italy
Prototype

Jorge Garcia Garay
Table lamp, Gotham
Iron, aluminium
Max. 100w bulb
h. 40cm (15 ¾ in) w. 20cm (7 ⅞ in) di. 20cm (7 ⅞ in)
Garcia Garay Iluminación Diseño, Spain

Martin Huwiler
Suspension light, Optic
Metal, steel cable, polycarbonate lens
100w bulb
di. 45cm (17 ¾ in)
Belux, Switzerland

108

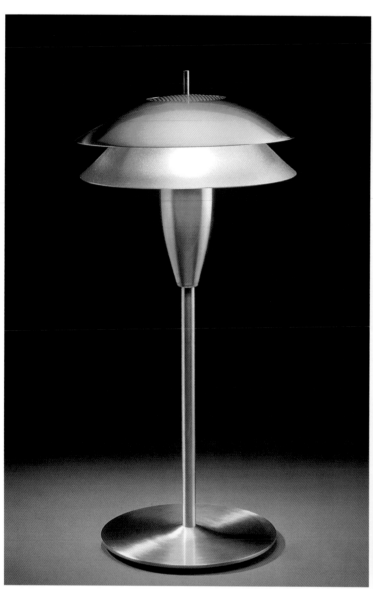

Anna Gili
Light painting, Dog
Aluminium, acrylic (Perspex)
3 x 18w neon bulbs
h. 193cm (75 ⅞ in) w. 145cm (57in) d. 21cm (8 ¼ in)
Slamp, Italy
One-off

Anna Gili
Table lamp, Monkey
Opaflex (glass and plastic mix)
100w incandescent bulb
h. 37.5cm (14 ⅞ in) w. 48.5cm (19in)
Slamp, Italy

Anna Gili
Floor lamp, Elephante
Opaflex (glass and plastic mix)
2 x 100w incandescent bulbs
h. 111cm (43 ⅝ in) w. 52cm (20½ in)
Slamp, Italy

Masamichi Katayama
Floor lamp, Naked
Chrome-plated steel
9w bulb
h. 125cm (49⅛ in) w. 12cm (4¾ in) d. 16cm (6¼ in)
Time & Style, Japan
Limited batch production

Bernhard Dessecker
Floor lamp, Stand Up For Your Light
Glass, stainless steel, plastic
250w halogen bulb or 35w CDM bulb
h. 190cm (74¾ in) w. 27cm (10⅝ in)
d. 16cm (6¼ in) di. 13cm (5⅛ in)
Ingo Maurer, Germany

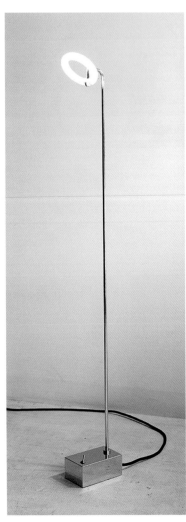

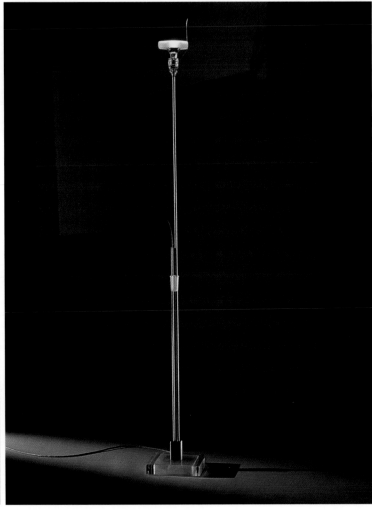

Rolf Sachs
Light sculpture, Felt Pen e t'ration
Felt
Neon
h. 102cm (40⅛ in) w. 22cm (8¾ in)
l. 32cm (12½ in)
Limited batch production

Rolf Sachs
Light sculpture, La Luna
Wood
Neon
h. 220cm (86⅝ in) w. 40cm (15¾ in) l. 5cm (2in)
Limited batch production

Frans Van Nieuwenborg
Suspension light, Canto Chiaro
Aluminium, polycarbonate
Fluorescent tube
h. variable l. 120cm (47⅛ in) d. 8cm (3⅛ in)
Van Nieuwenborg Industrial Design Consultancy
Group, The Netherlands
Limited batch production

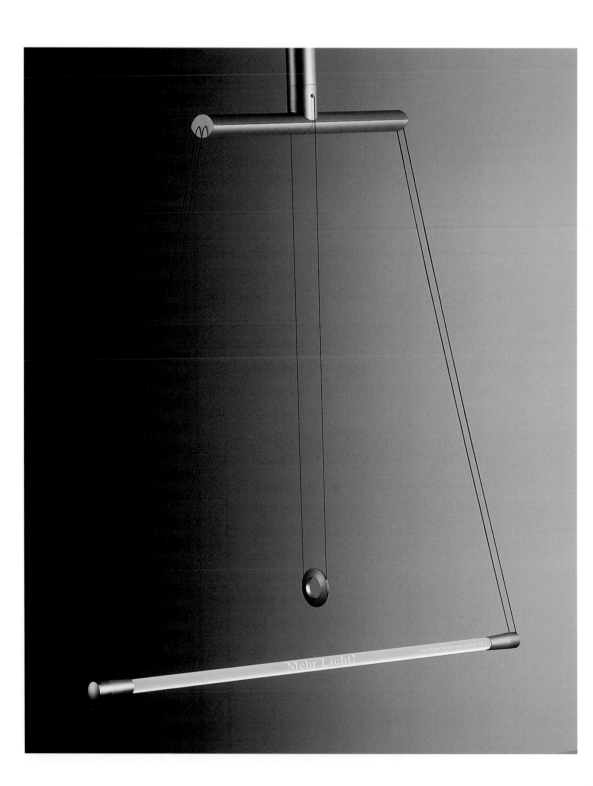

Alex Hochstrasser
Suspension light, Fluo
Lacquered metal, polyester
Max. 36w bulb
h. 50/200cm (19⅝/78⅝ in) l. 125cm (49⅛ in)
Metalarte, Spain

Iain Sinclair
Torch, Eon
Stainless steel, ABS
White light-emitting diodes
h. 0.25cm (⅛ in) w. 5.4cm (2⅛ in) l. 8.5cm (3⅜ in)
Torchco, UK

Sottsass Associati
Suspension light, Aero
Die-cast aluminium, acrylic, glass
2 x 54w bulbs
h. 5.6cm (2⅛ in) w. 33.6cm (13¼ in)
l. 125cm (49⅛ in)
Zumtobel Staff, Austria

Sigeaki Asahara
Adjustable spotlight, Krisma
Die-cast aluminium, chrome-plated steel
Max. 100w halogen or 20w fluorescent bulb
h. 17.5cm (6 ⅞ in) w. 18cm (7in) l. 9.5cm (3 ¾ in)
Lucitalia, Italy

Porsche Design
(F. A. Porsche and J. Tragatschnig)
Spotlight series, AIR
Cast aluminium
h. 12cm (4 ¾ in) l. 9.5cm (3 ¾ in) di. 7cm (2 ¾ in)
Antares Iluminacion, Spain

Franco Clivio
Spotlight, Stella
Cast aluminium
35–300w bulb
h. 31.3cm (12 ⅜ in) w. 19.2cm (7 ⅝ in)
di. 15.5cm (6 ⅛ in)
ERCO Leuchten, Germany

Charles Keller
High-bay reflector luminaire, COPA
Die-cast aluminium, polycarbonate
Various – from 32w bulb
h. 50.3cm (19 ¾ in) di. 31.5cm (12 ⅜ in)
Zumtobel Staff, Austria

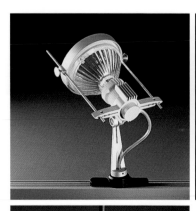

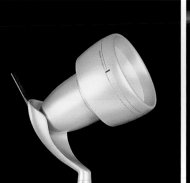

Urs and Carmen Greutmann
Table lamp, Eedisson
Iron, plastic
50w bulb
l. 90cm (35⅜ in)
Belux, Switzerland

Robert Foster
Table lamp, Blink
Nickel-plated steel, brass, ceramic
h. 40cm (15¾ in)
20w bulb
Fink! & Company, Australia

Ralph Ball
Floor lamp, Power Tower
Steel, plus sockets, flex and bulbs
60w bulbs
h. 200cm (78⅝ in) w. 30cm (11¾ in) d. 30cm (11¾ in)
Limited batch production

Danny Lane
Pair of floor lamps, Stands to Reason
Low iron float glass, stainless steel
50w halogen capsule
h. 199cm (78⅜ in) w. 22.5cm (8¾ in)
d. 22.5cm (8¾ in)
Danny Lane, UK
Limited batch production

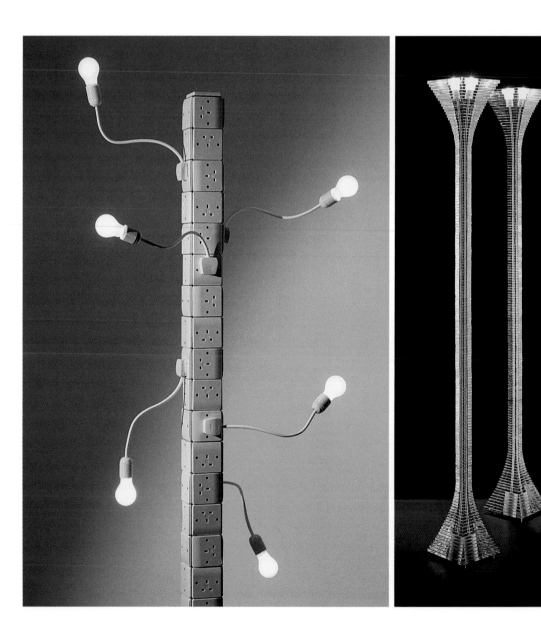

Power Tower, Ralph Ball

Ralph Ball's playful Power Tower is made of lighting flex, sockets and bulbs and is one of a series of designs that take the banal and the generic and create new products with an ironic twist.

Gianfranco Coltella
Floor lamp, Stalagmite
Recycled glass
Fibre optics
h. 180cm (71in) di. 25cm (9 ⅞ in)
Le Meduse di Coltella Gianfranco & C., Italy

Bohuslav Horak
Floor lamp, Kved
Aluminium, blown glass
25w bulb
h. 213cm (83 ⅞ in) di. 30cm (11 ¾ in)
Anthologie Quartett, Germany

OSCAR TUSQUETS BLANCA

EDITOR, THE INTERNATIONAL DESIGN YEARBOOK 1989/90

Here we are in the year 2000, the millennium is coming to an end, and we still haven't stopped enjoying ourselve: **nineties. After the mad, exorbitant, elaborate, obscene eighties, the nineties we have lived through seem reality been conservative, non-risk-taking and simply obsessed with commercialism.**

The economic crisis of the beginning of the decade called for prudence and profitability above all else. The mo: continuous research, started talking about marketing for the first time and suggesting that we draw inspiratic copying the Golf. All the lamp factories ask you for a Tizio; all the furniture makers for a Maralunga or, in my cas by impersonal multinationals.

Although it's a fact that very often economic euphoria does not signal a flourishing of the arts (you need only look case where an economic crisis has done so. It takes a lot to detect or recognize a difficult time for one of the art great era of rock? What about the great Italian film industry? What happened to great design in the United State: like Bertoia, Eames or Saarinen?

What is really remarkable about the design invented or produced in Italy is not that it is undergoing a period than forty years. It has always surprised me that in commercial American films, when the inevitable marriage cris Where did we go wrong?' instead of thinking about what they got right in keeping their love alive for so many yea!

[Translated from Spanish by Carmona UK Ltd]

s become commonplace to speak well of the development of design in the
onable, circumspect, strict and moral. But I fear that these years have in

rprising companies, those which had consolidated their prestige through
best-sellers made for the competition. All the car manufacturers are
her Varius chair. Companies with a glorious tradition have been taken over

zero input of the Arab countries, enriched by oil), I don't know of a single
hese invariably afflict them all. What is left of the great French songs, the
re are the companies like Knoll, Herman Miller? Where are the designers

s; the strange thing is that it has maintained such a high level for more
rs, the characters unfailingly ask themselves 'What happened to us?

Garouste and Bonetti
Floor lamp, Oriflamme
White gold on metal, silk
60–100w bulbs x 4
h. 180cm (71in) w. 20cm (7 ⅞ in) d. 50cm (19 ⅝ in)
Limited batch production

Aleksej Iskos
Chandelier, Waterfall
Plastic bags, water, 10 x 10w bulbs
h. 90cm (35 ⅜ in) w. 60cm (23 ⅝ in)
l. 60cm (23 ⅝ in)
Miscellaneous Design, Denmark
Limited batch production

Weyers & Borms
Lamp, Malix
Wood, glass
7w bulb
h. 28–30cm (11–11 ¾ in) d. 17–20cm (6 ⅝ –7 ⅞ in)
Limited batch production

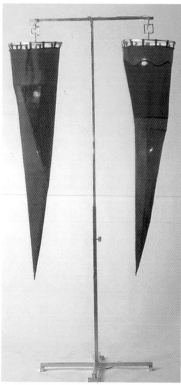

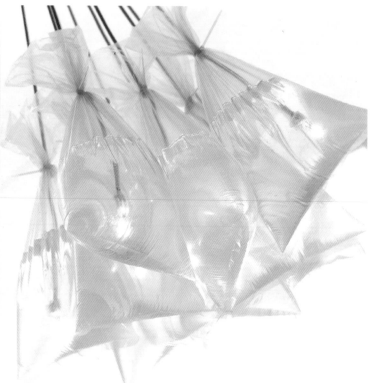

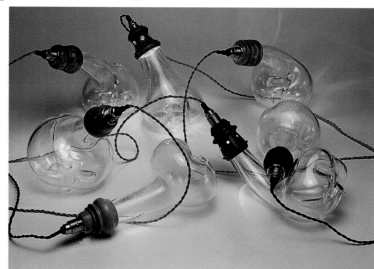

Mark Bond
Wall light, Rubber Light
Heat-proof rubber sheath, 40w bulb
h. 25cm (9 ⅞ in) w. 5cm (2in)
l. (cable) 260cm (102 ⅜ in)
Bond Projects UK
Limited batch production

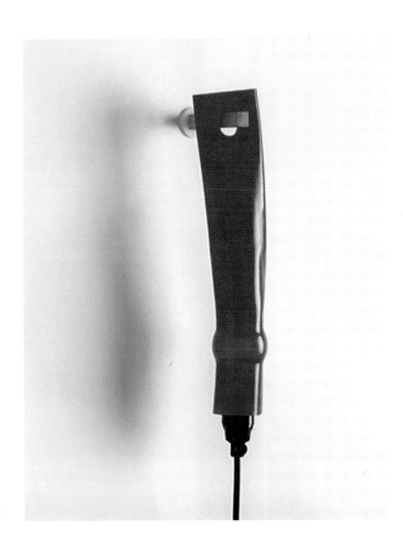

Rubber Light, Mark Bond

The rubber sheath of this light pulls firmly over the bulb and hangs over a wooden peg, screwed into a wall. It took Mark Bond several years to develop the design into a commercially viable product: much research time was spent sourcing a rubber material to withstand high temperatures. Eventually a manufacturer was found and they collaborated with the designer to produce a new material which is durable, safe and aesthetically pleasing.

Jacopo Foggini
Floor lamp, Dancing Sculpture
Methacrylate
75w bulb
h. 180cm (70⅞ in) di. 55–75cm (21⅝ – 29½ in)
Limited batch production

Sharon Marston
Floor lamp, Orange Cocoon
Woven nylon, monofilament
60w bulb
h. 150cm (59in) w. 35cm (13¾ in) d. 35cm (13¾ in)
Limited batch production

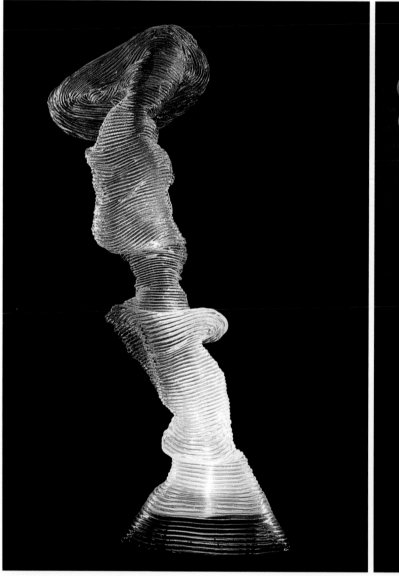

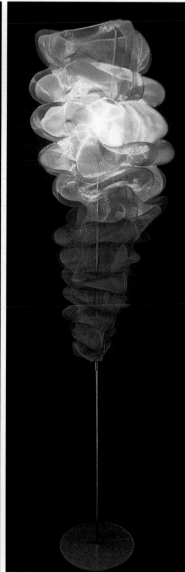

Dancing Sculpture, Jacopo Foggini

One of a limited edition of ten light sculptures by the Italian designer Jacopo Foggini created out of methacrylate, the plastic usually used to make car reflectors and fog lights. Each light takes a day to make and must be completed without stopping. The process is carried out partly by machine but Foggini colours all the resin himself and moulds it into organic shapes by hand.

El Ultimo Grito
Table lamp, La Lù
Wire, mild steel rod, electrical cable
9w low-energy bulb
h. 17cm (6⅝ in) di. 12cm (4¾ in)
El Ultimo Grito, UK
Limited batch production

Georgia Scott
Lamp from the Spike series
Aluminium mesh
Sylvania 'Hi Spot 50' bulb
h. 90cm (35⅜ in) w. 30cm (11¾ in)
Limited batch production

Gabriele Allendorf
Table lamp, Oberon
Stainless steel, plastic
40w or energy-saving bulb
h. 36cm (14⅛ in) w. 16cm (6¼ in) d. 16cm (6¼ in)
One-off

La Lù, El Ultimo Grito

The flex and the lampshade are one continuous line: the power cable is woven around a mild steel structure to create the lampshade.

TABLEWARE

'Dishes, plates, knives, forks etc., for use at meals' may be a definition of tableware, but this year's selection sees decorative and ornamental pieces outnumbering the prosaically useful.

Ingo Maurer's attraction to the bold – above the slick, plain or functionalist – can be seen in his selection of Borek Sipek's highly ornamental Murano glass vases, Takahide Sano's Cloud vase and examples from Michele de Lucchi's 'What are flower vases for?' series, while his playfulness and humour are reflected in the choice of the bread vase by Marcel Wanders, the Campana brothers' Bristles Fruit Bowl and Pischedda and Darmody's Confuse cups.

Although ceramic and glass are the preferred materials, Aki Kotkas' transformation of recycled PET bottles into drinking glasses, Olgoj Chorchoj's carbon fibre bowl and the injection-moulded polypropylene examples by Karim Rashid illustrate an interest, particularly among the younger designers, in working with less traditional tableware materials.

Despite the current vogue for crafts glass and ceramics, even the limited batch production pieces selected seem to take their inspiration from the world of mass production rather than crafts. Ronan Bouroullec's ceramic range using local clay, commissioned by the Vallauris Ceramics Museum, shows a successful collaboration between designer, craftspeople and factory. Like Vallauris, the Dutch company Cor Unum has produced ceramics since the early 1950s. Its most recent project involving a group of five Dutch architects utilizes both the latest CAD/CAM technology and the traditional production processes of rolling, pressing and moulding, undertaken by hand.

Perhaps it is no surprise that glass and transparency are popular this year, with their references to 1960s visions of the future. Finland's best-known glass company, Iittala, combines past and present in its Relations Concept designs. With a heritage extending back to 1881, Iittala has drawn on the talents of a group of contemporary designers, including Konstantin Grcic, Annaleena Hakatie and Marc Newson, and combined them with the skills of its master blowers and its glass-pressing techniques.

Konstantin Grcic
Glassware for the Relations range
(glasses, bowl, tray, ashtray, decanter)
Glass
h. 7.5–12.2cm (2¾–4⅝ in)
di. 6.4–7.7cm (2½–3in)
Hackman Designor, Iittala Glass, Finland

Marc Newson
Glasses for the Relations range
Glass
h. 5.5–11.5cm (2⅛–4½ in) di. 9.4cm (3¾ in)
Hackman Designor, Iittala Glass, Finland

Annaleena Hakatie
Glassware for the Relations range
(pitchers and bowl)
Glass
h. 7/13/17/20/29cm (2¾/5⅛/6⅝/7⅞/11⅜ in)
di. 5.3/8/8.2/8.8/17cm (2⅛/3⅛/3¼/3½/6⅝ in)
Hackman Designor, Iittala Glass, Finland

Relations Concept, Iittala

Iittala, Finland's best-known glass company founded in 1881, has a tradition of contemporary glass design and over the years has produced the work of great names such as Alvar Aalto – whose Savoy vase was launched sixty years ago – Kaj Franck and Tapio Wirkkala. The company's most recent project, 'Relations', includes a collection of pitchers from the Finnish designer Annaleena Hakatie; a series of drinks glasses that are one shape cut at three different heights from Marc Newson; and seven pieces by Konstantin Grcic which include a decanter, tray and stacking glasses, inspired by a glass-pressing machine the designer saw on a visit to the Iittala factory.

Michele de Lucchi
Vase, Liriope
Metal and blown Murano glass
h. 35cm (13¾ in)
Architetto Michele de Lucchi
(Produzione Privata), Italy
Limited batch production

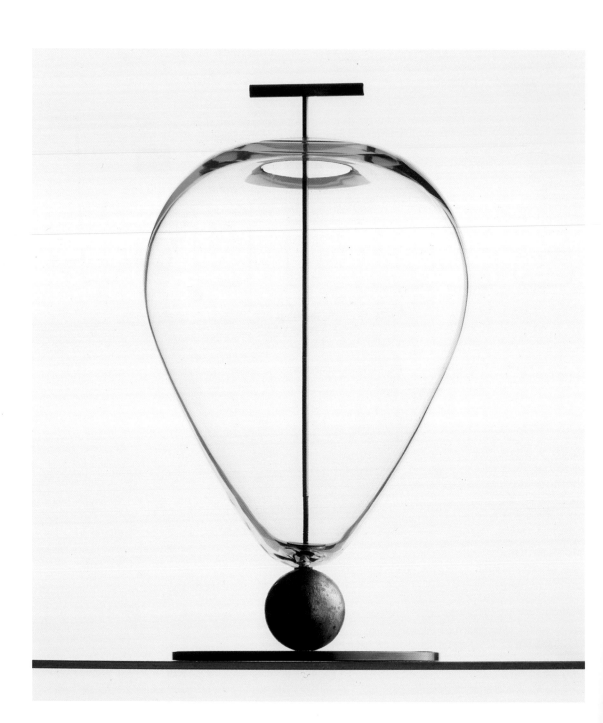

Michele de Lucchi
Vase, Artemisia
Metal and blown Murano glass
h. 34cm (13⅜ in)
Architetto Michele de Lucchi
(Produzione Privata), Italy
Limited batch production

Michele de Lucchi
Vase, Calicanthus
Metal and blown Murano glass
h. 32cm (12½ in)
Architetto Michele de Lucchi
(Produzione Privata), Italy
Limited batch production

Michele de Lucchi, vases

These are three of a collection of twelve blown Murano glass vases entitled 'What are flower vases for?' De Lucchi gives each a description: Artemisia – a vase to smell the aromas of grey; Calicanthus – a vase to remember the winter miracle; and Liriope – a vase for the search of sincerity. The collection forms part of Produzione Privata which the architect established in 1990 to enable himself to work more creatively and innovatively on small-scale decorative objects in glass, metal and ceramics.

Borek Sipek
Vase, Red Ball Unique
Bohemian crystal
h. 32cm (12 ½ in) di. 44cm (17 ⅛ in)
Steltman Galleries, Amsterdam, The Netherlands

Borek Sipek
Vase, Paur
Soda-potassium glass
h. 35cm (13 ¾ in) di. 19cm (7 ½ in)
Ajeto, Czech Glass Craft, Czech Republic
Limited batch production

Andrea Anastasio
Vase, Pesco
Glass, fluorescent rubber
h. 51cm (20 ⅛ in) di. 37cm (14 ⅝ in)
Design Gallery Milano, Italy

Borek Sípek

Very Baroque and Rococo, Sipek's glass vases continue to display the exuberance and
decoration which has been so much his style over the last two decades.

Ron Arad
Champagne glass
Glass
h. 24.5cm (9¾ in) di. (of base) 6cm (2¼ in)
Glaskoch, Germany

Andrea Anastasio
Vase, Ciuegio
Blown glass
h. 56cm (22in) di. 22cm (8¾ in)
Design Gallery Milano, Italy
Limited batch production

L'Anverre
Vase, Trepalle
Blown glass
h. 76cm (29⅞ in) di. 38cm (15in)
Zanotta, Italy

Emmanuel Babled
Vase, Oversized
Blown glass
h. max. 65cm (25½ in) di. max. 50cm (19⅝ in)
Limited batch production

Champagne glass, Ron Arad
The double skin of Arad's champagne glass ensures that any effervescence overflows
into an outer chamber, preventing drips or sticky fingers.

Enzo Mari
Whisky glasses, Conversazione
Lead crystal
h. 9.5cm (3¾in) di. 8cm (3⅛in)
Arnolfo di Cambio Compagnia Italiana del Cristallo,
Italy

Enzo Mari
Drinking glasses, Conversazione
Lead crystal
h. 13cm (5⅛in) di. 7cm (2¾in)
Arnolfo di Cambio Compagnia Italiana del Cristallo,
Italy

Carlo Moretti
Vases, Torre
Murano glass
h. 33–41cm (13–16⅛in) di. 16.5–17cm (6½–6⅝in)
Carlo Moretti, Italy
Limited batch production

Renaud Thiry
Reversible vase, Upside Down
Glass
h. 21cm (8¼in) di. 8/11cm (3⅛/4⅜in)
Cappellini, Italy (Progetto Ogetto Collection 1999)

Maarten Vrolijk
Vase, Fontana
Crystal
h. 21cm (8¼in) di. 38cm (15in)
Royal Leerdam Collection, 'Arum' Cristal,
The Netherlands
Limited batch production

Massimo Lunardon
Decanter and glasses, Presina
Glass, Borosilicate
h. 11/22cm (4⅜/8¾in) di. 7/9.5cm (2¾/3¾in)
Vayu, Italy

132

Aki Kotkas
Drinking glass
PET water bottles
h. 19cm (7½ in) di. 6.5cm (2⅝ in)
Limited batch production

Drinking glasses, Aki Kotkas

Aki Kotkas takes two empty PET water bottles to create a new drinking glass held together with the cap.

Isabel Hamm
Bowls, Twins
Blown glass
h. 7.5cm (2⅝ in) w. 17cm (6⅝ in)
d. 24cm (9½ in)
One-off

Isabel Hamm
Bowls, Set
Blown glass
h. 2.5–6cm (1–2¼ in)
di. 16/20/72cm (6¼ /7⅞ /28⅜ in)
Prototype

134

Arnout Visser and Erik-Jan Kwakkel
Four Flower Vase
Glass, rubber
h. 20cm (7 ⅞ in) w. 20cm (7 ⅞ in) l. 20cm (7 ⅞ in)
REEEL, The Netherlands
Limited batch production

Karim Rashid
Serving bowl, Rim Bowl
Injection-moulded polypropylene
h. 20.3cm (8in) d. 33cm (13in)
Umbra, Canada

Lena Bergström
Vase, Slitz
Crystal
h. 54.5cm (21½ in) w. 24.5cm (9 ¾ in)
Orrefors Kosta Boda, Sweden

Roberto and Ludovica Palomba
Glassware, Herb
Blown Murano glass
di. 50/65cm (19 ⅝ / 25 ½ in)
Allglass, Italy

Robert Foster
FINK! Explosive Vase
Explosive-formed anodized aluminium
h. 30cm (11 ¾ in) w. 10.5cm (4 ⅛ in) d. 6cm (2 ¼ in)
Fink! & Co., Australia

Ben van Berkel
Plate for Terra Incognita, Fragile
Glazed clay
h. 8cm (3⅛ in) di. 90cm (35⅜ in)
Cor Unum, The Netherlands
Limited batch production

Erick Van Egeraat
Container for Terra Incognita, Black Max
Glazed clay, platinum
h. 80cm (31½ in) di. 7–16cm (2¾–6¼ in)
Cor Unum, The Netherlands
Limited batch production

MVRDV/Winy Maas
Copypaste series for Terra Incognita
Glazed clay
Various sizes
Cor Unum, The Netherlands
Limited batch production

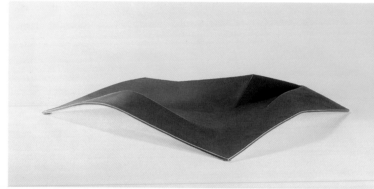

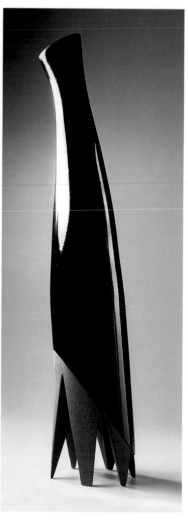

MVRDV/Winy Maas
Copypaste series for Terra Incognita
Glazed clay
Various sizes
Cor Unum, The Netherlands
Limited batch production

Copypaste Series, Cor Unum

Cor Unum (Latin for 'one heart') has been producing ceramics in both black and white clay since 1953 in 's-Hertogenbosch in The Netherlands. Today CAD/CAM technology supports the various production processes of rolling, pressing and moulding, which are primarily undertaken by hand, and most of their products are the result of commissioning well-known ceramicists, industrial designers, artists, architects and fashion designers to work on small, batch-produced collections. In 1998 the company invited five Dutch architects to design a ceramic container. MVRDV collaborated with ceramicist Winy Maas: the wet forms of the ceramic bowls were supplied by Maas and then pressed into a box that was far too small. Through this process a dish becomes a jug with a spout, or a vase pinched together in the centre, or a lopsided cup. Erick Van Egeraat's original Black Max IV container had a text applied to it: 'It is nonsense when architects claim that their work has nothing to do with fashion', a reflection about which Van Egeraat feels very strongly: however, technical circumstances prevented the text being applied. Ben van Berkel's Fragile could be a plate; as he comments: 'I was interested in the way objects could be placed on a given plane. It's simply a plateau. The idea was to create a thousand plateaux.'

Ronan Bouroullec
Vases
Ceramic
h. 9.5cm (3¾ in)
di. 29/34.5/57cm (11⅜ /13½ /22⅜ in)
Gilles Peyroulet & Cie, France

Ronan Bouroullec

The young French designer Ronan Bouroullec was the winner of the Best New Designer award at the ICFF in New York in 1999. One of his major projects is a commission from the Vallauris Ceramics Museum. Vallauris, a town in the South of France, was once famous for its ceramics, and fifty years ago work by Picasso and Le Corbusier was produced there. Bouroullec spent a year working with traditional materials and the skills of local craftspeople to create a very contemporary product range which uses the natural white or grey Vallauris clay.

Ronan Bouroullec
Bottle / decanter
Ceramic
h. 33.5cm (13 ¼ in) l. 10cm (3 ⅞ in)
di. 8.3cm (3 ¼ in)
Gilles Peyroulet & Cie, France

MARIO BELLINI

EDITOR, THE INTERNATIONAL DESIGN YEARBOOK 1990/91

I have always had a complex relationship with 'design' as a concept, as a discipline and as something spec

Go back and read my introduction to *The International Design Yearbook 1990/91*. Today, I wouldn't change mu
taken by this *Yearbook*, without any hopeless effort to confine it within methodological or theoretical framewor

Now, to say something in the *Yearbook* of the year 2000 means answering a question like 'What about desig
news, if you are on the hard, revolutionary-avantgardist side: **items (objects, furniture, tableware, etc.) relat**
designed and used during the second millennium, the first and all the ones before.

Good news for the same people (but actually bad for the academically oriented theoreticians): **'design' will con**
style', the multifaceted, multicultural, multiregional, transversal manifestations and style of our indefinable ti

self.

I can only agree with the very pragmatic and relaxed way in which 'design' is

e next millennium?' I would like to give you some good and bad news. The bad
e human body and human rites will remain – in a way – 'similar' to the ones

connote and represent a state of mind or, more brutally, a style; the 'design
esent and future.

Stephen Burks
Serving vases
Glass
h. 30.5/38/61cm (12/15/24in)
di. 23/38/30.5cm (9/15/12in)
Readymade, USA

Anna Gili
Goblet, Lion
Blown glass
h. 38cm (15in) di. 14cm (5½in)
Bisazza, Italy
Limited batch production

Hugo Timmermans
Vase/bowl, H2-0
Glass
h. 15/25cm (5⅞/9⅞ in) di. 25/30cm (9⅞/11¾ in)
Optic Product Development, The Netherlands

E00S
Vase, Artificial Plant
Rubber, metal, plastic
h. 50cm (19⅝ in) di. 12cm (4¾ in)
Prototype

Vase, E00S

A prototype plant pot with an integral and flexible support for plants such as orchids.

Takahide Sano
Vase, Kumo ('Cloud')
Sanded glass
h. 26cm (10¼ in) di. 18cm (7in)
Vayu, Italy
Limited batch production

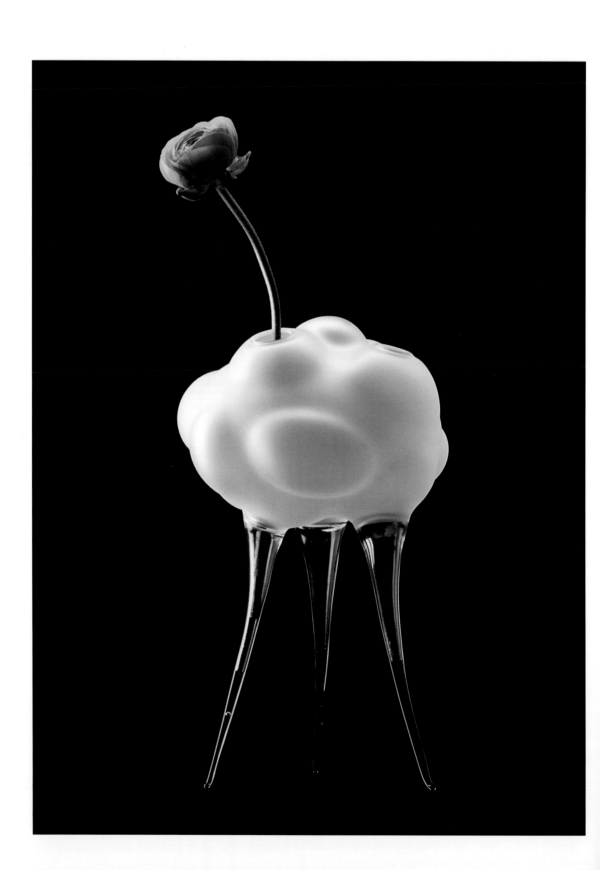

Masatoshi Sakaegi
Vase No. 1 from the Surface Tensions
Vessel series
Porcelain
h. 17.4–18cm (6 ⅞ –7in)
w. 11.6–16cm (4 ½ –6 ¼ in)
l. 10.1–12.6cm (3 ⅞ –5in)
Sakaegi Design Studio, Japan
Limited batch production

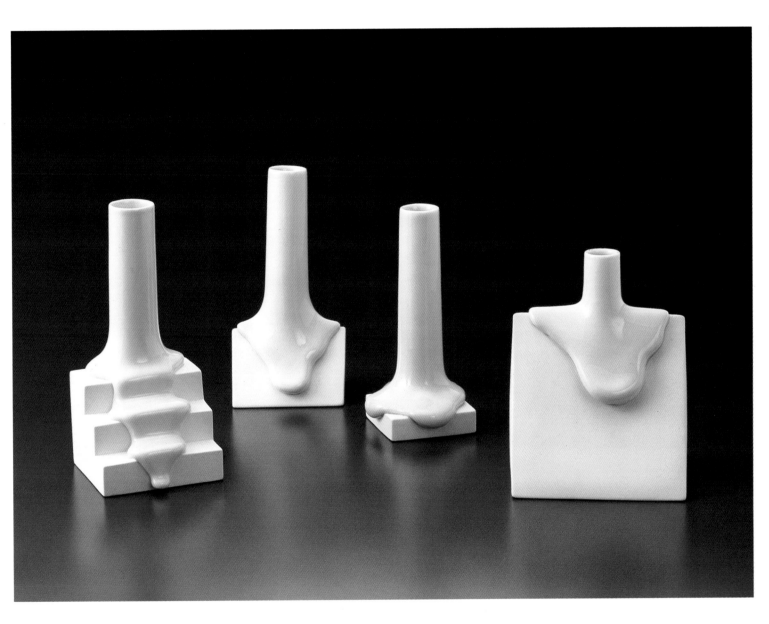

ANDRÉE PUTMAN

EDITOR, THE INTERNATIONAL DESIGN YEARBOOK 1992

146

Design is not dead, but in the last two decades we have been stuffed with information, bombarded by im
strange hunger for signature has turned design into a tool of fame. **We designers have become almost sp**
trends; aren't we overly respected animals? What is dangerous about the fashion cycle is the way in which
misused and finally rejected whatever their value. **My hope is that people will relax, and stop being so tense**
being design victims (fashion victims seem to have disappeared)! Why should a coffee pot need to be designe
trend has been used socially and is (or was) in danger of becoming arrogant.

a fascination for new ideas, and a

s or gurus, inventors of signs and

at first scorned, then adored, then

is 'in' and what is 'out' — let's avoid

ed by an architect? This fashionable

Fernando and Humberto Campana
Bristles Fruit Bowl
Plastic bristles, polystyrene
h. 12cm (4 ¾ in) w. 30cm (11 ¾ in) l. 30cm (11 ¾ in)
Campana Objetos, Brazil
Prototype

Andrea Branzi
Centrepiece, Izzika
Polished aluminium, interwoven glass rods
h. 6cm (2 ¼ in) w. 38cm (15in) d. 38cm (15in)
Zanotta, Italy

Sir Norman Foster
Rectangular tray, 90082
Stainless steel, pear wood
w. 49cm (19 ⅜ in) l. 65cm (25 ½ in)
Alessi, Italy

148

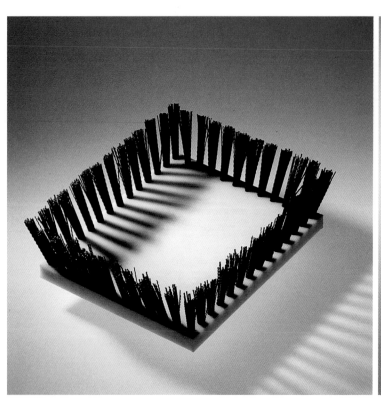

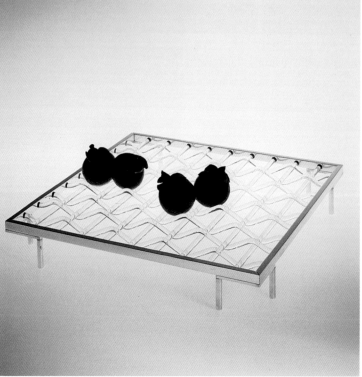

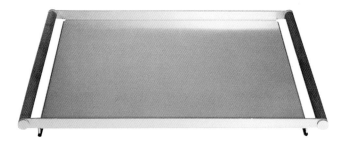

Fernando and Humberto Campana
Bristles Fruit Bowl

Ed Annink
Set of chopping boards, Brothers V
Duravit polyethylene anodized aluminium
Round: w. 29cm (11⅜ in) l. 37cm (14⅝ in) d. 1cm (⅜ in)
Rectangular: w. 16cm (6¼ in) l. 44cm (17⅜ in) d. 1cm (⅜ in)
Long: w. 9cm (3½ in) l. 60cm (23⅝ in) d. 1cm (⅜ in)
Driade, Italy

Eero Koivisto
Bowl, Smith
Polystyrene
h. 2cm (¾ in) di. 50cm (19⅝ in)
David Design, Sweden

Paolo Giordano
Bowls and tablet
Ceramic
Small: h. 6.5cm (2⅝ in) d. 10cm (3⅞ in) di. 9cm (3½ in)
Large: h. 7cm (2¾ in) d. 15cm (5⅞ in) di. 14cm (5½ in)
Tablet: h. 2.5cm (1in) w. 30cm (11¾ in) d. 15cm (5⅞ in)
I & I, Italy

Marta Laudani and Marco Romanelli
Plates, Mediterraneo
Gres
Small: h. 1.8cm (⅝ in) l. 21cm (8¼ in) d. 18.5cm (7¼ in)
Soup: h. 3.7cm (1⅜ in) l. 21cm (8¼ in) d. 19cm (7½ in)
Medium: h. 2.5cm (1in) l. 26cm (10¼ in) d. 24.5cm (9¾ in)
Large: h. 1.7cm (⅝ in) l. 33cm (13in) d. 30.5cm (12in)
Driade, Italy

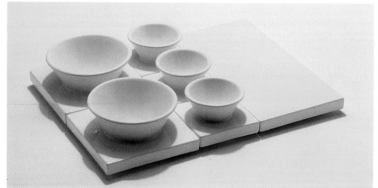

Salvatore Pischedda and Marie Darmody
Cup, Confuse
Ceramic
Cup: h. 5cm (2in) di. 8cm (3⅛ in)
Saucer: di 13.5cm (5¼ in)
Salvatore & Marie, Italy
Prototype

Borek Sipek
Porcelain tea set
Cup: h. 8cm (3⅛ in) w. 9cm (3½ in)
Sugar bowl: h. 9cm (3½ in) w. 17cm (6⅝ in)
Teapot: h. 18cm (7in) w. 22cm (8¾ in)
Milk jug: h. 17cm (6⅝ in) w. 9cm (3½ in)
Steltman Galleries, The Netherlands
Limited batch production

Erik-Jan Kwakkel
Cup, Double-cup
Porcelain
h. 11cm (4⅜ in) di. 9cm (3½ in)
REEEL, The Netherlands

Olgoj Chorchoj (Jan Nemecek and Michal Fronek)
Bowl, 40
Carbon fibre
di. 40/60cm (15¾/23⅝ in)
Tunnel, Czech Republic
Limited production

Bowl, Olgoj Chorchoj

Michal Fronek and Jan Nemecek are two Czech designers who founded the design group Olgoj Chorchoj (OC) in 1990.
Their limited-edition carbon-fibre bowl is one of a series of products using this extremely lightweight material.

Andrea Branzi
Mug with filter and saucer, Genetic Tales
Porcelain
h. 10cm (3 ⅞ in) di. 8.3cm (3 ¼ in)
Alessi, Italy

Christian Ghion
Vase, Ystas
Glass
h. 45cm (17 ¾ in) di. 15cm (5 ⅞ in)
One-off

Monica Guggisberg and Philip Baldwin
Faceted vase
Glass
h. 20cm (7 ⅞ in) di. 20cm (7 ⅞ in)
Verrerie de Nonfoux, Switzerland
One-off

Borek Sipek
Plate, TDF 11
Bohemian crystal, marble
di. 36cm (14 ⅛ in)
Steltman Galleries, The Netherlands
Limited batch production

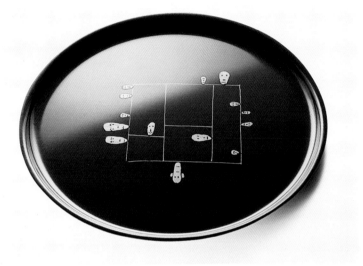

Anete Ring and Sara Rosenberg
Vase, Zen
Sand-cast aluminium
h. 13.5cm (5¼ in) w. 24.5cm (9¾ in)
d. 5.5cm (2⅛ in)
Rosenberg Ring Design, Brazil
Limited batch production

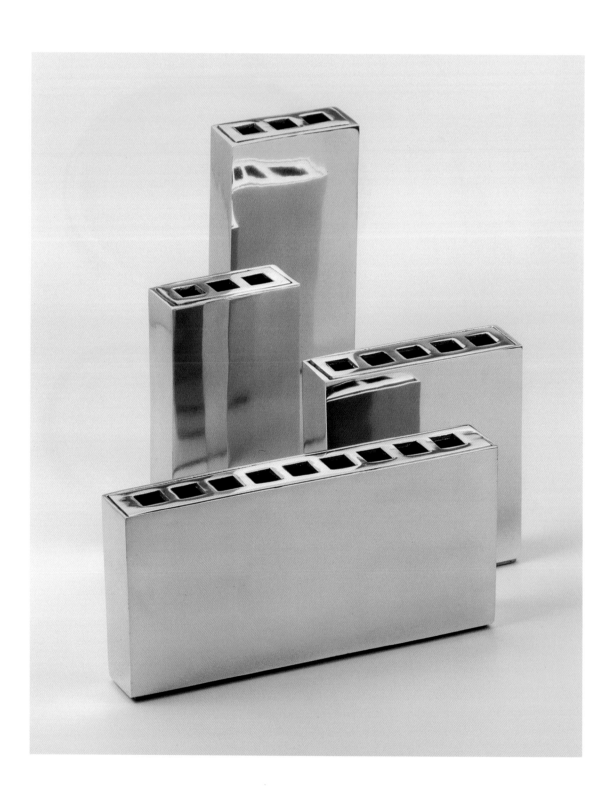

Anthony Di Bitonto
Candlestick/bud vase, Jojo
Extruded anodized aluminium
h. 10.2 / 15.3 / 20.3cm (4 / 6 / 8in)
di. 3.2–7cm (1¼ –2¾ in)
Benza Inc., USA

Eric LaRoye
Coffee-pot, Malgaro
Silver, Malgaro wood
h. 16.6cm (6½ in) w. 9.7cm (3⅞ in)
l. 17.5cm (6⅞ in)
Prototype

Pascal Mourgue
Vase, Les Trois Terres
Enamelled ceramic, aluminium
h. 21.5 / 26cm (8½ / 10¼ in) d. 4.5 / 6cm (1¾ / 2¼ in)
Ligne Roset, France

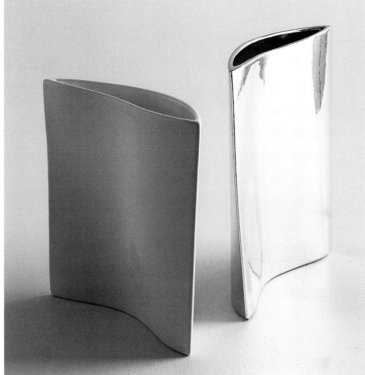

BOREK SÍPEK

EDITOR, THE INTERNATIONAL DESIGN YEARBOOK 1993

Speed! This one word probably epitomizes the essential change in design over the last fifteen years. Dictating thi
phone to make split-second decisions on projects in progress, it occurred to me how modern technology – it

The fax, now almost outdated, enabled us to react immediately in contacts with clients and the workplace. Th
in the street fifteen years ago. Drawings were done by hand or with Rapid-O-Graph, whereas no modern desig
magic. Indeed, many designers use computers as their basic tool.

During the economic boom of those earlier years the accent was upon prestige and opulence. Design becam
switched to design, and designers enjoyed a personality cult hitherto reserved for painters and sculptors. One did
recession, tastes changed and people sought more substantial and anonymous enhancement of their lifestyl

On the many occasions that I have roamed the Milan Salone with Ingo we have often been sickened by the she
always a few treasures which caught the attention.

Fashion is the fastest changing branch of design. **Writing about the last fifteen years in terms of fashion would
to no more than a slim volume. Design is somewhere in between, and designers may have to establish f
chair is conceived in a flash but the development process to the final product can take more than a year**

A great deal can change in fifteen years. It's a very short time!

e racing along the highway, interrupted at regular intervals by the mobile
ity – has had an impact on our craft.

ile phone, its shape and colour evolving each month, was not in evidence
o today is without an arsenal of advanced computers casting their 3D

ionable to the extent of replacing art objects in desirability. Galleries
a chair but became the proud owner of a Starck. With the onset of economic
ng the way for critics of ornament with their loathing of embellishment.

tity on offer. Everything had begun to look alike. There were, however,

compiling an encyclopedia. Architecture, on the other hand, would amount
selves where in the time-frame they wish to be placed. The idea for a good

Marcel Wanders
Disposable cutlery and bowl
Poplar wood
h. 4cm (1½ in) l. 13cm (5⅛ in) d. 4cm (1½ in)
Droog Design, The Netherlands for Oranienbaum
Prototype

Disposable bowl and cutlery and bread vase, Marcel Wanders
These two products were created for 'Couleur Locale', a project aimed at regenerating the local culture of Oranienbaum, Germany. The orange blossom sticking out of the bread vase is Marcel Wanders' reference to local orange trees which have been grown in wooden crates for the last 400 years, spending the winter indoors and living outside during the warmer months. The disposable bowl and cutlery are made from the wood of local poplar trees which are abundant and easily replaced.

Marcel Wanders
Bread vase, Oranienbaumer Viereck
Wholemeal orange loaf
h. 15cm (5 ⅞ in) w. 15cm (5 ⅞ in) d. 15cm (5 ⅞ in)
Droog Design, The Netherlands for Oranienbaum
Prototype

Katsuhiko Ogino
Cutlery, Project-21
Stainless steel
l. 20/20.5/21cm (7⅞/8⅛/8¼ in)
Tubameshinkou Industry, Japan

Cutlery, Project-21, Katsuhiko Ogino
This range of tableware is intended for people who have difficulty gripping traditional utensils. The cutlery may be grasped or held in different ways.

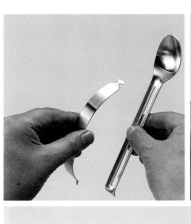   

Nina Tolstrup
Cutlery tool
Plastic
h. 8.5cm (3⅜ in) w. 3.5cm (1⅜ in) l. 21cm (8¼ in)
Prototype

Cutlery Tool, Nina Tolstrup
A four-in-one piece of cutlery combining knife, fork, spoon and teaspoon.

Randy Bell and Jose Perez for Herbst LaZar Bell, Inc.
Combined Flatware Utensil
Injected moulded polycarbonate
h. 1.3cm (½ in) w. 4cm (1½ in) l. 17.2cm (6¾ in)
Herbst LaZar Bell Inc., USA

Paola Navone
Salad/rice servers, Paloma
Polished stainless steel
Driade, Italy

Borek Sipek
Serving cutlery, TDF 00
Stainless steel
Steltman Galleries, The Netherlands
Limited batch production

TEXTILES

TEXTILES

Digital prints, fibre optics, plastics, polymers, polyurethane, resin, silicone, laminates – this year's textiles selection reflects how advances in new materials and technology are playing an increasingly important role in the work of textile designers.

It also highlights the artificiality of the boundaries between art, craft, design, and even engineering and science, as non-industrial artefacts – including one-off pieces by fibre artists, site-specific and bespoke pieces – feature alongside textiles designed for fashion, rugs and machine-made upholstery fabrics. Technology is also blurring the boundary between textiles and products – the 'wearable product' prototypes from Philips could equally well have featured in 'Textiles' as in the 'Products' chapter (see page 208).

In some countries the dichotomy between the crafts and industry has never been an issue, for example in Japan where textile designers and manufacturers combine century-old craft traditions with the latest materials and technology. In previous editions of *The International Design Yearbook* the work of Japanese textile designers has often featured heavily: this year it is clear that they continue to lead the way. Japan has no history of creating textiles for interiors, so it is from the fashion industry that new fabrics tend to emerge.

Ingo Maurer has chosen work by Yoshiki Hishinuma, one of the fourth generation of internationally acclaimed Japanese fashion designers, and Reiko Sudo of the Nuno Corporation who uses computers and advanced technologies to design complex weaves which appear handwoven and almost three-dimensional. Also featured are the one-off wall-based relief pieces and installations by Kyoko Kumai, one of Japan's leading textile artists whose work is exhibited in museums throughout the world, and Masako Hayashibe's pieces which use the traditional craft technique of crochet.

Perhaps a natural choice for Maurer is Sarah Taylor's textiles which combine the age-old craft of weaving with the cutting-edge technology of fibre optics, to produce threads of sparkling light shimmering across the weave. Capable of transmitting optical and digital information, fibre-optics technology is becoming increasingly interesting to designers and has been described by some textile experts as the medium of the future.

Salt
Knitted roman blinds, Creased Totems
Cotton, aluminium
h. 200cm (78⅜ in) w. 250cm (98⅜ in)
One-off

Creased Totems, Salt

Karina Holmes and June Swindell launched Salt in 1996 to bridge the gap between conceptual and one-off pieces and more commercial products. Using innovative combinations of materials and hand-weaving techniques, the duo create modular blinds, window treatments, sheers and screens which reflect an interest in natural and sculptural forms. Each piece allows light to pass through, while filtering out excess sunlight, obscuring unsightly views and providing privacy. The hand-knitted cotton Creased Totems blind with aluminium inserts plays with light and can filter it at different levels.

Sarah Taylor
Woven Fibre Optic Glove
Nylon monofilament, optical fibre
w. 12cm (4¾ in) l. 36cm (14⅛ in) d. 10cm (3⅞ in)
One-off

Kyoko Kumai
Wall hanging/sculpture, Blowing in the Wind
Stainless steel filaments
h. 13m (42¾ ft) w. 600cm (236⅛ in)
l. 600cm (236⅛ in) d. 500cm (196¾ in)
One-off

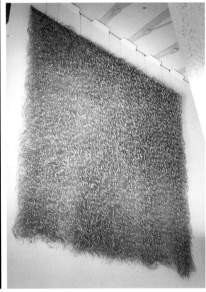

Woven Fibre Optic Glove, Sarah Taylor

Sarah Taylor weaves fibre-optic strands into fabrics. This one-off light-emitting glove was commissioned for permanent display in London's National Maritime Museum. Light is conducted along the length of the optical fibres using a light projector and rotating coloured discs to produce the effect of colour and movement. Fibre optics are perfect for fashion, furniture and interior design use as they do not emit UV light, or transmit heat or electricity. Part of Taylor's research project has been funded by the Japanese company Mitsubishi Rayon who see huge potential in the use of optical fibres.

Kyoko Kumai

Kyoko Kumai is one of Japan's leading textile artists and a self-taught weaver. For the past thirty years she has worked with industrial materials and since 1983 has exclusively used stainless steel to create her one-off pieces.

RON ARAD

EDITOR, THE INTERNATIONAL DESIGN YEARBOOK 1994

I cannot tell you about the state of design today – or in the last fifteen years. I have no urge to classify trend **design religion. Oscar Wilde once wrote: 'It is absurd to divide people into good or bad. People are either charmin**

Let's think of a new way to do *The International Design Yearbook* now that we know that only a handful of entrie us up to date with whatever.

When I was a guest editor in 1994, I tried (and failed) to convince the publisher to print each and every receive than my polite selection. Let's think of a new way of doing it (changes are always good). Please write with yo write to me (I was only a guest), not to Ingo (he is a guest too), but to Laurence King at 71 Great Russell Stree

RON ARAD

EDITOR, THE INTERNATIONAL DESIGN YEARBOOK 1994

and fads; I am deeply suspicious of people who do. **I do not subscribe to any**

r tedious.' I feel the same way about design – it either charms me or escapes me.

ally survive the year. Let's leave it to the dailies, weeklies and monthlies to keep

try. No vetoes. It would have made a far more valid document of a design year

eas (you might be from Madras, Milan, Bogotá or Berlin – international!). Don't

ndon WC1B 3BN, UK.

Chunghie Lee
Wall hanging/room divider, Work-98
Hand-woven hemp
h. 200cm (78⅝ in) w. 230cm (90½ in)
One-off

Emily Du Bois
Weaving, Ancestor 1
Tapa cloth, cotton thread
h. 71cm (28in) w. 61cm (24in) d. 1.3cm (½ in)
One-off

Ulf Moritz
Curtain fabric, Origami
Polyamide, polyester, acetate, cotton,
polyurethane
w. 130cm (51⅛ in)
Sahco Hesslein, Germany

Ulf Moritz
Upholstery fabrics, Elepunto and Elemento
Wool
w. 150cm (59in)
Sahco Hesslein, Germany

Masako Hayashibe
Textile, A Vessel Transmigrated II
Raw silk, whitewash
h. 15cm (5⅞ in) di. 30cm (11¾ in)
One-off

Masako Hayashibe
Textile, A Vessel Transmigrated I
Raw silk
h. 15cm (5⅞ in) di. 30cm (11¾ in)
One-off

170

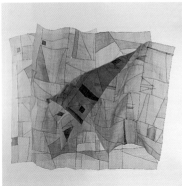   

A Vessel Transmigrated I & II, Masako Hayashibe
Masako Hayashibe uses the traditional craft technique of hand crochet to create
these vessels from raw silk; whitewash has been applied to the one above.

Yehudit Katz
Textile, Triptych-Moiré
Waxed linen, raw silk, celluloid
w. 220cm (86⅝ in) l. 180cm (70⅞ in) d. 15cm (5⅞ in)
One-off

Yehudit Katz
Wall hanging, Belts
Linen, raw silk, celluloid
w. 90cm (35⅜ in) d. 98cm (38⅝ in)
One-off

Peter Maly
Rugs, Pythagore and Euclide
Wool, stainless steel
w. 170-200cm (66⅞-78⅝ in)
l. 140-200cm (55⅛-78⅝ in)
Ligne Roset, France

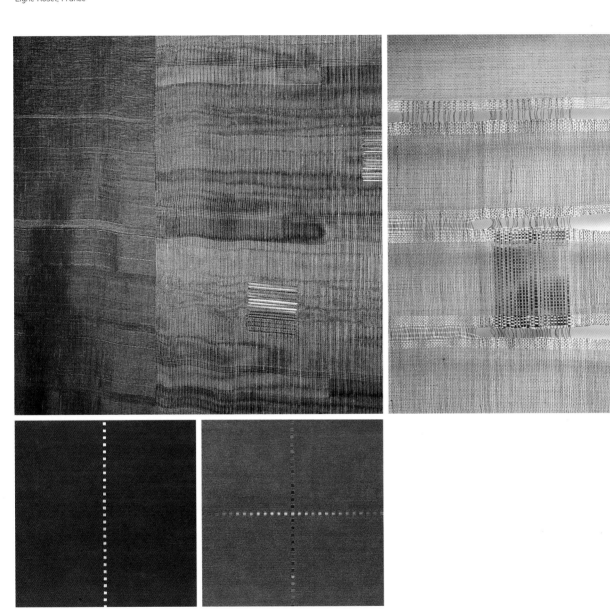

Asla Bekit, Daniel Henry, Sara Fredhave and
Sherife Ünal
Linen/linen-polyamide knits
Various sizes
La Cambre Ecole Nationale Supérieure des Arts
Visuels, Belgium – European Schools Network
From Masters of Linen
'Textile–Essence–Innovation' Exhibition

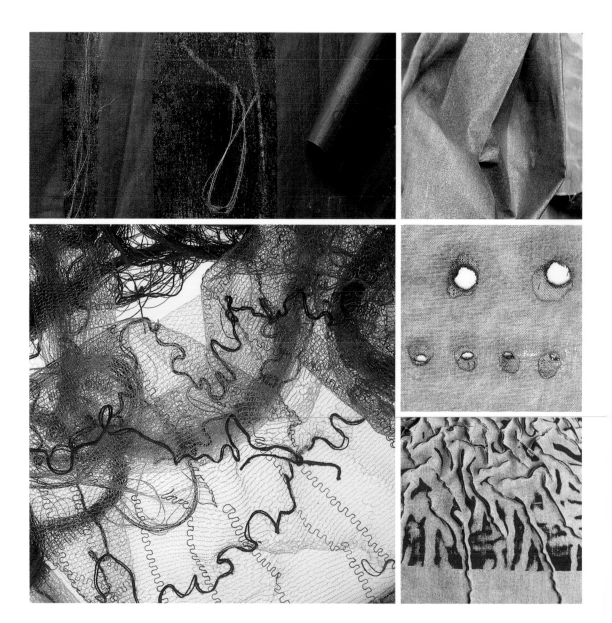

'Textile – Essence – Innovation', Ensav La Cambre

For the past nine years, eight European design schools have worked together on an annual textile project. Each year one of the schools collaborates with a professional partner to lead the project and in 1999 it was the turn of Ensav La Cambre in Brussels, working with Masters of Linen on 'Textile – Essence – Innovation'. Selected students spent a month working in La Cambre's textile studio experimenting with and combining new threads and technological treatments and applying these to create future visions for linen. Five pieces by the following students are shown here: Asla Bekit (top left and centre right) and Sherife Ünal (bottom left) from the Fachhochschule in Hanover; Daniel Henry from Ensav La Cambre, Brussels (bottom right), and Sara Fredhave of the Designskole, Copenhagen (top right).

Fabio Carlesso
Fabric, Rocko
Resin, fabric, silicone
w. 140cm (55⅛ in)
Blue Project, Italy
Limited batch production

Fabio Carlesso
Fabric, Rocko
Resin, fabric, silicone
w. 140cm (55⅛ in)
Blue Project, Italy
Limited batch production

Hiroko Suwa
Fabric, Tsumami Shibori
Polyester
w. 115cm (45¼ in) l. 115cm (45¼ in)
Nuno Corporation, Japan

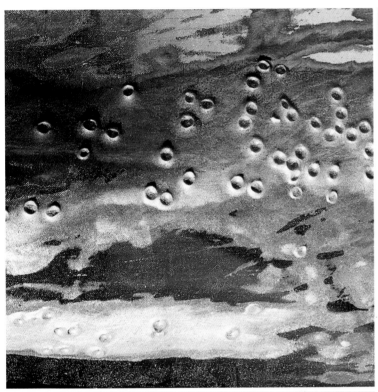

Fabio Carlesso
Fabric, Rocko
Resin, fabric, silicone
w. 140cm (55⅛ in)
Blue Project, Italy
Limited batch production

Fabio Carlesso
Fabric, Rocko
Resin, fabric, silicone
w. 140cm (55⅛ in)
Blue Project, Italy
Limited batch production

Santos & Adolfsdóttir
Fabric, sa003
Printed and laser-cut polyester polyamide
w. 160cm (63in)
Santos & Adolfsdóttir, UK

Jakob Schlaepfer for création baumann
Fabric, Elvino
90% wool, 10% viscose
w. 140cm (55⅛ in)
création baumann, Switzerland

174

Reiko Sudo and Yoko Ando
Fabric, Itomari
60% wool, 40% rayon
w. 74cm (29⅛ in)
Nuno Corporation, Japan

Itomari, Yoko Ando/Reiko Sudo, Nuno Corporation
Inspired by Japanese Temari – tiny toy threadballs, precision-wound in many colours and traditionally as precious as Fabergé eggs –
this woven wool and rayon fabric is felted under heat and pressure to create a surface of little balls.

Yoshiki Hishinuma
Fabric, 9WDMK622
Base-wrinkled polyester georgette laminated
with polyurethane film
(70% polyester, 30% polyurethane)
w. 70cm (27½ in) l. 20m (65½ ft)
Hishinuma Associates Co., Japan

Yoshiki Hishinuma

One of the fourth generation of internationally acclaimed Japanese fashion designers, Yoshiki Hishinuma has designed under his own label since 1994. Unable to find the fabrics he required, Hishinuma began designing and producing his own. Since his work first appeared in *The International Design Yearbook* it has evolved from designs that create an illusion of texture, to taking small areas of predominantly synthetic fabrics and using heat-setting techniques to create physical texture.

Yoshiki Hishinuma
Fabric, 9SHTD622
Base-shrunk 100% polyester taffeta
laminated with polyurethane film
w. 100cm (39⅜ in) l. 40m (131¼ ft)
Hishinuma Associates Co., Japan

Yoshiki Hishinuma
Fabric, 9WDMK407
Base-shrunk 100% polyester taffeta
laminated with polyurethane film
w. 100cm (39⅜ in) l. 40m (131¼ ft)
Hishinuma Associates Co., Japan

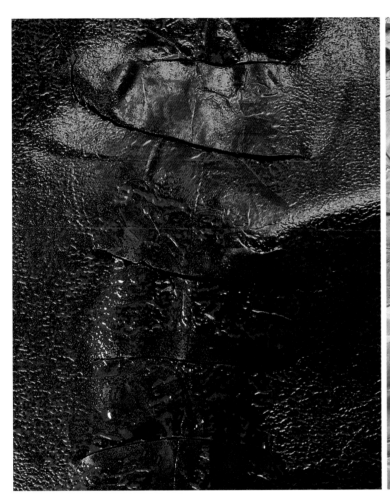

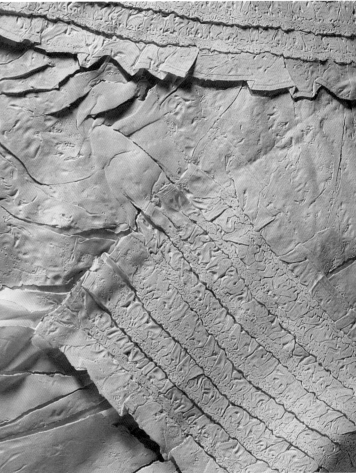

Yoshiki Hishinuma
Fabric, 9SHTD622
Base-shrunk 100% polyester taffeta
laminated with polyurethane film
w. 100cm (39⅜ in) l. 40m (131¼ ft)
Hishinuma Associates Co., Japan

Yoshiki Hishinuma
Fabric, 9WDMK407
Base-shrunk 100% polyester taffeta
laminated with polyurethane film
w. 100cm (39⅜ in) l. 40m (131¼ ft)
Hishinuma Associates Co., Japan

JEAN NOUVEL

EDITOR, THE INTERNATIONAL DESIGN YEARBOOK 1995

What changes have taken place in design in the last ten years? I asked myself this question while visiting the
Design is becoming largely style ... in the sense of concern for style, effects, anecdotes, the search for an art

Perhaps these small, simple things are essential for the survival of an economy…

More than ever I believe in the search for the essence; for a demanding design, with no concession to indulger

More than ever I believe that poetry is not incompatible with this attitude and, from Ron Arad to Ross Loveg

For that, thanks.

niture Fair. My impression is that increasingly the rigour lacks vigour.
rentiation as if these small anomalies could suffice to create an identity.

e picturesque. In any case, this is the only kind of design that interests me.

Alberto Meda to Ingo Maurer, these are the few who prove it.

Debbie Jane Buchan
Screen-printed surface design, Sparkle
Debbie Jane Buchan, UK

Helle Abild
Digitally printed fabric, Flowers for Summer IV
from y2k Quilt
Reactive dye printed on cotton
w. 101.6cm (40in) l. 178cm (70in)

Helle Abild
Digitally printed fabric, Green for Spring III
from y2k Quilt
Reactive dye printed on cotton
w. 101.6cm (40in) l. 178cm (70in)

Michael Sodeau
Rug, Walking on Water (detail)
Wool
w. 180cm (70⅞ in) l. 240cm (94½ in)
Christopher Farr, UK
Limited batch production

Studio Harry & Camila
Fabric, Gamma Speed
Bleached paper, rubber, fishnet,
hand-knotted synthetic ribbon, natural cords
w. 135cm (53⅛ in)
Prototype

Studio Harry & Camila
Fabric, Molecule
Synthetic stretch fabric, sequins
w. 135cm (53⅛ in)
Prototype

Studio Harry & Camila
Fabric, Dry Red Flower Purple Blood
Dried flowers, paint, rubber
w. 135cm (53⅛ in)
Prototype

Studio Harry & Camila
Fabric, Purple Flowers
Synthetic flowers, paper, rubber
w. 135cm (53⅛ in)
Prototype

180

Bute Design Studio
Upholstery fabric, Iona
85% wool, 15% nylon
w. 130cm (51⅛ in)
Bute Fabrics, UK

Bute Design Studio
Upholstery fabric, Melrose
93% wool, 7% nylon
w. 130cm (51⅛ in)
Bute Fabrics, UK

Bute Design Studio
Upholstery fabric, Dunbar
96% wool, 4% nylon
w. 138cm (54⅜ in)
Bute Fabrics, UK

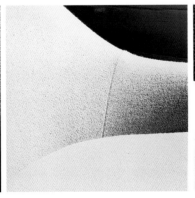

Bute Fabrics

Bute is a fabric-weaving company based on the island of the same name, off the west coast of Scotland. Founded in the late 1940s, it wove cloth for fashion houses like Hardy Amies until the 1960s when it started producing upholstery fabrics. In 1998 the company teamed up with the London-based furniture manufacturer SCP and a group of designers – Tom Dixon, Matthew Hilton, Jasper Morrison, Andrew Stafford and Terence Woodgate – to create a collection of furniture. The designers spent time going through Bute's archives and advised the company to make its fabrics much sharper, with more colour, texture and variety. Two of Bute's new fabrics are Dunbar and Melrose. Dunbar is a highly textural, contrast basket-weave fabric and was chosen by Terence Woodgate to upholster the angled headboard of his new bed, REM. Melrose is a medium texture reverse twist wool fabric produced in twenty-four different tones. It has been used on Woodgate's Sofa System and Andrew Stafford's newly launched Stafford armchair.

Fernando and Humberto Campana
Rug, Animado
Artificial grass, cow hide, rubber
w. 100cm (39 ⅜ in) l. 250cm (98 ⅜ in)
Campana Objetos, Brazil
One-off

182

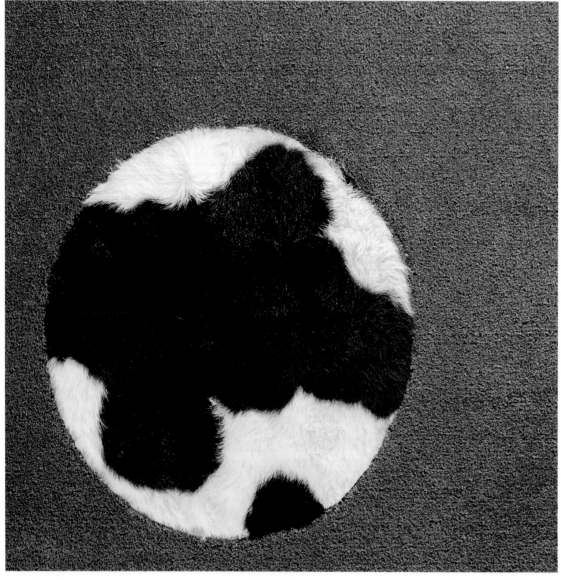

Kris Ruhs
Rugs
Wool
w. 200cm (78 ⅝ in) l. 300cm (118in)
Kam Sun Laupheim, Germany
Limited batch production

Stefano Giovannoni
Carpet, Pluto's Eyes
Wool
w. 185cm (72 ¾ in) l. 250cm (98 ⅜ in)
Asplund, Sweden

PRODUCTS

Now we know that technology works, it is losing interest as an end in itself. New technologies are launched, become obsolete and then extinct, almost before we start becoming familiar with them, and with so much 'stuff' competing for our attention, products need to appeal to us on other levels.

Take computers, for example. As the iMac proved when it single-handedly rescued Apple in 1998, in an overcrowded industry computers need to sell on looks and fashion. This year the iBook laptop has arrived, also designed by Jonathan Ive, and as with its older sibling, appearance will be a large factor in its success.

Product as friend or pet seems to be one way to stand out, and the duller the function the cuter the product. Philips and Alessi were the first manufacturers to introduce 'friendlier' styling and cute characters to the kitchen. This year sees Alessandro Mendini's Anna Time kitchen timer for Alessi, and Philips lets a cartoon pet escape into the office with its V-mail desk-top video camera. Inspired by the 'human condition of being alone at home', products as companions and entertainers is a theme in Pascal Anson's Stars in Your Eyes mirror and Gaby Klasmer's Doorman door stop, both part of the 'Home Alone' collection of objects created by a group of students and tutors from the Royal College of Art in London.

With grey boxes on the way out, what shapes will technology be taking? The television is fast disappearing into a flat panel on the wall, no longer powered by a bulky cathode ray tube but increasingly liquid crystal display (LCD) – the LC-20V2 is a new example from the designers at Sharp. Rotolo by Francesco Pellisari and Ron Arad has the ability to generate stereo sound from one, rather than two speakers and is unhampered by the usual tangle of messy cables. Prototype electronic clothing by Philips Design and Research demonstrates products merging with textiles and garments, while IDEO's prototype Message watches for Seiko are capable of sending and receiving verbal and written communications. Zuzu's Petals, Herbst LaZar Bell's solar-powered concept computer docking station, endeavours to humanize technology.

However, if technology is making our world increasingly complex, there are those designers who are looking for a far simpler life, as expressed in Cotelletto's Kannste Knicken beer mat/ashtray, Helena Mattila-Sorri's wall calendar, Nina Tolstrup's toilet roll/magazine holder, and Feldmann & Schultchen's birdcage.

Chifuyu Tanaka
Digital video camera, PV1
Magnesium, ABS, polycarbonate
h. 12.8cm (5in) w. 6.1cm (2⅜ in)
d. 10.8cm (4¼ in)
Canon, Japan

Jun Akabane, Hiroshi Kobayashi,
Arata Ono and Hideki Ito
Advanced Photo System camera, Pronea S
Polycarbonate
h. 8.7cm (3½ in) w. 11.6cm (4½ in) d. 9.1cm (3½ in)
Nikon, Japan

186

Seiji Kurokawa
Digital ViewCam, VL-DC5
Aluminium, plastic
h. 9.7cm (3¾ in) w. 14.4cm (5⅝ in) l. 6.5cm (2⅝ in)
Sharp Corporation, Japan

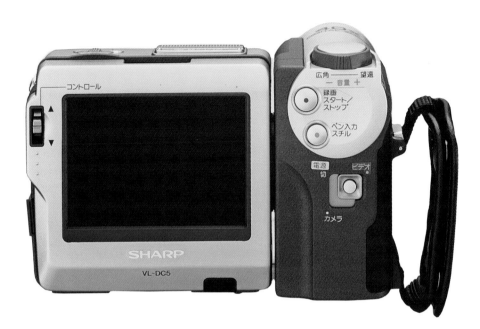

Andy Davey and Rochelle Smith
Laptop computer
Plastic
h. 3cm (1⅛ in) w. 30cm (11¾ in) l. 23cm (9in)
NEC Design, Japan
Prototype

Laptop Computer, Andy Davey and Rochelle Smith, NEC

This design came about through an investigation into laptop concepts that would be more flexible for individual users than those currently on the market. The prototype has a slide-off keyboard that reveals top access to replaceable peripherals, and any hard, floppy or compact disks can remain active via a stackable drive jacket system, allowing access at any time. The keyboard is operated remotely using infra-red, enabling the user to select their own comfortable working position.

Taisuke Saeki, Harumi Sakamoto,
Hiroyuki Mitsui and Iida Kouichi
20 inch LCD television, LC-20V2
Aluminium, ABS plastic
h. 43.5cm (17⅛ in) w. 71cm (28in) d. 18cm (7in)
Sharp Corporation, Japan

Hideki Kawai
Camera, IXUS M-1
Polycarbonate, ABS, stainless steel
h. 5.5cm (2⅛ in) w. 8.5cm (3⅜ in)
l. 3.5cm (1⅜ in)
Canon, Japan

Sharp Corporate Design Centre
Notebook-PC, PC-A 150
Magnesium, plastic
h. 2.1cm (⅞ in) w. 21.2cm (8¼ in)
l. 25.9cm (10¼ in)
Sharp Electronics, Germany

Sharp Corporate Design Centre
Portable MD player, MD-MS701H
Plastic
h. 2.9cm (1⅛ in) w. 8.7cm (3½ in)
l. 8.1cm (3¼ in)
Sharp Electronics, Germany

ALESSANDRO MENDINI

EDITOR, THE INTERNATIONAL DESIGN YEARBOOK 1996

190

I often ask myself which of my projects have the moral right to enter the new millennium. Which architec
threshold of the new era? What are the characteristics of the objects that are compatible with human dignity?

The answer is this: **the only architectural expressions, the only objects that can be justifiably admitted to the**
to human beings in a deep and broad manner. The short and too often sterile careers thus far enjoyed by the ob
withstanding the challenge of measuring themselves by the poetic standards set forth by ancient objects, the
of the soul in the material realm, an unobtrusive, respectful soul.

The degree of spirituality, the ethical calibre of a given project becomes the essential quality that authorizes ce
example, over the last twenty-five years the furniture industry has systematically espoused every school of the
They have been: Spatial, Surrealist, Folk, Political, Martial, Horror, Primitive, Wild, Vegetable, Sexual, Micro, M
Amoral, Moralist, Young, Popular, Traditional, Neo-Kitsch, Country, Ironic, Hyper-Decorative, Stylistic, Neo-Fi
Realistic, Techno-Playful, Technological, Brutalistic, Post Atomic, Aerodynamic, Indian, African, Third-W
Glamorous.

The kaleidoscope and labyrinth are, of course, organizational organisms, and eclecticism can be critically struc
painstaking attempt to bring about a fundamental behavioural transformation on an anthropological level.
foot in the old millennium and the other almost in the next. Of course, the debate regarding the ideal abod
ocean: always different and always the same. Aside from considerations of our actual physical habitations, v
or dreamed about: the home of our father, a friend or a lover...

Interior design and furnishings are destined to remain a jumbled soup of images, memories and ideas. It is i
lies hidden that kernel of poetry, that spiritual spark capable of animating the material realm. **The poetic appr**
standardized Utopian architecture and objects, with their cerebral, imaginary insubstantiality, positioned in
traditions, creating a situation in which the concept of habitation is transformed into a mirage.

cts, which objects of design, which objects in general are qualified to cross the

nnium are those that have been designed to have soul, that are capable of relating
ur design efforts, the habitations of the industrial age, must be capable of
ured places of anthropological ritual. In this way design becomes an expression

omena and not others to cross over with dignity into the next millennium. For
rackpot ideology. Furniture and objects have served an infinite variety of masters.
ographical, Ecological, Artistic, Hyper-Realistic, Instruments, Self-Produced,
Futuristic, Neo-Pop, Neo-Rational, Humble, Minimal, Neo-Tech, Primary, Native,
ıtal, Spiritual, Ritual, Totemic, Theatrical, Literary, Archaeological, Playful and

similar manner. The apparent chaos of the above list of adjectives demonstrates a
des of enormous effort, we are finally managing to take the giant step – with one
r be definitively resolved, nor should it be. It's rather like the waves upon the
a very well defined mental home, the net product of homes we have possessed

human trait that we must seek the redemption of any project undertaken: for here
sign strives to create an environment free of the harsh cruelty of constructed,
ions, immersed in space-time dimensions that invade and rupture past and future

Kazuki Isono
LCD Data Projector, VPL-X2000
PS plastic
h. 23.7cm (9 ⅜ in) w. 56.2cm (22⅛ in)
l. 64.9cm (25½ in)
Sony Corporation, Japan

Yoshinori Yamada
Compact MD/CD component system, CMT-MD1
Aluminium, glass, plastic
h. 21.5cm (8½ in) w. 24.5cm (9¾ in)
l. 56cm (22in)
Sony Corporation, Japan

Masakazu Kanatani
MD walkman, MZ-E44
ABS plastic
h. 1.8cm (⅝ in) w. 9.2cm (3⅝ in) l. 8.7cm (3½ in)
Sony Corporation, Japan

Tsutomu Kurokawa
Television stand, Quit
Chromed steel, wood, aluminium
h. 67/96/108cm (26⅜ /37¾ /42½ in)
w. 34cm (13⅜ in) d. 34cm (13⅜ in)
Time & Style, Japan
Limited production

Tangerine
Video Webphone
Plastic
h. 19.5cm (7¾ in) w. 3.4cm (1⅜ in)
d. 22cm (8¾ in)
Chaplet Systems Inc., Taiwan
Prototype

Video Webphone, Tangerine, Chaplet Systems Inc.
Aimed at the domestic and small/home office market, Tangerine's video webphone has
an optional 'Qwerty' keyboard and a height- and angle-adjustable colour LCD screen.
The position and angle of the camera can be easily adjusted to improve communication
of images and objects during telephone calls.

Yoshinori Inukai
Color Flatbed Scanner,
Canon CanoScan 620P ABS
h. 6.3cm (2½ in) w. 25.6cm (10in)
d. 37.3cm (14¾ in)
Canon, Japan

Peter Sheehan and Cathal Loughnane (Design
Partners)/Denis O'Keefe (Logitech)
Three button touch-sense mouse, WingMan
Force Feedback Mouse
h. 2.5cm (1in) w. 9cm (3½ in)
l. 12cm (4¾ in)
Logitech Engineers and Immersion Inc., USA

Greg Holderfield and
Josh Goldfarb/Herbst LaZar Bell Inc.
Paper shredder, GBC Shredmaster Shark 200
Injection-moulded plastic, cast aluminium
h. 10.2cm (4in) w. 6.4cm (2½ in) l. 30.5cm (12in)

Ken Wood and Roman Gebhard (Lunar Design)/Steve Kaneko,
Jim Stewart and Chris Tobey (Microsoft Corporation)
PC-based telephone, Microsoft Cordless Phone System
Injection-moulded ABS
Handset: h. 20cm (7⅞ in) w. 6cm (2¼ in) d. 5cm (2in)
Handset base: h. 10cm (4in) w. 11cm (4½ in) d. 13cm (5in)
Microsoft Corporation, USA

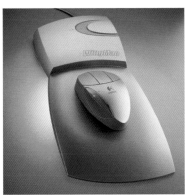

WingMan Force Feedback Mouse, Design Partners, Logitech Engineers and Immersion Inc.

This three-button mouse turns body motion into onscreen action for computer game players and Web users. Users can experience touch sensations such as gravity, recoil, slipping on ice, 'walking' up or down hills, wind, earthquakes and the motion of a train.

Shredmaster Shark 200, Herbst LaZar Bell Inc.

This paper shredder adjusts to fit most round or rectangular wastepaper baskets, while allowing ample space for other rubbish. It can process up to four pages at once and is slim enough to fit into a briefcase for business travel.

Anthony Mixides
Toaster, Tinker Toaster
Plastic
d. 24.5cm (9¾in) di. 18cm (7in)
Kingston University, UK
Prototype

Alessandro Mendini
Timer, Anna Time
Thermoplastic resin, chrome-plated zinc
(Zamak)
h. 12cm (4¾in) di. 10.5cm (4⅛in)
Alessi, Italy

Philips Design
Kitchen scales, Precision
ABS plastic, stainless steel
h. 4.5cm (1¾in) w. 21.5cm (8½in)
l. 25cm (9⅞in)
Philips Electronics/Philips Design,
The Netherlands

Tony McIntyre and Ian Dampney/Random
Technologies
Skate sharpener, Mosquito
Nylon (20% glass filled) or acetal,
artificial diamonds, nickel
h. 12.5cm (4⅞in) w. 4.5cm (1¾in) d. 5.6cm (2⅛in)
Mosquito Tribologies Corporation, Canada

Vincent Shum
Electronic Guest Book
Plastic
h. 136cm (53½in) di. 68cm (26¾in)
Nanyang Polytechnic G.S.I., Singapore
Prototype

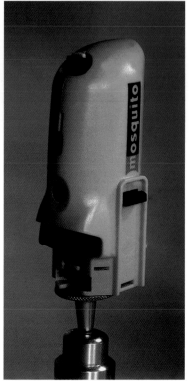

Philips Design
Desktop camera, V-mail Camera
(USB Desktop Video Camera)
ABS, polycarbonate,
chromed zinc (Zamak), Desmopan
h. 6cm (2¼in) w. 7.1cm (2¾in) l. 10.2cm (4in)
Philips Electronics/Philips Design,
The Netherlands

 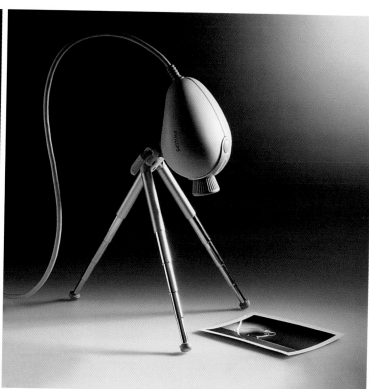

V-mail Camera, Philips

This video camera, which resembles a cartoon pet, is aimed at those who want to exhibit themselves on the Internet. It takes twenty-four pictures per second and records digital-quality sound to help with net conferences and video mail.

Roman Kovár
Sunglasses
Polypropylene
Standard size
Prototype

Shosaku Kawashima
Head-mounted display, Canon Glasses-type
Display GT270
Polycarbonate, titanium, polyester elastomer
h. 9.2cm (3 ⅝ in) w. 17.1cm (6 ⅝ in)
d. 19.5cm (7 ¾ in)
Canon, Japan

Puls Design
Ultrasound mobility aid, Sensix
Plastic
h. 4.1cm (1 ½ in) w. 21.5cm (8 ½ in)
l. 19.6cm (7 ¾ in)
Obrira Optik Brillen Rathenow, Germany

Simon Andrews
Mobile phone, Odyssey
ABS, silicone rubber
w. 6.5cm (2 ⅜ in) l. 10cm (3 ⅞ in)
d. 3.5cm (1 ¾ in)
Kingston University, UK
Prototype

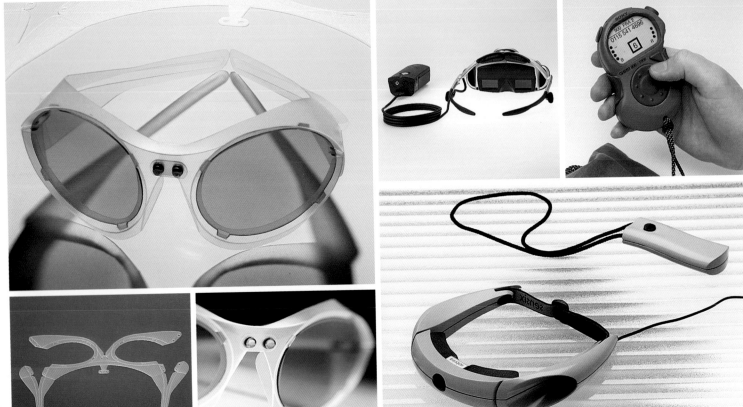

Glasses-type Display. Shosaku Kawashima. Canon

When connected to a television, video or DVD-player, this pair of glasses, constructed from flexible titanium alloy, makes it possible for the viewer to experience large-screen images. In a small room, or on a train or plane, the user has the experience of watching a 52-inch screen television from a distance of two metres (6 ½ feet).

Apple iBook
Jonathan Ive
Laptop computer, Apple iMac
Polycarbonate, rubber
h. 29.5cm (11⅝ in) l. 34.4cm (13½ in)
d. 4.6cm (1¾ in)
Apple, USA

Prima Ricerca and Sviluppo
Electric bicycle, Power Bike
Cast aluminium, carbon fibre
h. 85cm (33 ½ in) w. 43cm (17in) l. 165cm (65in)
Prima Ricerca & Sviluppo, Italy

Marc Newson
Ford 021C Concept 2
Carbon fibre
Engine type 1.6 litre Zetec-SE
Front wheel drive, 4 speed automatic transmission
Front seats: B+B Italia, Italy; analogue
instruments: Ikepod Watch Company, Switzerland
Ford, Italy

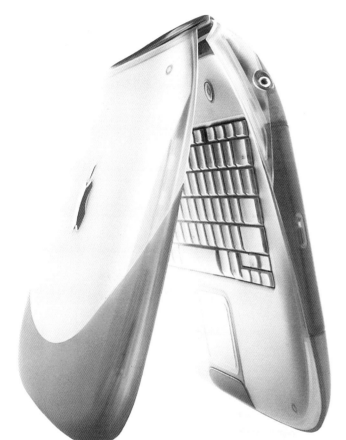

iBook, Jonathan Ive, Apple

The iBook is the portable version of the iMac, the hugely successful home computer
launched by Apple in 1998. It was due largely to the iMac that 1998 was Apple's first
profitable year since 1995. The iMac's ground-breaking design and colourful, translucent
casing took it into a class of its own. As a consequence, the computer industry is now
placing a greater emphasis on design and styling – the success of the iMac has proved that
computers do not have to be boring grey boxes. Like its predecessor, the iBook has been
styled by the British-born designer Jonathan Ive, and its success in its target market –
homes and schools – will probably be mainly due to its appearance. Technically, the iBook's
biggest novelty is wireless networking, which enables users to access the Internet up to 46
metres (150 feet) from where their hub or base station is connected to the telephone line.
Although wireless networking is not new, standard PC notebooks do not have a wireless
antenna built into the case.

RICHARD SAPPER

EDITOR, THE INTERNATIONAL DESIGN YEARBOOK 1998

For many years I have had on my table the blade of a Stone Age axe. It is probably more than 10,000 years ol
changed over the last decade and a half?' It also provides other answers, such as why we should care about

The blade has been cut from a heavy, impossibly hard stone I do not know but which resembles obsidian, and
have no idea how long it took to make, but it must have been months. And of these long months, more tha
work of art. As the great American graphic designer Paul Rand put it, a designer makes poetry out of prose.

This means that as soon as Stone Age man had discovered how to make an axe that worked, he wanted to m
something elementary, but also indefinable with rationale, productivity, cost effectiveness, numbers or pro

So I do not think that time can really change or influence design. But the things surrounding it, yes. Until
kitsch. Now we still have good design, but also acclaimed, famous, publicized but nevertheless still horrer

ovides for me, privately, the answer to the question 'How has design

design and what they are good for.

nd to an incredibly elegant, smooth form with a very sharp cutting edge. I

not gone into making a blade that works, but into making out of a tool a

tiful. Why? Because **the desire for beauty is something innate in us,**

es from somewhere else, a reflection of eternity.

decades ago, product design was either good or anonymous, nondescript

entic kitsch. This creates some confusion, I think.

200

Ross Lovegrove
Kettle
Stainless steel, plastic
h. 17.5cm (6 ⅞ in) di. 18cm (7in)
Hackman Designor, Finland

Metz und Kindler Produktdesign
Decorating set, Cream
Polypropylene, stainless steel, coated fabric
h. 40cm (15 ¾ in) w. 15cm (5 ⅞ in) d. 15cm (5 ⅞ in)
W.F. Kaiser, Germany

Enzo Mari
Gardening set
Polyamide
h. 29.5cm (11⅝ in) w. 5cm (2in)
Alessi, Italy

Feldmann & Schultchen
Bottle opener
Stainless steel
w. 4cm (1½ in) l. 12cm (4 ¾ in) d. 0.5cm (¼ in)
Prototype

Sofia Olsson
Can opener, ÖPPNA
Extruded anodized aluminium, steel
IKEA, Sweden

Carsten Joergensen
Garlic press, Allium
Teflon-plated aluminium
h. 4cm (1½ in) w. 3.5cm (1⅜ in) l. 16cm (6¼ in)
Inter Bodum, Switzerland

Enzo Mari
Gardening trowel
Cast aluminium
h. 31cm (12⅛ in) w. 8.5cm (3⅜ in)
Alessi, Italy

Yellow Circle
Kitchen wall scales, Integrale
Metal, polystyrene
h. 34cm (13⅜ in) w. 23cm (9in) l. 5cm (2in)
Soehnle Waagen, Germany

Jasper Morrison
Door handle and window pull, Gira
Brass, matt chrome finish
h. 5.1cm (2in) w. 14.3cm (5⅜in)
d. 6.9cm (2¾in)
Colombo Design, Italy

Richard Sapper
Door handle, Laser
Brass
h. 4.7cm (1⅞in) w. 6.3cm (2½in)
l. 13.8cm (5½in) d. 6.3cm (2½in)
Olivari B., Italy

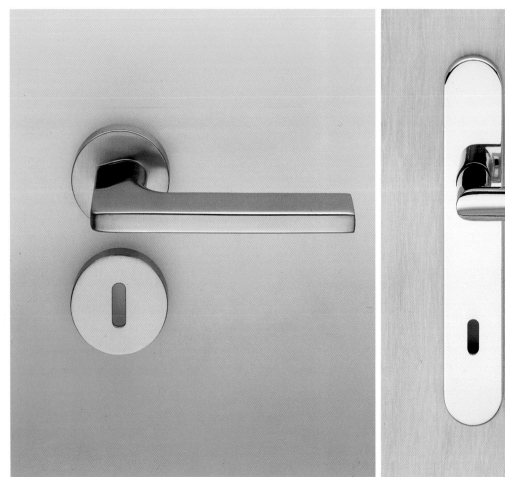

Pascal Anson
Light and mirror, Stars in Your Eyes
di. 40cm (15¾ in)
Post Design for Memphis, Italy

Peter Maly and Carsten Gollnick
Homeware collection, Le Rêve d'Edo
Blown glass, beech, moulded aluminium
h. 16–34cm (6¼ –13⅜ in)
di. 20–31cm (7⅞ –12⅛ in)
Ligne Roset, France

Gaby Klasmer
Door stop, Doorman
Stainless steel
h. 29cm (11⅜ in)
Post Design for Memphis, Italy

'Home Alone', RCA Furniture Design students and Post Design for Memphis
Two products from the 'Home Alone' project. Pascal Anson's ingenious and amusing Stars in Your Eyes literally produces the effect of stars in the pupils of the viewer's eyes when looking into the mirror. Gaby Klasmer's Doorman is a friendly-looking stainless steel door stop.

Thierry Gaugain, Patrick Jouin and Jean-Marie
Massaud
Mutable Floor
Aluminium, turf
w. 230cm (90½ in) d. 150cm (59in)
Luxlab, France
Prototype

204

Luxlab

Luxlab is a group of three young French designers who describe themselves as 'Idealists of the Domestic Interior'.
Mutable Floor is a garden for the interior – a pressed aluminium structure contains turf which is automatically nourished
and treated with anti-fungus protection; the shape of the lawn can be changed using air jacks and airbags housed in the
frame. The stainless steel fireplace with Pyrex duct and vacuum filter can be installed in a space without a chimney,
while the glass table contains water agitated by a hidden pump, and a lighting system which creates a moving projection
of light and shadow.

Susan Guempel and Urs Kamber (Svitalia)
Bookends
Anodized aluminium
h. 16/24cm (6¼ /9½ in)
w. 12/16cm (4¾ /6¼ in)
d. 21/16cm (8¼ /6¼ in)
Svitalia, Switzerland

Cotelletto
Beer mat/ashtray, Kannste Knicken
Cardboard
h. 9cm (3½ in) w. 9cm (3½ in) d. 0.2cm (⅜ in)
Prototype

Ross Menuez
Magazine rack, U-rack
Phenolic laminate
h. 25.5cm (10in) w. 23cm (9in) l. 28cm (11in)
Prototype & Production, USA
One-off

Theo Williams
Magnetic memo board, Big Mag
Lacquered stainless steel, magnets
h. 36cm (14⅛ in) w. 64cm (25⅛ in)
d. 3.5cm (1⅜ in)
Wireworks, UK

Rhoderik Moik-Tayali
Wardrobe, Häng Auf
Rope, steel
h. 3.5cm (39⅜ in) w. 30.5 (12in) l. 54cm (21¼ in)
Cotelletto, Germany

Kannste Knicken, Cotelletto
A beer mat that can be folded and used as a one-time ashtray.

Nina Tolstrup
Toilet roll / magazine holder
Stainless steel
h. 62cm (24 ⅜ in) w. 26cm (10 ¼ in)
d. 9cm (3 ½ in)
Habitat, UK

Jörg Ratzlaff
Toilet seat, Zenzit Madera
Laminated wood, aluminium
h. 4.3cm (1 ¾ in) di. 37.9cm (14 ⅝ in)
Pressalit, Denmark

Rolf Sachs
Refrigerator, Hot Cold
Oak, glass
h. 75cm (29 ½ in) w. 60cm (23 ⅝ in)
l. 180cm (70 ⅞ in)
Julius Hyde Furniture, UK
Limited batch production

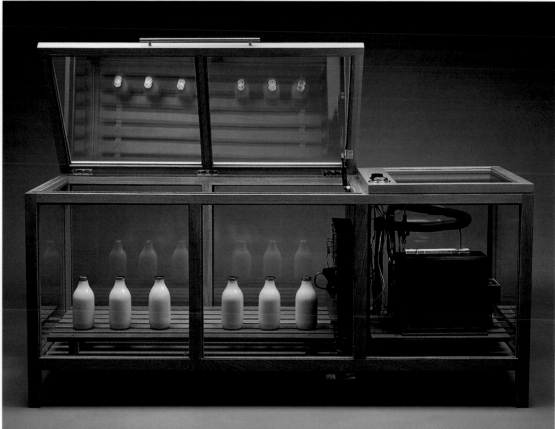

Zenzit Madera, Jörg Ratzlaff, Pressalit

A lavatory seat with a hinge section that creates a quick release and braking effect, allowing the seat to stand upright with no support and swing down slowly and quietly.

Hot Cold Refrigerator, Rolf Sachs

The glass walls of Rolf Sachs' refrigerator reveal two chambers – one houses a working compressor and the other a cold cabinet. Sachs wanted to display the aesthetic beauty of the engine as well as the contents of the refrigerator.

Yamaha Product Design Laboratory
Silent Electric Cello
Spruce, maple, ABS
h. 24.2cm (9½in) w. 43cm (17in) l. 126cm (49½in)
Yamaha Corporation, Japan

Alessandro Copetti
Loudspeaker, U-vola
KFC conglomerate
h. 42cm (16½in) di. 22cm (8¾in)
Copetti Design, Italy

Ron Arad
Self-adhesive CD holder, The Soundtrack
Thermoplastic resin
h. 0.75cm (¼in) l. 120.5cm (47¾in)
Alessi, Italy

Ron Arad and Francesco Pellisari
Loudspeaker, Rotolo
Wood
w. 20cm (7⅞in) di. 57.8cm (22¾in)
NAC Sound, Italy

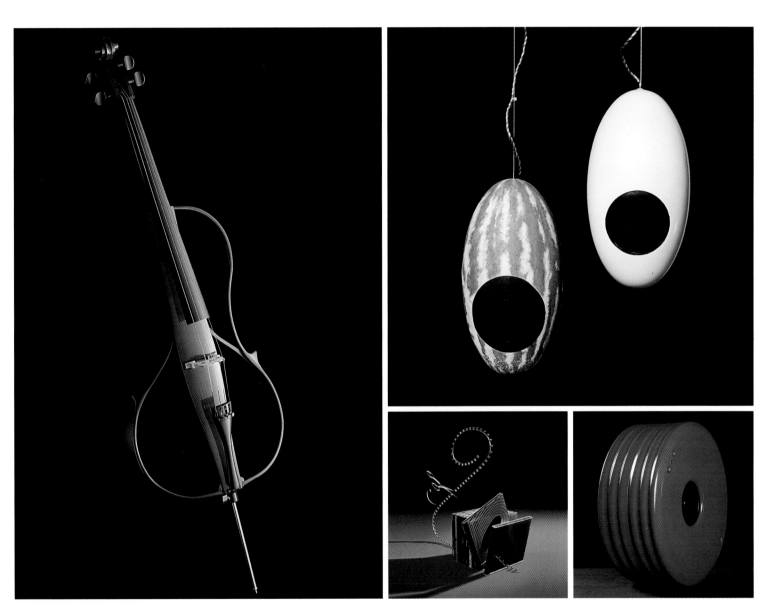

Silent Electric Cello, Yamaha Product Design Laboratory
For beginners and for use in practice sessions, this cello is designed 'to keep neighbours and relatives of musicians from tearing their hair out', by channelling most of the sound to an internal audio receiver and computer chip and then transmitting it to headphones worn by the player.

Philips Design/Philips Research
Electronic clothing, Sensor Sportswear
Fabric with printed and embroidered interfaces
Various sizes
Philips Design/Philips Research,
The Netherlands

Nick Crosbie and Craig Morrison
Rucksack
PVC
h. 38cm (15in) w. 28cm (11in) l. 9cm (3½in)
Inflate, UK

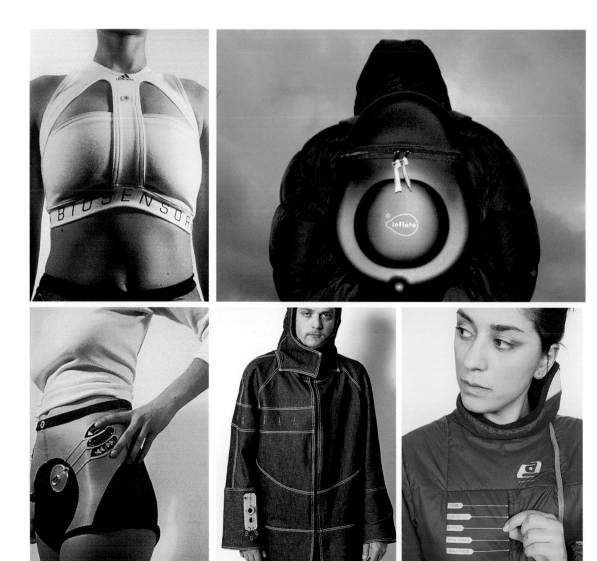

Electronic Clothing, Philips Design and Philips Research

Philips Design and Philips Research have come up with a range of prototype electronic clothing that integrate communication technologies into the garment construction. The collection provides enhanced functions in combination with high-performance knitted, woven and printed materials. Sensor Sportswear is bio-responsive performance clothing that can monitor body functions, as with Snowboarder Responsive Performance Wear which also features global positioning and flexible display functions, integrated in high-performance sports fabrics to provide increased visibility on the slopes. Stretch wool has been chosen for Imaginair-Airline Workwear, a cabin crew uniform incorporating flexible technologies for in-flight communications, and denim to integrate the audio functions for Audio Streetwear.

Denis Santachiara and Jeremy Magdalou
Rocking singing bird,
L'Uccellino ('The Little Bird')
Metal
Prototype

Susan Cohn
Cohndom Square Box
Plastic, aluminium, silver
Alessi, Italy

Titi Cusatelli
Book box, Salus Peccatorum
Prototype

Paolo and Carmine Deganello/Ernesto
and Giuseppe Bartolini
Necklace, Più di un cuore ('More than a Heart')
Silver
Atelier De Vecchi, Italy
Prototype

Naoko Shintani
Body sticking pocket, Segno
Prototype

Silvia Centeleghe
Garter, La signora quindici colpi
('The Fifteen Strike Lady')
Prototype

Alejandro Ruiz
Fake watch, È quasi ora ('It's Almost Time')
Prototype

Nedda El-Asmar
Silver box
Atelier De Vecchi, Italy
Prototype

Giuseppe Di Somma
Necklace, AMEN!
Acrylic
Prototype

Map (Maria Gallo and Patrizia Ledda)
Alaoua
Prototype

Randi Kristensen
Shell box, Conkidom
Prototype

Kicca D'Ercole
Necklace, Giocondom
Prototype

Condom Holders, Make Love With Design
The 'Make Love With Design' project, organized by the Comune di Milano, commissioned thirty-eight international designers to take up the challenge of persuading young people to carry condoms. A selection of them are shown here.

Tad Toulis (Lunar Design)
Electronic travel book, Travel Tote
PET
h. 15.2cm (6in) w. 15.2cm (6in) d. 5.1cm (2in)
Prototype

Martin Mengler / Magenta Design
Bed frame, Winx 300
Polyoxymethylene, glass-fibre reinforced plastic
resin, polyamide
h. 8cm (3⅛ in) l. 200cm (78⅝ in)
d. 100cm (39⅜ in)
Thomas Sitz-und Liegemöbel, Germany

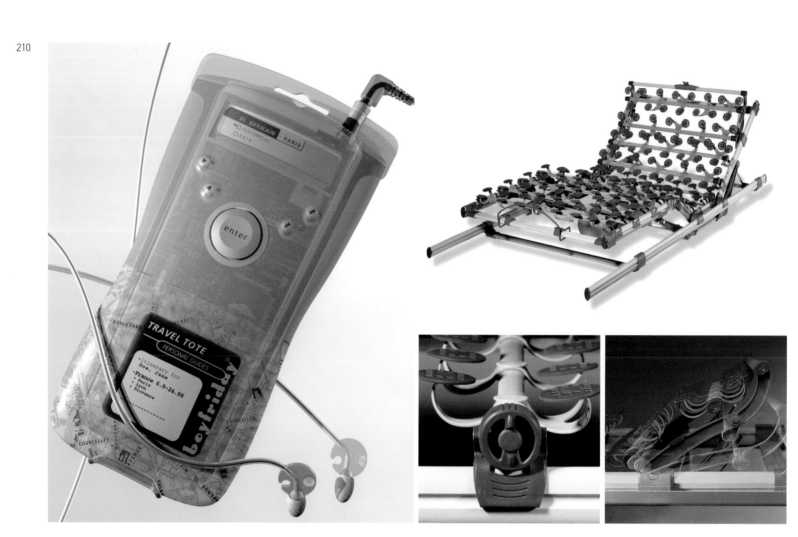

Travel Tote, Lunar Design

A prototype electronic 'guidebook' designed to provide travellers with information accessible via the Internet. Compact and lightweight, the Travel Tote dispenses with the need for a rucksack or suitcase full of travel books, audio tapes, maps and language translation devices. Comprising a miniature display, headset and PC board with modem, the guidebook allows the user to listen to information, look at maps and connect with the Web while on the move.

Sam Hecht/IDEO
E-mail watch, Post-it watch
Acid-etched glass, die-cast aluminium,
Neoprene, steel
h. 7cm (2¾ in) w. 3.8cm (1½ in) l. 7.8cm (3in)
Seiko Communications, Japan

Sam Hecht/IDEO
E-mail cyclist's watch, Lens
ABS, polycarbonate, silicone rubber, steel
h. 7cm (2¾ in) w. 3.2cm (1¼ in) l. 7.8cm (3in)
Seiko Communications, Japan

Naoto Fukasawa/IDEO
Pager watch, Flush
Die-cast aluminium, rubber
h. 7cm (2¾ in) w. 3.2cm (1¼ in) l. 7.8cm (3in)
Seiko Communications, Japan

Naoto Fukasawa and Sam Hecht/IDEO
Message watches, @ messagewatches
Die-cast aluminium, elasticized rubber
Digital: h. 7cm (2¾ in) w. 4.2cm (1¾ in)
l. 7.8cm (3in) d. 0.8cm (⅜ in)
Seiko Communications, Japan

Naoto Fukasawa and Sam Hecht/IDEO
Message watches, @ messagewatches
Die-cast aluminium, elasticized rubber
Analogue: h. 7cm (2¾ in) w. 3.2cm (1¼ in)
l. 7.8cm (3in) d. 1.2cm (½ in)
Seiko Communications, Japan

Marc Berthier
VHF radio, Tykho
Rubber
h. 8cm (3⅛ in) w. 3cm (1⅛ in) l. 14cm (5½ in)
Sperex, France

IDEO

The award-winning product-based design consultancy IDEO has been in business since 1991 and during that time has designed over 2000 medical, computer, telecom, industrial and consumer products. The design project for Seiko illustrates IDEO's forward-looking approach. @ messagewatches are one-off analogue and digital watches. The analogue version uses an LCD to display the message on the front edge of the watch for privacy, and a joystick button on the side provides navigation. The digital version takes its inspiration from train information displays and is worn under the wrist with messages scrolling along the horizontal length of the watch to maximize display space. The Post-it watch comes with a pencil that can be used to write on the etched surface of the face. The Lens watch has an LCD screen, enlarged by a magnifier lens which is also the watch surface. These prototypes use Frequency Modulated radio-wave technology which can receive e-mails from a website; unlike a pager, the cost of communication is the price of a local call. Transmission sites have been set up in Portland and other parts of the United States. The Flush pager watch receives messages in the same way a pager does: the sender telephones a call centre and the message is then transmitted to the surface of the watch.

Josh Goldfarb, Jon Lindholm and Simon Yan
Herbst LaZar Bell Inc.
Computer docking station, Zuzu's Petals
Aluminium, Santoprene, acrylic
h. 38cm (15in) w. 15.2cm (6in)
Prototype

Karen Chekerdjian
Set of four clothes hangers, Mobil
Acrylic
h. 4.5–7cm (1¾–2¾in) w. 4.1–7cm (1½–2¾in)
Edra, Italy

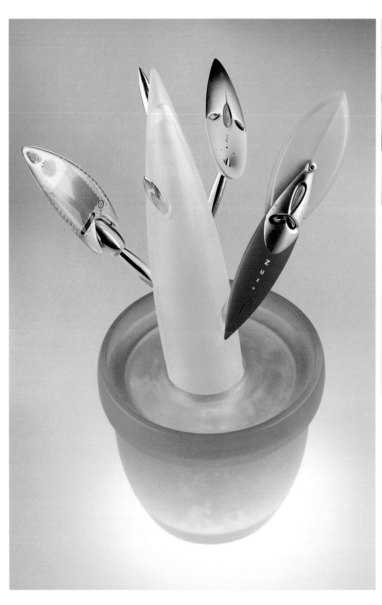

Zuzu's Petals Computer Docking Station, Herbst LaZar Bell Inc.
The concept for this solar-powered, palm-sized docking station grew from the designers'
desire to humanize technology and create a computer that grows and changes with the
consumer, dispensing with the need to purchase additional products. The 'leaves' or
'petals' are made of a soft membrane which can be worn by the user and then returned
to the main 'stem' for the information to be downloaded.

Kazuo Kawasaki
Folding wheelchair, CARNA
Titanium, aluminium
h. 85/90cm (33½/35⅜ in)
w. 58/64cm (22⅞/25⅛ in)
d. 90/95cm (35⅜/37⅜ in)
SIG Workshop, Japan

Sunways GmbH
Solar cell, POWER
Silicone
w. 10cm (3⅞ in) d. 10cm (3⅞ in)
Sunways, Germany

Olafur Thordarson
Wine rack, Delirium Tremens
Resin
h. 83.2cm (32¾ in) w. 33cm (13in)
d. 30.5cm (12in)
Dingaling Studio, USA
Limited batch production

Kuno Prey
Documents folder/filing box,
Inorder 1/Inorder 2
Polypropylene
h. 26.5cm (10⅜ in) w. 37cm (14⅝ in)
d. 0.3–3.5cm (⅛–1⅜ in)
Nava Design, Italy

Kazuo Kawasaki
Portable computer, Intertop
Metal, plastic
h. 2.9cm (1⅛ in) w. 21cm (8¼ in) d. 15cm (5⅞ in)
Fujitsu, Japan

Doug Halley
Air-integrated diving computer
Polycarbonate, polyurethane, aluminium,
silicone rubber, die-cast magnesium
w. 8.5cm (3⅜ in) l. 19cm (7½ in) d. 3cm (1⅛ in)
Glasgow School of Art, UK
Prototype

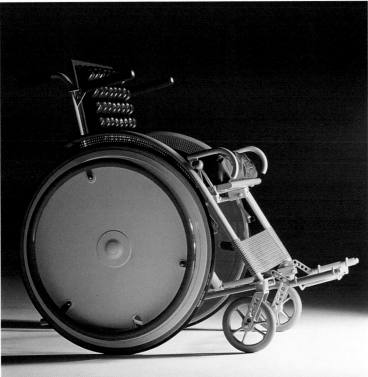

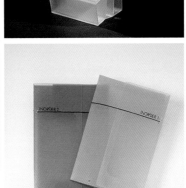

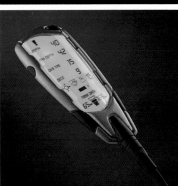

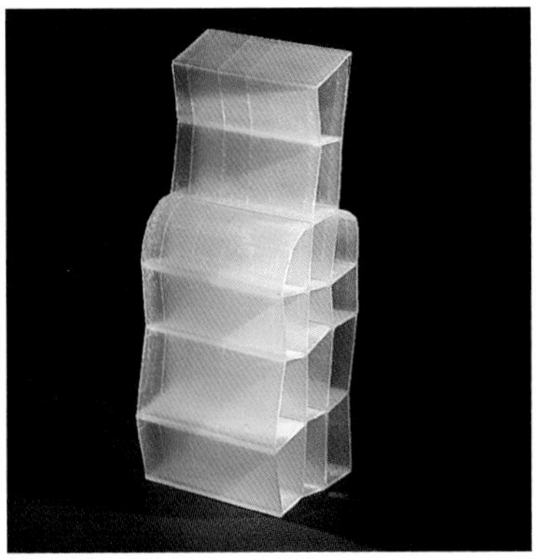

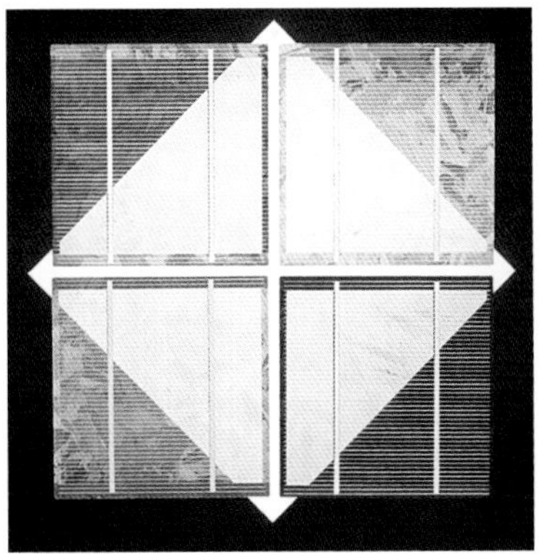

Transparent Solar Cell

Using a newly developed, patented manufacturing process, the POWER solar cells achieve a record output efficiency of 16 per cent. The transparent version affords 30 per cent maximum transparency and can be integrated into window façades and roof glazing. The new process is also ecologically friendly, completely dispensing with the chemicals required in traditional glass-texturing processes.

JASPER MORRISON

Every space has an atmosphere, empty or full. The quality of a space filled with objects depends both on the qu objects. **Objectality is equivalent to personality, it's the character and spirit of things. It's what attracts us t**

Objectality consists of a balance of different variables: form/void; materials/lack of materials; discr status/avoidance of status; degree and type of emotion evoked; object sex appeal; colour/lack of colour. Thes which we are by now trained to judge in the first few seconds of seeing an object. Having evaluated these varia disliking an object.

If we like an object, and consider it desirable, we begin an evaluation of secondary objectality variables: cost; qu expression of our own personality.

If an object meets all our requirements of these variables we usually end up living with it. Once we have it at h its objectality has been. Some objects with a high initial objectality count quickly fall from favour due to s expected it to; it doesn't express our personality as we expected it would; it's just another stupid object we c acquired without too much evaluation, may, over time, assume high objectality counts through faithful servi

In the end what we demand of objects is that they result in a positive addition to our living space, enric meaningful experience of the way we live. This, the *science of objectality*, is the occupation of *design*.

e empty space and on the 'objectality' of the

s us from, an object.

scretion; expression of function; expression of
rimary components of an object's objectality,
brain comes to its conclusion of liking or

nstruction; usefulness; longevity of usefulness;

uickly find out how accurate our evaluation of
reseen deficiency; it doesn't work as we
y need. Other objects, which we may have
ugh qualities which only time and use reveal.

quality of everyday life and making a more

Vico Magistretti
Kitchen, Cinqueterre
Anodized aluminium, beech, stainless steel
h. 138/214.8/240.4cm (54⅜/84½/94⅝ in)
w. 75/90/105/120/135cm (29½/35⅜/41⅜/47⅛/53⅛ in)
d. 60cm (23⅜ in)
Schiffini, Italy

Jasper Morrison
Kitchen
Oak, silkscreen painted glass, stainless steel
Various sizes
Units, Italy

Mikael Warnhammar
Kitchen, VÄRDE
Birch, stainless steel, glass
Various sizes
IKEA, Sweden

Enzo Mari
Desk set, Scrittura
Porcelain, steel
h. 3.1–14.3cm (1⅛–5⅜ in)
w. 4.5–15.7cm (1¾–6⅛ in)
l. 18.4–40cm (7¼–15¾ in)
di. 2.9–15.3cm (1⅛–6in)
Rosenthal, Germany

Antonio Citterio
Kitchen, Arclinea
Stainless steel, frosted glass
Various sizes
Arclinea, Italy

Gerd Wilsdorf
Oven, Modul B
Stainless steel
h. 162cm (63¾ in) w. 69.2cm (27¼ in)
d. 68.6cm (27in)
Siemens Electrogeräte, Germany

Antonia Astori
Kitchen, Anice
Stainless steel, aluminium, glass
h. 86/91cm (33⅞ in/35¾ in)
l. 210.7cm (83in)
d. 64.5cm (25¾ in)
Driade, Italy

Matali Crasset
Pet Tray
Polypropylene
h. 8.5cm (3⅜ in) w. 23cm (9in) l. 38cm (15in)
Authentics, Germany

Dick van Hoff
Coat hook
Aluminium
h. 12cm (4¾ in) w. 60cm (23⅜ in)
REEEL, The Netherlands

Gerd Wilsdorf
Cooktop with gas hob, Modul E1
Stainless steel
h. 100cm (39⅜ in) w. 150cm (59in)
d. 68cm (26¾ in)
Siemens Electrogeräte, Germany

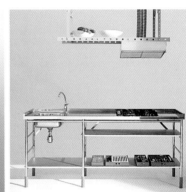
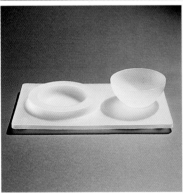

Claudio Silvestrin
Washbasins and bath from the I Fiumi range,
Adige, Po, Rubicone
Stone
Washbasin, Adige: h. 80cm (31½ in)
d. 60cm (23½ in)
Bath, Po: h. 50cm (19⅝ in) l. 190cm (74¾ in)
d. 130cm (51⅛ in)
Washbasin, Rubicone: h. 80cm (31½ in)
d. 60cm (23½ in)
Boffi, Italy

I Fiumi, Claudio Silvestrin

The I Fiumi ('Rivers') bathroom collection is the result of a collaboration between
the minimalist architect Claudio Silvestrin, Boffi and Zantedeschi Marmi, the Italian
stone-cutting firm. The made-to-order elliptical bath Po is carved from one piece
of Lecce stone.

Arni Aromaa and Sauli Suomela
Washbasin
Steel, acrylic, glass fibre
h. 120cm (47⅛ in) w. 120cm (47⅛ in)
d. 47cm (18½ in)
Oras, Finland
Prototype

Javier Ruiz-Tapiador Trallero
Washbasin, Albeus
Ceramic
w. 80cm (31½ in) d. 50cm (19⅝ in)
Rapsel, Italy

Marcel Wanders
Bird House
Porcelain, wood
h. 18cm (7in) l. 30cm (11¾ in) d. 25cm (9⅞ in)
Droog Design, The Netherlands for
Oranienbaum
Prototype

Carl Clerkin
Cleaning unit, Mr Clean
Laminated birch ply, steel, skateboard wheels
h. 50cm (19⅝ in) w. 30cm (11¾ in)
d. 40cm (15¾ in)
One-off

Harri Koskinen
Container/stool, Fatty-Containers
Birch plywood, metal
h. 40cm (15¾ in) w. 40cm (15¾ in)
l. 20/40cm (7⅞ /15¾ in)
Schmidinger Modul Wohn & Objektbedarf,
Austria

Chris Bundy
Clock
Steel, porcelain enamel
w. 5cm (2in) di. 28.6cm (11¼ in)
Erie Ceramic Arts Company, USA

Feldmann+Schultchen
Birdcage, Netcage
Nylon net, steel, aluminium, wood
h. 80cm (31½ in) di. 40cm (15¾ in)
Prototype

Jasper Startup
Fan, Wind
Rattan, metal
h. 30cm (11 ¾ in) di. 25cm (9 ⅞ in)
Startup Design, UK

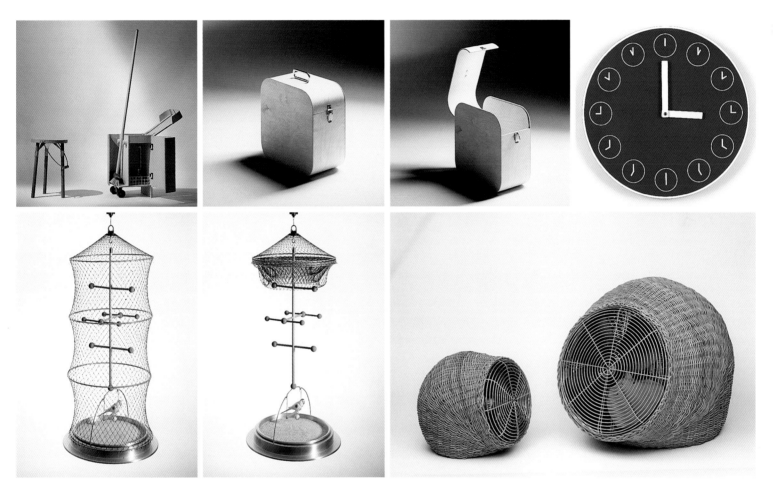

Birdcage, Feldmann+Schultchen
This prototype birdcage was developed in collaboration with ornithologists. The flexible net prevents birds suffering skull and wing injuries which occur frequently with rigid cages. The mesh allows the cage to be easily cleaned and provides a surface for the birds to climb vertically as well as horizontally.

Ettore Sottsass
Mirror, Più o meno iside
Mirror, lacquered metal
h. 225cm (88⅝ in) w. 90cm (35⅜ in)
d. 100cm (39⅜ in)
Post Design for Memphis, Italy
Limited batch production

Setsu Ito
Plant-pot holder, Trifoglio
Steel
h. 90cm (35⅜ in) di. 50cm (19⅝ in)
Ravarini Castoldi & C, Italy

222

Jan Padrnos
CD holder, Brutal
Steel
h. 44cm (17⅜ in) w. 44cm (17⅜ in)
d. 26cm (10¼ in)
Tunnel, Czech Republic
Limited batch production

Pascal Bauer
CD holder, CD Roll
Anodized aluminium, polypropylene
h. 60–120cm (23⅝–47⅛ in)
Ycami, Italy

Helena Mattila-Sorri
Wall calendar, In The Air
Silver rope, paper
h. 80cm (31½ in) w. 7cm (2¾ in)
Everyday Design, Finland
Limited batch production

In The Air Wall Calendar, Helena Mattila-Sorri

This monthly calendar has a roll of paper for each day which reveals a different poem, thought or proverb on themes such as love and life.

Philippe Starck
Mirror, CAADRE
Metal, crystal glass
h. 195cm (76¾ in) w. 105cm (41⅜ in)
Fiam Italia, Italy

Philippe Starck
Dumb-bells, POAA
Matt nickel-finished brass
l. 20cm (7⅞ in)
weight 2/3kg (4½ / 6½ lb)
XO, France

Philippe Starck

Starck, certainly the best-known designer of the late twentieth century, continues to transform everyday objects. Starck's POAA dumb-bells in matt nickel-finished brass were designed to be both decorative and useful in the rooms of the Sanderson Hotel which opened in 1999, one of two London hotels that Ian Schrager commissioned Starck to design.

BIOGRAPHIES

Helle Abild was born in Copenhagen in 1964 and graduated from the Danish Design School in 1989. She specializes in computer designs of printed, knitted and woven textiles for the fashion market, as well as woven fabric for the contract market. She has worked for CAPUT.com in Copenhagen, Jhane Barnes Textiles in New York and for CNET.com and Deepa Textiles in San Francisco. 180

Werner Aisslinger was born in Berlin in 1964. He founded his own design company in 1993 and has since worked on furniture projects for Italian companies such as Magis, Cappellini and Porro. He has also carried out corporate architecture concepts and projects for Lufthansa and Mercedes Benz. 46

Jun Akabane, **Hiroshi Kobayashi**, **Arata Ono** and **Hideki Ito** all work for the Nikon Corporation. Akabane, Kobayashi and Ono studied at Chiba University; Ito attended the Musashino Art University. 186

Gunilla Allard was born in 1957. She worked as a stage designer and property manager for the film industry during the early 1980s, then studied interior architecture at the University College of Arts, Crafts and Design in Stockholm. Today she works as a stage designer and furniture designer. She was awarded the Excellent Swedish Form prize in 1991, 1992 and 1996. 80

Harry Allen received a Masters degree in industrial design from the Pratt Institute, New York, then worked for Prescriptives Cosmetics before opening his own studio. His interior design projects include the Murray Moss shop in New York, the Dragonfly Selects jewellery store in Taiwan, and new offices for *Metropolis* magazine and the Guggenheim Museum, New York. He has designed a medicine chest for Magis, various articles for Wireworks and lighting for George Kovacs and IKEA. 57

Gabriele Allendorf was born in Munich in 1956. She studied interior design at the Academy of Fine Arts in Nuremberg, then set up her own studio in Munich designing a collection of lights, one-offs, light environments and lighting for films, theatres and exhibitions. Clients include BMW, Hewlett Packard and Zumtobel Staff. She lectures on lighting at colleges in Munich and Coburg. 123

Andrea Anastasio was born in Rome in 1961. He studied at the University of Rome, and received a Masters degree in philosophy from the University of Venice. During the early 1990s he produced glassware for Le Cadre Gallery, Hong Kong, Memphis and Sawaya & Moroni, as well as glass lamps for Artemide. He moved to India in 1993 but still designs items for Italian outlets. He is also involved with Rahul Mehrotra Associates in Bombay, working on architectural projects for private residences. 19, 130, 131

Yoko Ando was born in Shibuya, Tokyo. He trained as a graphic artist at the Musashino Art University and is currently working for Nuno Corporation. He has exhibited his work within Japan and at the 'L'Asie en Rose' fashion show in Manila, The Philippines. 175

Simon Andrews received a Bachelors degree in furniture and product design from Kingston University, UK. Whilst studying he also worked freelance for clients including H.M. Prison Services, Sony and IKEA. He achieved first place in the Student Award 1998, which formed part of the International Design Resource Awards. 196

Ed Annink was born in The Hague in 1957. He studied jewellery, interior, furniture and product design and in 1985 set up 'Ontwerpwerk', a practice involved in international graphics, product and environmental design. Clients include Anthologie Quartett, Authentics, Droog Design, O'Neill, Shell and DMD. 149

Pascal Anson was born in London in 1973. He studied at Kingston University, receiving a Bachelors degree in product and furniture design, and has just completed a Masters degree at the Royal College of Art. He has exhibited his work in the UK, Japan and Italy and in 1999 won the Victoria and Albert Museum Hoardings Competition. 203

L'Anverre Atelier is a Belgian design group whose members are Sem Schanzer, Armin Homolka, Marc Melis and Myryam Garouche. They work primarily in glass but are also involved in Fine Art, graphic design and sculpture as well as music, photography and films. 131

Ron Arad was born in Tel Aviv in 1951. He studied at the Jerusalem Academy of Art, and from 1974 to 1979 at the Architectural Association, London. In 1981 he founded One Off with Caroline Thorman. In 1988 he won the Tel Aviv Opera Foyer Interior Competition with C. Norton and S. McAdam. As well as the design and construction of the new One Off design studio in Chalk Farm, London, in 1991, projects have included furniture design for Poltronova, Vitra, Moroso and Driade; the interiors of the restaurants Belgo and Belgo Centraal in London; and the winning competition entry for the Adidas Stadium in Paris (unbuilt). In 1994 Arad established the Ron Arad Studio in Como to continue the production of limited-edition handmade pieces. He is currently Professor of Furniture Design and Industrial Design at the Royal College of Art in London. 37, 131, 207

Antoni Arola was born in Tarragona, Spain in 1960. He studied at the EINA in Barcelona where he is now a lecturer. From 1984 to 1990 he worked with Alberto Lievore and Jorge Pensi, then joined Associate Designers where he was responsible for interior and industrial design projects. He opened his own studio in 1994. 92

Arni Aromaa and **Sauli Suomela** both studied at the University of Art and Design in Helsinki (UIAH), receiving Masters degrees in 1998. Their industrial design office, Pentagon Ltd, concentrates on product development, design concepts and strategic design. Both are part-time teachers in the department of product and strategic design at UIAH. 220

Sigeaki Asahara was born in Tokyo in 1948 and studied in Turin, Italy. Since 1973 he has worked as a freelance industrial designer in Tokyo. His work has received much acclaim including the iF Best of Category award, Hanover in 1992. 114

Teppo Asikainen see Valvomo

Antonia Astori began her career by designing system furniture for Driade. In 1984 she collaborated with Marithé and François Girbaud on a chain of stores in Paris, Brussels, Montreal, San Francisco and Milan. In 1987 she enlarged and remodelled the Driade Factory. This design was the model for further renovations for its outlets in Milan, Berlin and Tokyo, as well as for Bang & Olufsen in Munich. Astori continues to design furniture and is also active in exhibition design. 217

Shin and **Tomoko Azumi** studied industrial design at Kyoto City University of Art and the Royal College of Art, London. They founded Azumi's in 1995, undertaking projects for British, Italian and Japanese clients. In 1996 they were finalists in the Blueprint/100% Design Awards. 40

Radim Babák and **Jan Tucek** were born in Brno in 1972 and Liberec, Czech Republic in 1973, respectively. Both studied at the Academy of Applied Arts in Prague. Babák has worked in the studios of Borek Sipek and Jiri Pelcl. They designed a collection of lights, PUR, in 1998 which has been produced by Tunnel. 103

Emmanuel Babled was born in France in 1967, and today lives in Milan and Venice. He studied at the Istituto Europeo di Disegno in Milan, then worked with Prospero Rasulo and Gianni Veneziano at Studio Oxido in Milan. He has been working as a freelance designer since the early 1990s for clients such as Fine Factory, Steel, Casprini, Wedgwood, Waterford Crystal Ltd, Kundalini and Rosenthal. Since 1995 he has also been an independent producer of Murano glass vases and ceramic items. 131

Philip Baldwin see Monica Guggisberg

Georg Baldele trained at the Academy of Applied Arts, Vienna where he received a Masters degree in product design. From 1996 to 1998 he attended the Royal College of Art in London where he studied under Ron Arad and Floris van der Broeke. He has been the recipient of various awards including the Blueprint/100% Design Awards Special Prize in 1998. 106

Enrico Baleri was born in Albino, Italy in 1942. He studied architecture at Milan Polytechnic, and while still a student was invited by Dino Gavina to open a furnishing centre in Bergamo. In 1968 he founded a research group in Milan and has since designed collections and furniture for Gavina, Flos, Knoll International and Alias, a firm he set up in 1979. He was art director for Alias until 1983. In 1984 he and his wife Marilisa Baleri Decimo started Baleri Italia, collaborating with Hans Hollein, Alessandro Mendini and other designers. Since 1986 Baleri has been active in the fields of architecture, image and communication, promotional graphics and industrial design. 96

Ralph Ball studied furniture design at Leeds College of Art, UK and received a Masters degree from the Royal College of Art, London where he is now Senior Tutor. He has taught at various design schools in the UK and from 1981 to 1984 was a designer with Foster Associates. Today he is part of the Naylor-Ball Design Partnership. 60, 105, 116

Pascal Bauer is an industrial, interior and furniture designer and has also worked on set design. His work can be found in the permanent collection of the Guggenheim Museum, New York. 223

Asla Bekit was born in Eritrea in 1970 and is currently studying textile and product design at the Fachhochschule für Design und Medien, Hanover. Projects undertaken during the last term included the concept for a new hotel, a telecom competition for EXPO 2000 and a new design for IKEA. 172

Mathias Bengtsson received a Bachelors degree from the Danish Design School, Copenhagen and a Masters degree from the Royal College of Art, London. He has exhibited his work throughout Scandinavia, at the Stedelijk Museum in The Netherlands, and in the Post Design Exhibition at the Memphis Gallery in Milan in 1999. 61

Randall Bell is Senior Vice President of Herbst LaZar Bell. He received a degree in industrial design from the University of Illinois, then worked for companies such as Healthcare, Amoco, Tyco Toys and the US Postal Department before joining HLB. He holds over forty patents for housewares, office and personal care products. 163

Mario Bellini was born in 1935 and graduated in architecture from Milan Polytechnic in 1959. He began to design products and furniture in 1963. Completed architectural projects include the office building of the AEM Thermoelectric Power Plant at Cassano d'Abba; the Milan Trade Fair Extension; the Tokyo Design Centre; the Schmidtbank Headquarters in Germany; the Arsoa Company Headquarters in Yamanashi-ken and the Natuzzi Americas Inc. Headquarters in North Carolina. He is currently undertaking projects in Russia and Dubai. 30

Ricardo Bello Dias worked for various architectural practices before joining Lissoni Associati in 1992. After a period in London he returned to Lissoni as consultant and head of art direction. He left in 1996 to found Studio bd, which became Codice 31 the following year. 86

Sebastian Bergne studied industrial design at the Central School of Art and Design and at the Royal College of Art, London and worked in Hong Kong and Milan before forming his own practice, Bergne: Design for Manufacture, in 1990. His clients include Cassina, Vitra, Oluce, Authentics and Driade. He is a lecturer at the Royal College of Art. 88

Lena Bergström studied in the textile department of the National College of Arts, Crafts and Design in Stockholm, then moved to the University of Art and Design in Helsinki. In 1989 she studied computer-aided textile production in Belgium, and two years later travelled to Japan where she served an apprenticeship in carpet design. She has been working at Orrefors since 1994. 135

Marc Berthier is a partner in the Paris-based Design Plan Studio. Primarily an industrial designer, he received the Premio Compasso d'Oro in 1991 and 1994; the Form design award in Germany in 1995, 1997 and 1998; the Design Plus in 1999 and has also been awarded the Grand Prix National de la Création Industrielle by the French Ministry of Culture. 211

Jurgen Bey teaches at the Design Academy in Eindhoven and is a guest lecturer at the Hogeschool voor de Kunsten, Utrecht. His designs include garden seats for Oranienbaum, Germany in association with Droog Design, a light shade and the Kokon furniture series for Droog Design and garden design for the Princessenhof Museum of Ceramics in Leeuwarden. 61, 64, 65, 99

Mark Bond trained in furniture design at Ravensbourne College of Design and at the Royal College of Art, London. He has worked for ASA designers and for Conran Associates where for three years he headed the interior design department. He now works independently for clients such as the Design Museum, the Barbican Centre, Habitat and Viaduct Furniture. He is also co-director of Bond Projects UK which produces a range of furniture. 121

Christoph Böninger was born in Düsseldorf, Germany in 1957. He studied industrial design in Munich and Los Angeles and worked for Schlagheck & Schultes Design, Munich from 1983 to 1987. In 1987 he joined Siemens Corporation, New York as Manager, Industrial Design. Since 1997 he has been the Vice President of Siemens Design & Messe GmbH. 81

Reno Bonzon was born in France in 1954. He studied in Paris and is currently working on the design of furniture using aluminium, wood and steel. 96

Pierre Bouguennec was born in Brittany and moved to New York in 1987 where he trained as a cabinet-maker before starting in practice as an architect. Since 1989 he has worked in his own studio, Boum Design, on interior design, furniture and lighting projects. In 1998 his lamp Plug In was manufactured by Ligne Roset in France and won two awards at the Furniture Fair in Paris. 41

Ronan Bouroullec was born in Quimper, Brittany in 1971. He graduated in applied and decorative art and has worked on a freelance basis since 1995 designing objects and furniture for Cappellini, Units, Christian Liaigre, Domeau et Pères, Ex Novo, Ligne Roset, Ardi, Galerie Néotù and La Monnaie de Paris. He was awarded Best New Designer at the International Contemporary Fair in New York in 1999. 88, 138, 139

Jaime Bouzaglo was born in Alcázar, Morocco where he began his studies in architecture. He moved to Quebec in 1982 and founded his own studio in 1990, designing restaurants, boutiques and furniture. 38

Anja and **Stefan Böwer** were both born in Osnabrück, Germany and trained in the Architecture and Design Division of the Academy of Fine Arts, Munich and the Architecture Division of the Technische Universität in Berlin, respectively. Stefan worked for Silvestrin Design, Van Berkal & Bos, Konstantin Grcic and Sieger Design. Anja completed a Diploma at the Hochschule der Künste in Berlin and gained experience in various architectural practices. They started their professional collaboration in 1998. 72

Andrea Branzi was born in Florence in 1938. He studied architecture, then founded the avant-garde group Archizoom Associates together with Gilberto Corretti, Paolo Deganello and Massimo Morozzi in 1966. From 1974 to 1976 he was involved with Global Tools, and in the late 1970s set up CDM, a Milan-based group of design consultants. He worked with Studio Alchimia and Memphis from the outset, designing furniture and objects and preparing shows and publications. He founded the Domus Academy in 1983 and has been its Cultural Director and Vice President. In 1987 Branzi won the Compasso d'Oro prize in recognition of his whole career. 148, 153

Ralf Braun was born in Heinsberg, Germany in 1971. He trained as a cabinet-maker but later studied product design and architecture at the Fachhochschule in Aachen, receiving a diploma in 1998. Since 1996 he has worked as a freelance product designer for clients such as Siemens Design & Messe and Sirona Dental. He is a founder member of Cotelletto and of Braun-Wagner Design. 205

Jan Bremermann was born in 1961. He has worked as an architect and industrial designer in Berlin since 1990 and has designed and built a studio space for the Berlin-based jewellery designer C. F. Daw. He currently practises under the name Bremermann and Partners. 101

Jan Broekstra was born in 1964. He lives and works in Arnhem, The Netherlands, where he designs and makes prototypes in porcelain for JKN Arnhem. In 1997 he designed a service, Vaan Frits, for Rosenthal Studioline. 91

Debbie Jane Buchan was born in 1973. She has a Masters degree in art and design and a Bachelors degree in surface decoration. Her work was selected for the New Designers Exhibition in London in 1995 and it has also been shown in Scotland and Japan. 180

Chris Bundy graduated from Hamilton College, New York in 1982 with a Bachelors degree in Fine Arts. He worked as President for Toxic Arts Inc. designing furniture and interior and display systems for retail companies. He is currently a partner in Prototype and Production, creating a wide range of product designs. He recently completed the interior design for the Standard Listening Room, a bar in New York. 221

Rolf Bürger was born in 1958. He studied product design in Münster, Germany, then co-founded the HELIX-Akantus design group. 91

Stephen Burks was born in 1969. He studied architecture at the Illinois Institute of Technology and product design at IIT's Institute of Design, and also attended Columbia University's Graduate School of Architecture. Before launching Readymade, he worked as a designer at Prescriptives, Siegel & Gale, IDEE Co. (Tokyo), Fitch Inc. (Boston), the Arnell Group and Swatch Creative Lab, Milan. He exhibited his work at the Néotù Showroom in New York in 1999. 26, 142

Christof Burtscher and **Patrizia Bertolini** were born in Austria in 1964 and Italy in 1962, respectively. Burtscher trained as a master joiner and wood carver, then studied carpentry and sculpture at the European Design Institute in Milan. Bertolini studied industrial design at the Istituto Superiore per le Industrie Artistiche in Rome, then Fine Art and industrial design at the European Design Institute. They have worked together since 1991 and have had their own studio in Bolzano since 1995, specializing in furniture design. 76

Sigi Bussinger was born in Munich, Germany in 1965. Since 1989 he has been working as a sculptor and performing artist. 100

Julia Büttelmann was born in 1961. She is a master of bookbinding and also designs furniture from paper and pasteboard. 49

Antonio Cagianelli graduated from the University of Florence in 1989, then continued his research in Paris where he participated in a show at the Galleria Kamien, followed a year later by his first collection in resin at the Galleria Inov. This gave rise to Plastic Emotion, a collection of everyday articles for the home. He is currently working with the Galleria Clara Cremini in Paris and for Edizioni Galleria Colombari, Alessi and Daum. 38

Fernando and **Humberto Campana** have worked together in São Paulo since 1984. Humberto trained as a lawyer and Fernando, his brother, graduated as an architect. In 1998 the Museum of Modern Art in New York dedicated an exhibition to their work entitled 'Progetto 66'. They collaborate with manufacturers such as OLuce and Edra. 45, 47, 102, 148, 182

Chiara Cantono studied architecture and industrial design at Milan Polytechnic and opened her own design studio in 1993. In 1997 she created a furniture collection using Kevlar and carbon fibre, and the following year designed Alicia, a collection of lamps which react to light like fibre optics. She has collaborated with companies such as Brunati Italia and Busnelli Industrial Group. 50, 92

Fabio Carlesso works as a graphic and interior designer, and designs furniture in resin and plastic. He also works as consultant and collaborator with various textile designers and architects. 173

Achille Castiglioni, born in Milan in 1918, began his career after the Second World War with his brothers Livio and Pier Giacomo. He is well known for interiors, furniture and lighting, and his clients include Flos, Phonola, Bernini, Cassina, de Padova, FontanaArte, Interflex, Kartell, Marcatré, Olivetti, Up & Up and Zanotta. Castiglioni has been honoured nine times with the Compasso d'Oro. He was Professor of Industrial Design and Decoration at the University of Milan from 1969 to 1993. Exhibitions include shows at the Galeria d'Arte Moderna e Contemporanea in 1996; at the Vitra Design Museum in Weil am Rhein and the Museum of Modern Art in New York in 1997; and at the Niitsu Art Museum in 1998. 39, 45

Silvia Centeleghe was born in Argentina. She studied industrial design in Argentina and received a Masters degree in design from the Domus Academy, Milan. For the last eighteen years she has worked in various areas of design including graphics, industrial design and art direction. 209

Alan Chadwick was born in Dublin in 1957. He studied at the Ecole Camondo in Paris, then collaborated on interior design projects, furnishings and restaurants for the La Villette and Louvre Museums. Today he works in Europe and in the USA where he has designed a line of children's furniture. He began his collaboration with Baleri Italia in 1998. 82

Daniel Charny was born in Jerusalem in 1966. He graduated from the Bezalel Academy of Arts and Design, then taught in the industrial design department. From 1995 to 1997 he studied at the Royal College of Art, London. He has his own studio in London and is a full-time tutor at the Royal College of Art. In 1999 he took part in the Post Design Exhibition at the Memphis Gallery in Milan. 21

Karen Chekerdjian was born in Beirut in 1970. She worked with advertising agency Leo Burnett-Beirut from 1991 until 1993 when, with two associates, she founded Mind the Gap, a communications and graphic design agency based in Beirut. She has designed products on a freelance basis since 1996. 212

Peter Christian established Stuart Design Partnership with Ruth Stuart in 1996. They design furniture and lighting for various UK-based manufacturers. 107

Antonio Citterio was born in Meda, Italy, in 1950. He studied at Milan Polytechnic and in 1973 set up a studio with Paolo Nava. They were awarded the Compasso d'Oro in 1979. In 1987 Terry Dwan became a partner in Studio Citterio Dwan, and the company has undertaken many interior design projects, including schemes for Esprit and offices and showrooms for Vitra. Among the work realized in Japan, in partnership with Toshiyuki Kita, is the headquarters in Kobe for World Company, the Corente Building in Tokyo, and, in 1992, the Diago headquarters in Tokyo. Recent projects include the Madison Avenue flagship store in Avenue Montaigne, Paris and a textile factory building near Milan. 78, 217

Richard Clack was educated at Kingston Polytechnic in Surrey, UK, then worked for the design consultancy ASA. He now has his own company and works for IKEA as a contract freelancer. 23

Claesson Koivisto Rune was formed by Mårten Claesson, Eero Koivisto and Ola Rune who met at the University College of Arts, Crafts and Design in Stockholm. All three partners teach at various institutions in Sweden and Ola Rune was head teacher at the Beckmans School of Design in Stockholm from 1997 to 1998. Mårten Claesson is also a freelance architecture and design writer for publications including the newspaper *Svenska Dagbladet City* and the magazines *Form* and *Forum*. 149

Carl Clerkin was born in London in 1973. He started his training with a foundation course at Central St Martin's College of Art and Design, then received a Bachelors degree in furniture design from Middlesex University. He completed a Masters degree at the Royal College of Art in 1998 and has since worked as a freelance furniture and product designer. 88, 221

Franco Clivio was born in 1942. He studied at the Hochschule für Gestaltung in Ulm where he later worked as an assistant lecturer. Since 1968 he has been responsible for product design for the Gardena company in Ulm. He also works freelance for clients such as Erco, Lamy and Siemens. Since 1980 he has taught product design at the Höhere Schule für Gestaltung in Zurich. 114

Nigel Coates was born in 1949 in Malvern, UK. He studied at Nottingham University and the Architectural Association, London, founding Branson Coates with Doug Branson in 1985. The practice has completed over twenty projects in Japan and the fit-out of a series of shops in London, notably Jigsaw and Liberty. The practice undertakes a range of projects, including objects and furniture, buildings, interiors and exhibitions and landscape design. Recent projects include the Geffrye Museum extension in Hackney, London and the National Centre for Popular Music in Sheffield. Coates taught at the Architectural Association from 1978 to 1986, and is currently Professor of Architectural Design at the Royal College of Art. 54, 55

Susan Cohn is an Australian jeweller and designer. She founded her own gold- and silversmithing workshop, Workshop 3000, in 1980. 209

Gianfranco Coltella was born in Saluzzo, Italy in 1959. He studied design in Milan then worked for Gregotti Associati, De Pas, D'Urbino and Lomazzi and Olivetti. He currently teaches design at the European Institute in Turin. 117

Comma was founded by David Khouri and Roberto Guzman. Khouri moved to New York from California to attend Columbia University graduate school, receiving Masters degrees in architecture and in historic preservation. Prior to co-founding Comma he worked for Bohn Associates, designing retail and showroom projects. Guzman also attended Columbia University, graduating with a Masters degree in architecture in 1987. He has worked for various architects including Kohn Pedersen Fox and Peter Marino. 19, 22

Alessandro Copetti studied at the University of Venice and in the School of Architecture of the Royal Academy of Fine Arts in Copenhagen. On his return to Italy he established Alessandro Copetti Design and Architecture Office to work on product, graphic and interior design and planning. In 1998 he founded Blasotti and Copetti Design with the aim of producing a new line of furniture. In 1999 Copetti was awarded the Premio Ambiente for his U-Vola speaker. 207

Matali Crasset was born in Châlons-en-Champagne, France and studied at the Ecole Nationale Supérieure de Création Industrielle. She collaborated with Denis Santachiara in Milan and with Philippe Starck on the Thomson Multimedia products, founding her own studio in 1998. She holds seminars at the Ecole Nationale Supérieure des Arts Décoratifs in Paris, the Danish Design School in Copenhagen and the Domus Academy in Milan. 217

Nick Crosbie was born in 1971. He has a degree in industrial design from Central Saint Martin's College of Art and Design and a Masters degree from the Royal College of Art, London. He set up Inflate in 1995 with brothers Michael and Mark Sodeau. Michael left in 1997 but the company increased in size to include eight members. In 1998 they collaborated with Craig Morrison on a range of PVC bags and also launched a UK designer distribution service representing products from Eurolounge and Jam, amongst others. In 1999 Inflate collaborated with Ron Arad on the Memo chair. 37, 208

Titi Cusatelli was born in Milan in 1965. She graduated in industrial design from the Istituto Europeo di Disegno then worked for various Italian designers, founding her own industrial and graphic design studio in 1990. She has designed sportswear, tableware, furniture and toys. Recently her design for a bicycle was nominated for the Compasso d'Oro Award. 209

Marie Darmody see Salvatore & Marie

Andy Davey is principal of TKO Product Design which he founded in 1990. He graduated from the Royal College of Art, London and has since designed for NEC, Canon and Sony, amongst others, as well as creating eyewear for Seiko, lights for Daiko and toys for Hasbro. His Freeplay clockwork radio won the 1996 BBC Design Award for Best Product and Best of Category in the consumer products section of ID's annual design review. 188

Lionel Dean qualified as an engineer before undertaking a Masters degree at the Royal College of Art, London. He works independently for international clients. 91

Andrea de Benedetto was born in Bolzano, Italy in 1972. She received a Bachelors degree in industrial design from the University of Plymouth, UK and has recently completed a Masters degree in the same subject at the Royal College of Art, London. From 1991 to 1993 she worked for Silk Cut Graphic Design Studio. In 1999 she took part in the Post Design Exhibition at the Memphis Gallery in Milan. 88

Paolo Deganello was born in Este, Italy in 1940 and studied architecture at the University of Florence. An architect, designer and teacher, he was one of the founders of the radical design group Archizoom in 1966. He has designed furniture and lighting for companies such as Cassina, Driade, Venini and Zanotta. 209

Michele de Lucchi was born in Ferrara, Italy in 1951 and graduated from Florence University in 1975. During his student years he founded the Gruppo Cavart, a group concerned with avant-garde and conceptual architecture. He designed for Alchimia until the establishment of Memphis in 1981 and was responsible for the design of the Memphis exhibitions and a series of new household appliances. In 1986 he founded and promoted Solid, a group of young designers developing new design concepts, and in 1990 Produzione Privata, a production company for experimental objects. De Lucchi has been design chief for all of Olivetti's office products, special applications and office systems since 1992. 78, 83, 91, 128, 129

Kicca D'Ercole was born in Barletta, Italy in 1961. She works in Rome in the fields of design, graphics and web design. 209

Bernhard Dessecker was born in 1961 in Munich. He studied interior architecture and from 1983 to 1984 worked at Studio Morsa in New York. Since 1984 he has been a freelance designer collaborating with the design team of Ingo Maurer. 110

Anthony Di Bitonto was born in Canada in 1965. He received a degree in architecture from McGill University in 1987 and subsequently practised in Montreal. In 1992 he moved to New York where he was awarded a graduate degree in industrial design from the Pratt Institute. He now works for Smart Design as a product designer in the fields of housewares, consumer electronics, and medical and scientific equipment. 155

Nick Dine was born in New York in 1966 and studied at the Rhode Island School of Design and the Royal College of Art, London (furniture department). He worked in London for two years, then returned to New York in 1993, setting up his own interior architecture and product design firm, Dinersan. Its most recent commissions include an exclusive boutique in SoHo as well as several residences in New York. 23

Tom Dixon was born in Sfax, Tunisia in 1959 and moved to the UK when he was four years old. He formed Creative Salvage with Nick Jones and Mark Brazier-Jones in 1985. His studio, Space, is where his prototypes and commissioned works – stage sets, furniture, sculpture, illuminated sculpture, architectural installations, chandeliers and other objects – are made. His clients include Cappellini, Comme des Garçons, Nigel Coates, Ralph Lauren, Vivienne Westwood and Terence Conran. In 1994 Dixon opened the Space shop. He is currently head of design at Habitat UK. 61

Dante Donegani and **Giovanni Lauda** were born in Italy in 1957 and 1956, respectively. Donegani graduated from the Faculty of Architecture in Florence, then worked for Corporate Identity Olivetti. He has collaborated with firms such as Memphis, Stildomus and Luceplan. Lauda has a degree in architecture and works in the fields of interior, exhibition and industrial design for companies such as Artas, Play Line and Sedie and Company. He was a member of Morozzi and Partners until 1994. Donegani & Lauda was established in 1993. 20

Jan Dranger graduated from the Royal College of Art and Design, Stockholm in 1968 and co-founded Innovator Design Company which designed interiors for shops and commercial areas as well as furniture. He worked on paper furniture during the 1970s, and later began research into the use of plastic, producing a new furniture collection in Milan in 1982. Since the mid-80s Dranger has collaborated with IKEA. He received the Ecology Design Award at the iF Hanover in 1999 for the softAir seating. 47

Emily Du Bois received a Masters degree from the California College of Arts and Crafts, Oakland. She carried out postgraduate studies at the Indian Institute of Hand Loom Technology in Varanasi, India and is at present a Lecturer at the University of California, Davis in the department of environmental design. She holds the NEA Individual Artist Fellowship as well as the California Arts Council Fellowship. 170

Donato D'Urbino and **Paolo Lomazzi** were born in Milan in 1935 and 1936, respectively. In the 1960s they created a series of inflatable designs which culminated in their inflatable chair Blow in 1967. They have designed for Acerbis, Artemide, Driade, Disform and others, and have extended their work to include architecture, product and lighting design. 39, 80

François Duris was born in 1972. From 1997 to 1998 he trained at the Ecole Nationale Supérieure des Arts Décoratifs, Paris and began to develop his Trellis shelving system. He has worked for Vichy and L'Oreal and collaborated on the packaging for L'Eau d'Issey 2000 for Issey Miyake. From 1995 to 1998 he worked with Martine Duris Coloriste. 27

Charles Eames (1907–1978) was one of the most influential furniture designers of the twentieth century. He was born in St Louis, Missouri and studied architecture at Washington University from 1924 to 1926, before setting up his own practice in 1930. In 1936 he received a scholarship to study at Cranbrook Academy of Art, Michigan where he met Ray Kaisèr (1912–1988). The couple, who married in 1941, collaborated on a number of design projects, experimenting with new techniques and materials, notably moulded plywood. Herman Miller produced the Eames' furniture designs from 1946. The fibreglass shell chair was designed in 1948 and the wire chair in 1952. 35

Hugo Eccles trained at the Royal College of Art, London before working for IDEO Product Development Europe and then Ross Lovegrove's Studio X. He now runs a London-based design company specializing in products, furniture and interiors. 38

Jan Eisermann was born in 1963. He trained as a joiner and worked and taught in Papua New Guinea for three years. Upon his return to Germany he studied in the department of design, University of Applied Sciences, Cologne. He is currently working as a freelance designer and is a member of kraut royal, a cooperation between Eisermann, formfiction and fremdkörper. He lectures at the Academy of Crafts and Design in Münster. 22

Nedda El-Asmar was born in Belgium in 1968. She studied jewellery design and silversmithing at the Royal Academy of Fine Arts, Antwerp, then took a Masters degree at the Royal College of Art, London. She currently works as a freelance silversmith and designer for companies in France and Belgium. 209

El Ultimo Grito is a design and product development company specializing in furniture, lighting and interiors. It was set up in London in 1997 by Roberto Feo, Rosario Hurtado and Francisco Santos. 67, 123

EOOS was founded by Martin Bergmann, Gernot Bohmann and Harald Gründl who studied together at the Academy of Applied Arts in Vienna from 1988 to 1994. They started their collaboration in 1990, forming EOOS in 1995, and specialize in product, furniture and architectural design. 143

Falt Design was founded by Francesco Tibaldi and Alessandro La Spada. The studio is involved in interior planning, design and consultancy for clients including Richard Ginori, Arosio, Kundalini and Nippon Brox Co., Osaka. Tibaldi studied at the Istituto Europeo di Disegno in Rome and worked for Aldo Cibic and Anna Gili. La Spada graduated from the Interior Design Institute in Milan. Before co-founding Falt Design he worked at Studio Sawaya and Moroni. 53

André Feldmann and Arne Jacob Schultchen were born in 1964 and 1965, respectively and have worked as a team since they met at the Hochschule für Bildende Künste, Hamburg from which they graduated in industrial design in 1992/93. Their work ranges from product design, furniture, lighting and interior design to graphics, packaging, exhibition design and experimental works. 201, 221

Emmanuel Fenasse was born in 1959 and graduated from the Ecole Nationale Supérieure de Création Industrielle in Paris in 1990. He works as a furniture and interior designer and has recently completed a showroom in Strasbourg. He designs for the label 3Designers with Mansu Farman-Farmaian and Laurence Hamelin. 49

Uwe Fischer was born in 1958. He founded Ginbande with Klaus-Achim Heine in 1985. Both partners studied at the Hochschule für Gestaltung, Offenbach, specializing in industrial design and visual communication, respectively. Ginbande works on corporate identities for public and private companies, and its experimental two- and three-dimensional pieces are regularly exhibited. 97

Jacopo Foggini was born in Turin in 1966. He was awarded Best Young Designer at the Salon de La Lumière in Paris in 1993 and has since built up an international reputation for his sculptural methacrylate lamps. He has held one-man shows in Germany, Italy and the UK, and his installation for Romeo Gigli won critical acclaim during the 1997 Milan Furniture Fair. 122

Monica Förster was born in 1966 and is currently living in Stockholm where she works as a product and film set designer. She studied at the University College of Arts, Crafts and Design, Stockholm. In 1999 she exhibited her work with David Design at the Milan Furniture Fair. 90

Sir Norman Foster was born in Manchester, UK in 1935 and studied architecture and city planning at the University of Manchester and at Yale University. He established Team 4 in 1963 – with his late wife, Wendy, and Su and Richard Rogers – and founded Foster Associates in 1967. Today he is famous for his high-tech designs, such as the Hong Kong and Shanghai Bank (1979–85) and Stansted Airport (1981–89). Other projects include the Sackler Galleries at the Royal Academy of Arts, London, which was named the RIBA building of the year in 1993; the Centre d'Art Cultural, Nîmes; the remodelling of the Reichstag in Berlin; headquarters for Commerzbank in Frankfurt; and the airport at Chek Lap Kok for Hong Kong. He is currently working on the new Wembley Stadium in London and is also active in furniture and product design. 148

Robert Foster is a trained silversmith and for the past fifteen years has created functional objects in aluminium and stainless steel. He recently expanded his work to include furniture, light fittings and theatrical sets and started to produce tableware under the name 'Fink'. 115, 135

Sara Fredhave was born in 1973 and is currently studying fashion design at the Danish Design School in Copenhagen. Her work was exhibited in collaboration with the 'Masters of Linen' at the 1999 Spring Premier Vision. 172

Michal Fronek and **Jan Nemecek** were born in 1966 and 1963, respectively. Both studied at the Academy of Applied Arts in Prague under Borek Sipek. They began their collaboration as the design group Olgoj Chorchoj and have completed numerous interior design projects in Prague. Artel II was founded in 1993. They were responsible for designing the interior fittings in Vaclav Havel's Prague house. Other commissions include a fire staircase at the Academy of Fine Arts; a jeans shop and sports shop in Bratislava; and the reconstruction and interior of a penthouse for *Elle* magazine (all 1996). 152

Naoto Fukasawa was born in Kofu, Japan in 1956 and graduated from Tama Art University. He was Chief Designer at the Seiko Corporation before joining IDEO San Francisco. He returned to Japan in 1996 to become director of IDEO, Japan. He has lectured at the Royal College of Art, London and at Tama Art University, and currently teaches at Matsushita Design. 211

John Gabbertas trained as a cabinet-maker and set up his own company five years ago. He now works for some of the leading UK and European furniture manufacturers. He was the recipient of the Seating in Practice award for his $3^{1/8}$ range of chairs and tables at the 1998 SIT Fair in London. 66

Jorge Garcia Garay was born in Buenos Aires and has worked in Barcelona since 1979 as the director of Garcia Garay Design. He is involved almost exclusively with lighting design. 108

Garouste & Bonetti have worked together since 1980 producing furniture, textiles and jewellery. Elizabeth Garouste was born in Marcilly sur Eure, France and studied set design at the Ecole Camondo in Paris. Mattia Bonetti was born and trained as a designer in Lugano, Switzerland, then worked as a textile designer, style consultant and photographer. 120

Frank Gärtner trained in mechanical engineering in Lörrach, Germany. He went on to study under Professor Richard Sapper, amongst others, at the Academy of Fine Arts in Stuttgart. He founded Studio GID (Gärtner Industrial Design) in 1997. 105

Thierry Gaugain see Luxlab

Frank O. Gehry was born in Toronto in 1930 and moved to Los Angeles in 1947. He received his Bachelor of Architecture degree from the University of Southern California, and studied city planning at the Harvard University Graduate School of Design. He established his architectural practice in 1962 and has since risen to fame with buildings in the USA, Europe and Asia, most recently the Guggenheim Museum in Bilbao. Current projects include the Experience Music Project in Seattle, Washington; the Bard College Centre for the Performing Arts in Annandale-on-Hudson, New York; and the Walt Disney Concert Hall in Los Angeles. 33

Roman Gebhard was born in Ulm, Germany. He studied industrial design at the Art Center College of Design in Pasadena and in Europe, graduating in 1995 with a Bachelors degree in industrial design. He joined Lunar Design in 1996 and has worked on commissions for Microsoft and Hewlett-Packard. 193

Christian Ghion was born in Montmorency, France in 1958. He graduated from E.C.M. (Etude et Création de Mobilier), Paris in 1987 and since then has worked with Patrick Nadeau. Since 1998 he has concentrated on industrial and interior design for European and Japanese companies including Cinna/Roset, Néotù, 3 Suisses, Idée, Tendo and Thierry Mugler. 153

Anna Gili graduated from the Istituto Superiore delle Industrie Artistiche in Florence. She has designed objects for Alessi; tiles for Inax, Tokyo; ceramic pots for Richard Ginori; carpets, tapestries and furniture for Cassina, glass vases for Salviati and Bisazza, as well as furniture and textiles for Cappellini. In 1999 she designed a light installation, 'Noah's Ark', for the Milan Furniture Fair. 109, 142

Paolo Giordano was born in Naples in 1954. He studied architecture at the Milan Polytechnic, graduating in 1978, then worked as a graphic designer and photographer for Italian and international magazines. In 1992 he began working as a designer and design consultant for companies in Italy and abroad. Following a trip to India he produced a collection of painted wood items for Alessi/Twergi as well as his own range of metal furniture called 'Asia Edition', and founded I+I which produces home accessories handmade in India. 150

Stefano Giovannoni was born in La Spezia, Italy in 1954 and graduated from the architecture department of the University of Florence in 1978. From 1978 to 1990 he lectured and carried out research at Florence University and also taught at the Domus Academy in Milan and at the Institute of Design in Reggio Emilia. He is the founding member of King-Kong Production, which is concerned with avant-garde research in design, interiors, fashion and architecture. Clients include Alessi, Cappellini, Arredaesse and Tisca France. 183, 200

Ernesto Gismondi was born in San Remo, Italy in 1931. He studied at Milan Polytechnic and the Higher School of Engineering, Rome. In 1959, with Sergio Mazza, he founded Artemide SpA, of which he is the President and Managing Director. He has designed lights for Artemide since 1970 and was involved in the development of Memphis in 1981. 91

Natanel Gluska was born in Israel in 1957 but currently works in Zurich and in Lefkada, Greece. He studied in Israel, The Hague and at the Rietveld Academy, Amsterdam (1985 to 1989). His most recent projects include the interior of a club in Zurich, chairs for the Union Bank of Switzerland, Zurich (both 1999) and chairs for the Sanderson Hotel, London and Donna Karan's shop, Madison Avenue, New York (both 2000). 63

Josh Goldfarb received a degree in industrial design from the University of Cincinnati, College of Architecture, Art and Planning in 1995. He currently works for Herbst LaZar Bell. He has received numerous awards including the ID Annual Design Review, Industrial Design Excellence Awards, and the Good Design Award from the Chicago Athenaeum Museum. 193, 212

Carsten Gollnick was born in Berlin in 1966 and received a Masters degree in industrial design from the Hochschule für Bildende Künste, Brunswick. He is co-founder of Yo Creative Answers design agency and has his own product design company in Hamburg. Projects include porcelain products for Arzberg, home accessories for Ligne Roset in cooperation with Peter Maly, cutlery for Carl Mertens; carpets for JAB and items for Mont Blanc. He has received the iF Product Design Award and the FORM 99 Prize. 203

Konstantin Grcic was born in Munich in 1965. He attended the John Makepeace School for Craftsmen in Wood, then studied furniture design at the Royal College of Art, London. He worked in the office of Jasper Morrison before founding his own studio in Munich. He has been commissioned to produce furniture designs for the Munich Tourist Information Office in collaboration with David Chipperfield, as well as exhibition concepts for Authentics in Germany, Italy and France. Clients include Agape, Cappellini, Flos, Iittala, Moormann, Montina, SCP and Wireworks. 77, 80, 126

Urs Greutmann was born in 1959 and trained in architectural drawing and industrial design. He has run his own studio since 1985, specializing in interior, lighting, furniture and exhibition design. 115

Davide Groppi was born in Piacenza, Italy in 1963. He works as lighting designer for clients such as Tecno, Boffi and Feroom. In 1999 he started to teach industrial design at Milan Polytechnic. 100

Pawel Grunert was born in Warsaw in 1965 and studied at the Academy of Art and Furniture Design. He has taken part in exhibitions in Japan and Europe and was the winner of the 1996 International Furniture Design Fair in Asahikawa. He currently collaborates with Edizioni Galleria Colombari. 63

Gitta Gschwendtner was born in 1972 in Würzburg, Germany. She holds a Bachelors degree in furniture and product design from Kingston University, Surrey and a Masters degree in furniture design from the Royal College of Art, London. Since 1998 she has worked as a freelance furniture, product and interior designer. 51

Monica Guggisberg and Philip Baldwin are an American/Swiss couple who have been working together for fifteen years. They both trained in Sweden at the Orrefors Glass School and later in the studio of Ann Wolff and Wilke Adolfsson. In 1982 they established their own design and hot glass studio near Lausanne, Switzerland. 153

Roberto Guzman see Comma

Knut and Marianne Hagberg are a brother and sister team. They trained as architects in Copenhagen and have worked together since 1979. They were awarded the Excellent Swedish Design Prize in 1984 for their Talus chair, in 1988 for the Puzzel children's furniture, in 1993 for the Line plate and in 1998 for the Patrull child's stool. They collaborate with IKEA. 23

Annaleena Hakatie was educated at the University of Art and Design in Helsinki and undertook special studies at the Orrefors Glass School and the Pilchuck Glass School. She has held one-man shows in Helsinki and in Sweden, and exhibited her work at the Venice-International Glass Biennale (1998–9). She has been a part-time lecturer at the University of Art and Design in Helsinki and today works for Iittala Glass. 127

Ashley Hall was born in Cardiff, Wales in 1967. He studied furniture design at Nottingham Trent University and then the Royal College of Art, London, graduating in 1992. He designs products, furniture and lighting both for his own production and for manufacturers such as Designease, RSVP, Anthologie Quartett, Stephen Philips Design and SKK Lighting. 52

Doug Halley was born in Glasgow, Scotland in 1976. He has studied industrial design and recently graduated from the Glasgow School of Art with a Bachelors degree in product design. He has worked with Cassina in Milan. 213

Isabel Hamm studied ceramic design in Germany, then from 1996 to 1998 took a Masters degree in glass and ceramics at the Royal College of Art, London. Before moving to London she had her own studio in Cologne and received commissions from Apple and Fairform. 89, 134

Noa Hanyu was born in Kanagawa, Japan in 1965. He graduated from the department of product design at Tama Art University, Tokyo, then worked at GK Planning and Design from 1989 to 1990. Awards for his work include the Grand Prix of the Japan Craft Expo and the Grand Prix of the Takaoka Craft Competition (both 1996). 62

Masako Hayashibe was born in Tokyo in 1940. She became interested in textile weaving while studying in Stockholm and in 1976 returned to Japan and set up the Spiral workshop. She has exhibited her work at the National Museum of Modern Art in Tokyo. 170

Sam Hecht was born in London in 1969. After studying at the Royal College of Art he worked as an interior and industrial designer. He moved to Tel Aviv and joined the Studia group, then to San Francisco where he began his collaboration with IDEO. He completed projects for AT&T and NEC as well as designing office interiors for IDEO, then worked for IDEO in Japan with clients such as NEC, Seiko and Matsushita. He is currently head of Industrial Design at IDEO, London. 211

Albert Heer was born in Switzerland in 1962. After training as a draughtsman he studied architecture in Zurich and worked as a freelance architect. Today he has an office in Zurich with a partner, working on architectural as well as industrial, furniture and interior design commissions. 47

Christian Heimberger has worked for Paschen & Companie for several years. He served an apprenticeship as a carpenter before studying arts and crafts in Hildesheim and finally taking a degree as a wood technician, joiner and interior designer. He worked as a structural engineering designer and as a freelance furniture designer before joining Paschen. 73

Achim Heine was born in 1955. He founded the design project Ginbande in 1985 which he ran until its closure ten years later. Today he works as a product designer based in Berlin and Frankfurt with clients such as Thonet, Vitra and Wogg, and as a partner in the graphic design firm Heine/Lenz/Zizka. He is Professor of Conceptual Design at the Hochschule der Künste in Berlin. 24

Daniel Henry is studying textile design at L'Ecole Nationale Supérieure des Arts Visuels/La Cambre in Brussels. His work in collaboration with 'Masters of Linen' was exhibited at the 1999 Spring Premier Vision and he will be researching linen for them again in 2000 in Berlin. He is currently working for Belgian textile manufacturer Liebaert. 172

Anette Hermann was born in 1970. After graduating from the Danish Design School in Copenhagen she worked for the design group Light Stories. She opened her own studio in 1998. 105

Matthew Hilton was born in Hastings, UK in 1957. He studied furniture design at Kingston Polytechnic, Surrey, until 1979, then worked for several years as an industrial designer in London. In 1984 he began designing furniture for SCP, Disform, XO, Idee, Alterego and Driade. 31, 57

Yoshiki Hishinuma was born in Sendai, Japan in 1958. He started a course at the Bunk College of Fashion in Tokyo but left after a year to work freelance, having gained experience with Miyake Design Studio. He founded his own company, Hishinuma Associates Co. Ltd, in 1987. He has since started a label for womenswear, Yoshiki Hisinuma, and has shown the collection in Paris. In 1999 a retrospective of his work was held at the Haags Gemeentemuseum, The Hague. 176, 177

Alex Hochstrasser was born in Switzerland in 1973. He studied industrial design at the Hochschule für Gestaltung und Kunst in Zurich and has worked for design consultancies in Barcelona, New York and Tokyo. 113

Greg Holderfield is Director of Industrial Design at Herbst LaZar Bell. He obtained a Bachelors degree in industrial design from the University of Illinois in Urbana-Champaign, then worked for IBM, Motorola, Zenith Electronics and Colgate before joining HLB. He has lectured in industrial design across the USA and is currently working at the Institute of Design in Chicago. 193

Bohuslav Horak was born in Pardubice in the Czech Republic in 1954 and attended both the Zizkov Art School of Prague and the Academy of Applied Arts. In 1987 he became a member of the design group Atika and in 1990 set up his own studio. Many of his designs are produced by Anthologie Quartett. 117

Wayne Hudson was born in Burnie, Tasmania in 1948 and is currently undertaking studies for a doctorate in Fine Art at the School of Art, University of Tasmania. He trained as an upholsterer before becoming involved in furniture design and Fine Art. 49

Richard Hutten graduated in industrial design from the Design Academy in Eindhoven in 1991 and set up his own studio. Philippe Starck selected two of his products for the interiors of the Delano Hotel in Miami and the Mondrian Hotel in Los Angeles. Hutten taught product design at the Art School in Maastricht from 1996 to 1998. 96

Martin Huwiler was born in Zurich in 1960. He studied product design at the School of Design in Zurich and carried out research work on ecology and design. He has been a self-employed designer for the last ten years, specializing in product design and architecture. 108

Inflate see Nick Crosbie

Yoshinori Inukai was born in Nagoya, Japan in 1964. He graduated from Kanaza College of Art in 1996 and joined Canon shortly afterwards. He has received numerous national awards and in 1999 received the iF Award in Germany as well as the IDEA 99 Bronze Prize, USA. 193

Aleksej Iskos was born in Khar'kov, Ukraine. He studied architecture and trained as a teacher, moving to Denmark in 1991 and graduating from the Institute of Industrial Design at Denmark's Design School in Copenhagen in 1996. He set up his own design group, Light Stories, in 1997. 120

Setsu Ito was born in Yamaguchi, Japan in 1964. He obtained a Masters degree in product design from the University of Tsukuba. He has undertaken design research projects for the TDK Corporation, NEC Electric Co. and Nissan Motor Co., and in 1989 worked for Studio Alchimia in Milan. Since 1989 he has collaborated with Angelo Mangiarotti and has become a consultant designer for the TDK Corporation with Bruno Gregori. 222

Ichiro Iwasaki was born in Tokyo in 1965. He graduated in industrial design from the Salesian Polytechnic in Tokyo. In 1986 he joined Sony Corporation as head of the audio-visual department. He moved to Italy in 1991 and worked for MH Design and Studio Matteo Thun. He now has his own practice involved in product design. 107

Hans Sandgren Jakobsen was born in 1963. He trained as a cabinet-maker before studying furniture design at the Danish Design School in Copenhagen. He has worked in Nanna Ditzel's drawing office since 1991 and is also a member of the design group Spring. Freelance clients include Via America, Fritz Hansen and Fredericia Stolefabrik. 36

Carsten Joergensen was born in Denmark in 1948. He was educated at Copenhagen School of Art where he studied painting and graphic illustration and later taught. From 1969 to 1970 he was a designer at Royal Copenhagen. In 1974 he started his collaboration with Bodum Company, initially as a freelance designer. He subsequently founded a department within the company, and moved with it to Lucerne in 1983. 201

Ehlén Johansson has worked as an in-house designer for many product areas of IKEA. She is a graduate of the product design department of the School of Design and Crafts in Gothenburg. She also works for Pelikan & Co. in Copenhagen. 81

Hella Jongerius was born in De Meern, The Netherlands in 1963 and studied at the Academy of Industrial Design, Eindhoven. She began working with Droog Design in the early 1990s. She also designs for Dry-Tech 1, the Hema Dutch department store, Makkum and Cappellini. She recently designed the interior of the Museum of Modern Art restaurant in New York. Since 1998 she has taught design at the Design Academy, Eindhoven. 78

Patrick Jouin see Luxlab

Masakazu Kanatani is an industrial designer currently working for Sony Design Centre, Japan. 192

Peter Karpf was born in Copenhagen in 1940. He worked as a carpenter before entering the Academy of Arts and Crafts in 1961 to study furniture design. He has collaborated with the textile artist Nina Koppel, with furniture and industrial designer Grete Jalk and with the architect Arne Jacobsen. He has developed many furniture and lighting products. In 1989 he wrote an architectural manifesto and formed the Alfabetica Group. 36

Masamichi Katayama was born in Okayama, Japan in 1966. He worked for various design offices then began to work freelance in 1991. In 1992, with Tsutomu Kurokawa, he established H Design, a practice concerned with interior and furniture design projects, including retail outlets in Japan and a range of furniture produced by manufacturers such as Thonet and Aidec Co. Ltd. 110

Yehudit Katz was born in Israel and graduated from the Bezalel Academy of Arts and Design, Jerusalem. He received a postgraduate degree from the Ateneum School of Art in Helsinki and has since designed textiles for various mills in Israel and abroad. He has taught weaving at the Art Centre of Jerusalem and is Senior Lecturer at the Shenkar College in Ramat Gan. 171

Hideki Kawai was born in Nagoya, Japan in 1967. He graduated from the Aichi College of Art in 1989 and joined Canon. 189

Kazuo Kawasaki graduated from the Kanazawa College of Arts, then joined Toshiba. He opened Kazuo Kawasaki Design Studio, and four years later, eX-Design Inc., working on business strategies, traditional crafts, interior design and computer hardware design. In 1996 Kawasaki was appointed Professor for the School of Design and Architecture at the Nagoya City University. 213

Shosaku Kawashima was born in Kanagawa, Japan in 1966. He graduated from the Asagaya College of Art in Tokyo in 1984 and joined Olympus shortly afterwards. Since 1992 he has been working for Canon. 196

Charles Keller trained in the aircraft construction industry before studying industrial design at the School of Applied Art in Zurich. He has worked as a lighting consultant on numerous projects including a new exhibition building in Basle and a laboratory building at the Swiss Federal Institute of Technology. He has also designed lights for Zumtobel. 114

David Khouri see Comma

Toshiyuki Kita was born in Osaka in 1942 and graduated in industrial design from the Naniwa College in 1964. He established his own design studio in Osaka and began working both in Milan and Japan, focusing on domestic environments and interior design. In 1989 he was presented with the Delta de Oro award in Spain. He designed the chairs and interior for the rotating theatre in the Japanese Pavilion at Expo '92, Seville. 53, 91

Gabriel Klasmer was educated at the Bezalel Academy of Arts and Design, Jerusalem and at the Royal College of Art, London where he is now Senior Tutor in Industrial and Furniture Design. He took part in the 'Home Alone' show at the Memphis Gallery during the Milan Furniture Fair in 1999. 203

Stefanie Klein has a Diploma in industrial design from the Hochschule der Künste, Berlin. She trained as a product designer in Berlin and worked for Frog Design, moving to London in 1997 to work for Isis. She now designs for Starfish. 87

Ubald Klug was born in Zurich. He studied at the Kunstgewerbeschule and since 1966 has run his own architecture, interior design and product design office in Paris. 76

Michael Koenig was born in 1971 in Würselen, Germany. He trained as a cabinet-maker and furniture designer, working on a freelance basis for clients in Aachen such as Cotelletto and Freiraum. He has lectured at the University of Aachen since 1997 and currently designs for Habitat UK, Wireworks and Zanotta. 38

Eero Koivisto see Claesson Koivisto Rune

Matijs Korpershoek was born in Leeuwarden, The Netherlands in 1969, and studied in Eindhoven at the Academy of Industrial Design, graduating in 1996. His two graduation projects were awarded the Industrial Product Quality Award (Dutch furniture award) 1997 and the Talent Trophy of the Annual Advertising Awards 1998. He has worked for Droog Design since 1996. 107

Harri Koskinen was born in Karstula, Finland in 1970 and studied product and strategic design at the University of Art and Design, Helsinki. Since 1998 he has been chief designer for Hackman Designor, Iittala Glass. 221

Aki Kotkas was born in 1974. He is currently studying at the University of Industrial Arts in Helsinki. 133

Roman Kovár was born in Czechoslovakia in 1976. He studied at the Academy of Arts, Architecture and Design in Prague. 196

Randi Kristensen was born in Denmark in 1959 but today lives in Milan. She began a collaboration with Studio Sowden In 1984. Since 1992 she has taken part in many exhibitions in Milan and Europe and is active in domestic product design. She has taught at the Carrara Academy of Fine Arts in Bergamo. 209

Kyoko Kumai was born in Tokyo, Japan in 1943 and graduated from Tokyo National University of Arts. In 1994 she was the subject of a solo exhibition at the Museum of Modern Art in New York. This was followed in 1995 by 'Textile and New Technology 2010', held in London and The Netherlands. She was awarded the Bronze Prize at the 9th International Tapestry Triennial in Lódz, Poland in 1998. 167

Tsutomu Kurokawa was born in Aichi, Japan in 1962. He studied design in Nagoya and trained in the offices of Ics Inc. and Super Potato Co. In 1992, with Masamichi Katayama, he established H Design to work on interior and furniture design projects including a series of boutiques in Japan. 192

Erik-Jan Kwakkel was born in Delfzijl, The Netherlands in 1965. He trained at the Hogeschool voor de Kunsten Arnhem, in the faculties of Fine Art and Three-dimensional Design. Since then he has worked as a jewellery designer and ceramicist. In 1997 he was appointed guest designer for a series of unique pieces at the crystal works of Royal Leerdam BV. 135, 151

Danny Lane was born in Urbana, Illinois in 1955. He moved to the UK in 1975 to work with the stained-glass artist Patrick Reyntiens, then studied painting at Central St Martin's College of Art and Design in London. In 1983 he co-founded Glassworks with John Creighton and began a three-year association with Ron Arad. In 1988 he started producing work for Fiam Italia. He was commissioned by the Victoria and Albert Museum, London in 1994 to install a glass balustrade in its new Glass Gallery. In 1998 he produced a water sculpture for the Conrad International Hotel in Cairo. In 1999 Lane held an exhibition in London entitled 'Breaking Tradition'. 116

Sophie Larger graduated from the Ecole Nationale Supérieure des Arts Décoratifs, Paris in 1997 and has recently completed a Masters degree in furniture design. She has exhibited with VIA in Paris and has created designs for Ligne Roset. 49

Eric LaRoye was born in 1947. From 1989 to 1994 he was a student at St-Lucas, Karel de Grote Art School in the department of jewellery and silversmithing. He was given an honourable prize in the International Jewellery Design Competition in Tokyo in 1998, and the following year received the Henry van de Velde Award for best product. 155

Marta Laudani and **Marco Romanelli** work together as interior and product designers with practices in Rome and Milan. Laudani graduated in Rome in 1979. Romanelli took a Masters degree in design after graduating in architecture in 1983. He worked for Mario Bellini until 1985 when he became freelance. He was editor at *Domus* magazine from 1986 to 1994 and has been a design editor at *Abitare* since 1995. He works as a consultant for Driade and is art director at Montina and Oluce. Laudani and Romanelli currently work for Atlantide, Cleto Munari, Montina and Oluce. 150

Ferruccio Laviani was born in Cremona, Italy in 1960. He graduated from the Faculty of Architecture at Milan Polytechnic in 1986 and in the same year exhibited his work in the Memphis show '12 Nuovi'. He was a founder member of the Solid Group before leaving to join Michele de Lucchi's studio. Since 1991 he has worked for the Imel Company as well as freelance for clients such as Foscarini, Emmemobili, Gruppo Industriale Busnelli and Moroso. 45

Chunghie Lee is a fashion and textile designer who was born in Korea in 1945. He has degrees from the Hong-Ik University in Seoul where he is now a lecturer in the department of fibre arts. He was awarded the Fulbright Exchange Scholarship to Rhode Island School of Design in 1994 to research textile design. 170

Mark Lee was born in Taipei in Taiwan but today lives and works in New York. He designs ambient light sources using paper, fabric, metal and leaves. 92

Pierpaolo Lenoci was born in Novara, Italy in 1967 and studied industrial design in Milan. He worked in the studio of Denis Santachiara as well as spending periods with Magis and with Andries Van Onck before starting a freelance practice collaborating with firms such as Progetti Brunati, Dovetusai, Costantino and Fantasia. 79

Martin Leuthold was born in Switzerland in 1953. He started his career as an embroidery designer and today leads a team of designers working on the Schlaepfer fabrics range. Since joining Schlaepfer in 1973 he has received numerous awards for his work including first prize at the International Competition for textile design in Stuttgart and the Swiss Design Award (both 1995). 174

Ulrika Liffner was born in Jönköping, Sweden. She studied Fine Arts and ceramics before moving to London to take a Bachelors degree in product design at Central St Martin's College of Art and Design. She is currently studying for a Masters degree at the Royal College of Art. In 1999 she worked with Dinersan in New York and also took part in the Post Design Exhibition at the Memphis Gallery in Milan. 21

Maya Lin was born in Athens, Ohio in 1959 and graduated from Yale University School of Architecture in 1986. She came to public prominence in 1981 with her award-winning design for the Vietnam Veterans' Memorial in Washington, DC. In 1986 she established her own studio in New York. Her recent work includes an apartment in New York for Peter Norton of Norton Utilities; a library and chapel for the Children's Defense Fund in Clinton, Tennessee; and a series of furniture for Knoll International. 38

Jon Lindholm has a Bachelors degree in design from Arizona University. He worked in Europe and the Far East before joining Herbst LaZar Bell. His distinctions include Industrial Design Excellence Awards, an Appliance Manufacturer Annual Design Award and a Good Design Award from the Chicago Athenaeum Museum. 212

Jonas Lindvall trained as an interior architect at the Hochschule der Künste in Gothenburg, and also studied at the Royal College of Art in London and the Royal Academy in Copenhagen. He runs Vertigo Architects in Malmö, Sweden and has designed for Swecode, David Design and Kockums. Architectural projects include restaurants, offices, retail and domestic projects in Sweden including the Flos Scandinavia showroom and office, and the concept for McDonald's restaurants in Gothenburg. 72

Piero Lissoni was born in 1956. He studied architecture at Milan Polytechnic and formed his own company with Nicoletta Canesi in 1984. He has worked with Boffi Cucine as art director since 1986 and was awarded the Compasso d'Oro in 1991 for the Esprit kitchen. In 1995 he became the art director for Cappellini and started his collaboration with Cassina and Nemo. In 1996 Lissoni was appointed art director for Units. He started a collaboration with Benetton in 1998. Recent interior design projects include the headquarters of Welonda; two hairdressing salons; two new showrooms for Cappellini; the Allegri showroom and the Boffi Bagni showroom in Milan. 56

Mary Little graduated from the Royal College of Art, London. Her first series of experimental upholstery, 'Coat of Arms', was shown in London in 1994 and a piece was purchased by the Victoria and Albert Museum. In 1997 she formed Bius with Peter Wheeler, designing one-offs, limited editions and production furniture. 50

Vera Lopes studied political science and belles-lettres in Porto Alegre. After living in Europe for a while, she returned to São Paulo, Brazil and founded Atelier Ferro & Fogo, designing objects made from iron and stainless steel. She works for architects in Brazil and since 1994 has designed candles and lights with Maria Pessoa. 88

Jeremy Lord was born in 1950. In the early 1970s he designed and built amplification and lighting systems for pop groups and discos, then worked with theatrical lighting and audio-visual systems, becoming a freelance designer in the late 1970s. He worked for a short time in medical electronics, then in 1994 set up Colour Light Company to develop and manufacture his designs. A version of his Chromawalls formed an installation at the Museum of Contemporary Arts, Los Angeles in 1998. 104

Ross Lovegrove was born in Wales in 1958. He graduated from Manchester Polytechnic in 1980 with a degree in industrial design, later receiving a Masters from the Royal College of Art, London. In 1984 he moved to Paris to work for Knoll International and became a member of the Atelier de Nîmes with Gérard Barrau, Jean Nouvel, Martine Bedin and Philippe Starck. In 1986 he co-founded Lovegrove and Brown Design Studio, later replaced by Lovegrove Studio X. Current projects include the Airbus A3XX, a first-class interior for Japan Airlines and a diversification programme for Tag Heuer in Switzerland. 44, 201

Massimo Lunardon, born in Marostica in 1964, is an artist and designer working primarily in glass. He received a Masters degree in industrial design from the Domus Academy, and has since collaborated with designers including Andrea Anastasio, Ron Arad, Marc Newson and Javier Mariscal. He has exhibited his work throughout Europe, most recently at the Glass Biennale in Venice (1998/99), as well as in the USA in the 'New Glass Review' at the Corning Museum of Glass, New York (1997). 132

Luxlab was formed in 1998 by three French designers. Thierry Gaugain graduated from the Ecole Nationale Supérieure de Création Industrielle, Paris in 1991 and worked with Philippe Starck on the Thomson multimedia products and the Aprilia 6.5 motorcycle. Patrick Jouin also studied at ENSCI, then joined the Tim Thom design studio of Thomson multimedia. Since 1995 he has been a member of the Starck studio. Freelance clients include Fermob, Proto Design and Ligne Roset. Jean-Marie Massaud graduated from ENSCI in 1990. He opened his own furniture and industrial design studio in 1994 and designs for Authentics, Baccarate, Magis and Yamaha. 204

Vico Magistretti was born in Milan in 1920 and graduated from Milan Polytechnic with a degree in architecture in 1945. His furniture, lamps and other designs have been produced by Alias, Artemide, Cassina, de Padova, Fiat, Knoll International and Rosenthal. Since 1967 he has been a member of the Academy of San Luca in Rome. He has been the recipient of major awards, including the Gold Medal at the Milan Triennale in 1951, the Compasso d'Oro First Prize in 1967 and 1979, and the Gold Medal of the Society of International Artists and Designers in 1986. He was awarded the Compasso d'Oro for his whole career in 1995, the iF Product Design Award in 1998 for Vicoduo and the IDEA 98 USA for Vicodun. 79, 83, 216

Peter Maly is the head of Peter Maly Studio in Hamburg working on product and interior design. The practice designs international furniture collections as well as producing concepts and designs for trade fairs and exhibitions. Clients include COR, Behr, Interlübke, Thonet and Ligne Roset. 171, 203

Cecilie Manz was born in Denmark in 1972 and studied furniture design at the Danish Design School, Copenhagen and interior architecture and furniture design at the University of Art and Design in Helsinki. She worked for Studio Yrho Wiherheimo in Helsinki, then formed her own studio in 1998. She recently held a retrospective, 'Form – Transformation', with Bodil and Richard Manz at the Danish Art and Craft Museum in Copenhagen. 69, 70

Map Design and Communication is a Milan-based consultancy founded in 1997 by Patrizia Ledda and Maria Gallo. The company is active in the design of furniture, tableware, giftware and packaging, and recently coordinated a new line of wedding gifts for Acquachiara and a candle collection for Covo. It organized the condom-holder exhibition 'Make Love With Design' in Milan in 1999. 209

Enzo Mari was born in Novara, Italy in 1932 and studied at the Academy of Fine Art in Milan. In 1963 he co-ordinated the Italian group Nuove Tendenze and in 1972 participated in 'Italy: the New Domestic Landscape' at the Museum of Modern Art, New York. Mari is involved with town planning and teaching. He has been awarded the Compasso d'Oro on three occasions: for design research by an individual (1967); for the Delfina chair (1979) and for the Tonietta chair for Zanotta (1987). Since 1993 he has collaborated with the KPM (Royal Porcelain Works) in Berlin, and in 1996 staged the 'Arbeiten in Berlin' exhibition at Charlottenburg Castle. 132, 201, 216

Sharon Marston graduated from Middlesex University, UK with a Bachelors degree in jewellery design. She then worked in the props and costume departments of various theatre companies before joining the studio of fashion designer Bella Freud. Since 1995 she has worked for other designers such as Owen Gaster and Michiko Koshino as a freelance pattern cutter. In 1997 she set up her own business as a three-dimensional textile designer. 122

Jean-Marie Massaud see Luxlab

Helena Mattila-Sorri was born in Finland in 1953. She founded her own company, Everyday Design, in 1995. 224

F. Maurer was born in 1962 in Vienna. Since 1989 he has worked as a freelance designer, specializing in product development, presentations and interior concepts as well as furniture and lighting objects. He has collaborated with Anthologie Quartett, Ingo Maurer, Artificial Design and Objects and Authentics. 107

Tony McIntyre was born in Toronto in 1950. He studied at the Architectural Association, London where he later taught, and has also lectured at the Royal College of Art and the University of Turin. He worked for several major UK practices before founding Mosquito in 1997. 194

Alessandro Mendini was born in Milan in 1931. For many years he has been the theorist of avant-garde design, co-founding the Global Tools Group and collaborating with Studio Alchimia during the 1970s. An architect, furniture and product designer, he is art director of Swatch Lab of Milan and of Alessi. His many awards include the Compasso d'Oro, an honour from the Architectural League of New York, and the distinction of Chevalier des Arts et des Lettres. In 1990 he set up Atelier Mendini with his brother, the architect, Francesco Mendini. The atelier's projects include Alessi House, Milan; a tower in Hiroshima; the Groninger Museum in The Netherlands; a theatre in Arezzo, Italy; and the McDonald's Headquarters in Milan. 194

Martin Mengler was born in 1963. He trained as a cabinet-maker and later studied industrial design at the Fachhochschule in Darmstadt. He worked for several companies before becoming head of the industrial design department at Magenta Design. His Winx300 bed system was voted one of the Top Ten designs at the iF Product Design Awards in Hanover in 1999. 210

Ross Menuez was born in New York in 1965. He studied sculpture and anthropology at Hunter College then became interested in metalwork. Since 1992 he has created several series of furniture, lighting and accessories using stainless steel. He is currently working on a showroom interior and furniture for the couture house Maurizio Galante in Paris; office furniture for the film director Ridley Scott; and a new collection of one-offs and production pieces for an exhibition in Cologne. 56, 205

Evelyne Merkx is a Dutch interior designer who studied at the Rietveld Academy. She has her own business in partnership with Patrice Girod and is working on the renovation of the Main Hall of the Concert Building in Amsterdam as well as the refurbishment of the Hema department store. Her most recent commission is a new shopping and bar/catering section at Schiphol Airport. 66

Metz und Kindler Produktdesign was founded by Guido Metz, Matthias Schlett and Michael Kindler, three product designers from the University of Darmstadt. The company is active in public design and tableware, and works for manufacturers such as Authentics, Alessi and WMF. In 1992 and 1995 three projects won the exhibition at the Braun Design Prize and in 1997 the Die Enyklopen cutlery was awarded the Sabattini Prize and the Knut ladle received a Design Plus award. 201

Ligia Miguez was born in 1959 in São Paulo and is currently working on a line of objects in aluminium, wood and steel. 96

Anthony Mixides was born in London in 1976. He has recently completed a degree in furniture and product design at Kingston University and while studying worked for clients such as Sony and IKEA. 194

Marre Moerel was born in Breda, The Netherlands in 1966. She studied fashion design and sculpture at Rotterdam Academy of Art, then in 1987 was selected for the student exchange programme and moved to Exeter, UK where she received a Bachelors degree in sculpture in 1989. She studied furniture design at the Royal College of Art, graduating in 1991, then in 1993 moved to New York where she works as a freelance furniture designer and artist. She has taught furniture design at Parsons School of Design since 1995. 95

Rhodrick Moik-Tayali was born in Lusaka, Zambia in 1972. He was trained as an orthopaedic technician but since 1996 has worked as a freelance product and interior designer for Cotelletto in Aachen, Germany. 205

Carlo Moretti was born in Murano, Italy in 1934 and today lives in Venice. He attended law school in Padua, then in 1958 established the Carlo Moretti company with his brother Giovanni. They work in Murano crystal and their designs can be found in the major museums in Italy, Europe and the USA. Carlo Moretti is the sole administrator of Immobiliare Murano srl which opened the Contemporary Museum of Glass in Murano. 132

Ulf Moritz graduated in 1960 from the Textilingenieurschule, Krefeld, Germany and worked as a textile designer for Weverij de Ploeg before setting up his own design studio in 1970. His work includes collection co-ordination, corporate identity, art direction, exhibition stands and architectural projects. He has collaborated with Felice Rossi, Montis, Ruckstuhl, Interlübke and Interline Nova. The textile collection Ulf Moritz by Sahco Hesslein was established in 1986. Since 1971 he has been a professor at the Academy of Industrial Design in Eindhoven. 170

Craig Morrison started his career in the music industry, designing Latex costumes for the band Meat Beat Manifesto, and has since worked similarly with the Spice Girls and Frankie Goes to Hollywood. He is currently working with design company Inflate on a co-designed luggage range as well as on a series of products for the Millennium Dome, London. 208

Jasper Morrison was born in London in 1959. He studied design at Kingston Polytechnic Design School, The Royal College of Art, and the Hochschule der Künste, Berlin. In 1986 he set up his Office for Design in London. He has designed furniture and products for companies including Alessi, Alias, Cappellini, Flos, FSB, Magis, SCP, Rosenthal and Vitra. In 1995 his office was awarded the contract to design the new Hanover tram for Expo 2000. The first vehicle was presented to the public in 1997 at the Hanover Industrial Fair and was awarded the iF Transportation Design Prize and the Ecology Award. 23, 32, 202, 216

Pascal Mourgue was born in Neuilly-sur-Seine, Paris in 1943. He studied sculpture at the Ecole Boulle, then graduated from the Ecole Nationale Supérieure des Arts Décoratifs. He worked as a freelance designer during the 1980s, collaborating with Fermob, Artelano, Ligne Roset, Toulemonde-Bochart, Scarabat and Cassina. He has designed sailing ships for Cartier, crystal for Baccarat, shops for Ligne Roset and graphics for the Musée de la Poste in Paris. 155

Eddy Mundy was born in 1973. He served an apprenticeship as an engineer before studying industrial design and technology at Loughborough University, UK. He has worked for Land Rover and BMW and is currently studying for a Masters degree in industrial and furniture design at the Royal College of Art, London. He took part in the Post Design exhibition at the Memphis Gallery in Milan in 1999. 21

MVRDV is the interior design and architecture firm of Winy Maas, Jacob van Rijs and Nathalie de Vries. Based in Rotterdam, they specialize in architecture and urban planning, and their projects include the gatekeeper's house of the Hoge Veluwe National Park; the main offices of the broadcasting organizations VPRO and RVU in Hilversum; and a block of flats in Amsterdam. 136, 137

Paola Navone was born in Turin in 1950, and graduated in architecture from Turin Polytechnic. She worked for Alessandro Mendini, Ettore Sottsass and Andrea Branzi, and as part of the experimental groups Global Tools and Alchimia. She was consultant art director to Centrokappa form 1975 to 1979, and has also acted as a consultant to Abet Laminati. Other clients include Alessi, Knoll International and Fiat Auto. In 1988 she founded the manufacturing company Mondo with Giulio Cappellini. 163

Maxine Naylor received a Bachelors degree in furniture design from Middlesex Polytechnic and a Masters degree in furniture design and timber technology from Buckinghamshire College. She has lectured widely, and was a course tutor at the Royal College of Art, London from 1995 to 1998. 87

Julie Nelson was born in 1963. She studied three-dimensional design at Middlesex Polytechnic, concentrating on ceramic and metal sculpture. She has since set up her own studio working on interior and commercial projects and in film and television. She launched her first series of organic sculptural lamps, 'Anthropoid', in 1995. 94

Jan Nemecek see Michal Fronek

Marc Newson was born in Sydney, Australia. He studied jewellery design and sculpture and started experimenting in furniture design. In 1987 he moved to Japan where his designs were put into production by Idee. He set up a studio in Paris in 1991, working for clients such as Cappellini and Moroso, and formed a joint venture, Ikepod Watch Company. Since the mid-1990s he has been responsible for the interior design of a series of restaurants, including Coast in London, Mash & Air in Manchester and Osman in Cologne. In 1997 Newson moved to London and set up Marc Newson Ltd, designing for Alessi, Iittala and Magis. He recently designed the livery and interior of the $40 million Falcon 9008 long-range private jet. 127

N2 is named after the highway which runs between Basle and Lucerne in Switzerland. It was set up in 1997 by Jörg Boner, Christian Deuber, Paolo Fasulo, Kuno Nüssli and This Reber to focus on furniture design. 68

Katsuhiko Ogino was born in 1944 and graduated from the Musashino University of Art in 1966. He was a lecturer at the Japan Design School until 1969, then established various practices: Mono-Pro Kogei (1972), Humpty Dumpty Ltd (1976) and Time Studio Ltd (1978). In 1986 he was made a member of the Craft Centre, Japan, of which he is now director. In 1997 he became an adviser for the Kumamoto Prefectural Traditional Crafts Centre. 160

Olgoj Chorchoj see Michal Fronek and Jan Nemecek

Sofia Olsson is currently studying and works on a freelance basis for IKEA. 201

Jan Padrnos was born in Kutná Hora in the Czech Republic in 1967. He studied mechanical engineering but became interested in product and furniture design as well as architecture whilst working in an architectural studio during the early 1990s. In 1996 he left Prague, establishing his own studio in Trebic in 1998. 223

Roberto Palomba and **Ludovica Serafini** established their design and architecture studio in 1994. They have worked on several hotel designs and the restructuring of the Nazareno Gabrielli shops in Monza and Pisa, as well as a series of new shops in Dubai. They are involved in set design for television and ballet productions, and urban planning. Palomba and Serafini act as art directors for numerous firms, including AllGlass, and as consultants for the corporate image and public relations of the Finnish sauna firm Effegibi's. 18, 92, 135

Verner Panton (1926–1998) was born in Denmark and studied architecture at the Royal Art Academy in Copenhagen from 1947 to 1951. He worked with Arne Jacobsen on experimental furniture from 1950 to 1952, then opened his own studio in Binningen, Switzerland in 1955. His Cardboard House (1957) and Plastic House (1960) established his reputation. His 1960 Stacking Chair was produced by Herman Miller from 1967, and he designed the first one-piece, cantilever plastic chair, known as the Panton Chair, for Vitra in 1969. His range of work also included lighting, carpets, textiles and exhibition design. In 1999 a major retrospective of his work was held at the Design Museum in London. 35

Francesco Pellisari is an Italian acoustic designer who has recently won much acclaim for his omnidirectional speakers. His company NAC Sound makes a wide range of hi-tech hanging ceramic speakers. 207

Maurizio Peregalli was born in Varese, Italy in 1951. He studied in Milan where he began to work on fashion shops and showrooms. His projects include the design of the Giorgio Armani boutiques in Milan and London, and the image of the Emporio Armani chain. In 1984 he founded the furniture collection Zeus for which he currently works as partner and art director. He is also a director of Noto which produces Zeus. 78

Gaetano Pesce was born in La Spezia, Italy in 1939, and studied architecture and industrial design at the University of Venice. He established Gruppo N in Padua and a studio with Milena Vettore in 1961. In 1969 he designed a self-inflating furniture series for Cassina and Busnelli, and in 1971 established the company Bracciodiferro. He was commissioned to design a skyscraper in New York in 1978 and moved there in 1983, maintaining a studio in Paris. In 1995 he was commissioned to design the New York offices for Chiat Day. He is a professor at the Cooper Union School of Architecture and Art, New York and at the Institut d'Architecture et d'Etudes Urbaines in Strasbourg. 104

Maria Pessoa was born in São Paulo and attended the Escola Brazil and the Dalton de Luca studio. She currently works with Vera Lopes designing sculptural lights and candles. 88

Karl Pircher was born in Bolzano, Italy in 1963. He studied mechanical engineering at the Istituto Tecnico di Bolzano and product design at the University of Applied Arts in Vienna. In 1999 he took part in the Post Design Exhibition at the Memphis Gallery in Milan. 21

Salvatore Pischedda see Salvatore & Marie

Ferdinand A. Porsche was born in 1935 in Stuttgart. He studied design in Ulm then from 1960 worked in the design studios of Porsche KG, becoming manager in 1962 and developing the Formula 1 racing car and the Porsche 904 and 911. He founded Porsche Design in 1972, moving the studio to Zell am See in 1974. 114

Tim Power is an American architect and designer who has lived in Milan since 1990. He has worked in the studios of Sottsass Associati, Superstudio and I.O.O.A., and set up his own studio in 1995. Clients include Zeritalia, Cassina/Interdecor, BRF, Poltronova, WMF, Rosenthal and FontanaArte. He has recently begun to work on interior and architecture projects. 20

Gregory Prade was born in Oklahoma, USA in 1959. He is a freelance designer and project consultant and develops, produces and markets his own designs from his studio in Munich, Germany. 89

Kuno Prey was born in San Candido, Italy in 1958. He has his own studio and is a design consultant for numerous international companies. His products have won international awards including three Premio Compasso d'Oro prizes. He lectured at the Domus Academy from 1983 to 1984 and in 1993 became Professor of Product Design at the Bauhaus-Universität, Weimar in the Faculty of Art and Design. 213

Puls Design & Konstruktion was founded by Dieter Fornoff, Eberhard Klett and Andreas Ries to create products with a distinctive form using new technologies and ecological, economic materials. 196

Radi Designers was founded by Florence Doléac Stadler, Laurent Massaloux, Olivier Sidet, Robert Stadler and Claudio Colucci. Florence Stadler was a design consultant for Sommer Allibert until 1996. Massaloux and Sidet both worked for Philippe Starck in 1996 and then in the design department of Thomson Multimedia. Robert Stadler was born in Austria and taught at the Academy of Applied Arts in Vienna from 1994 to 1997. Radi is now based in Paris with an office in Tokyo headed by Colucci, who previously worked as a designer for Idee. 98

Dieter Rams was born in Wiesbaden, Germany in 1942. He studied architecture and interior design, then carpentry. In 1955 he started working for Braun AG and began to design products, becoming head of the product design department in 1961. He also designed furniture for Otto Zapf. Rams has been Professor of Industrial Design at the Hochschule für bildende Künste in Hamburg since 1981. 71

Karim Rashid graduated in industrial design from Carleton University in Ottawa, Canada in 1982. After graduate studies in Italy he moved to Milan for a one-year scholarship in the studio of Rodolfo Bonetto. He worked with KAN Industrial Designers in Toronto, designing projects ranging from high-tech products to furniture and also designing the Babel and North clothing collections from 1985 to 1990. Rashid was a full-time Associate Professor of Industrial Design at the University of Arts in Philadelphia for six years. Since 1992 he has been principal designer for Karim Rashid Industrial Design in New York. 20, 135

Jörg Ratzlaff is an industrial designer who lives in Hamburg. He has worked for clients such as Pressalit, Coca Cola, IBM, NEC, Samsung, Sharp and Villeroy and Boch. 206

Matthias Rexforth was born in 1963 and graduated with a diploma in product design from the University of Kassel in 1994. He specializes in furniture, exhibition and architectural design. 69

Fernando Rihl see Christopher Procter

Anete Ring studied architecture at the Institute of Technology in Israel and has since designed residences and interiors. He works with Sara Rosenberg, producing unique pieces in cast aluminium and brass, and took part in the 'Brazil Faz' design exhibition in Milan in 1996. 154

Marco Romanelli see Marta Laudani

Sara Rosenberg graduated with a Masters degree in Fine Arts from the University of São Paulo and later studied at the Kunstgewerbeschule in Zurich. 154

Kris Ruhs was born in New York in 1952. His work has been exhibited in galleries in Italy, New York and Florida, and he contributed to the exhibition 'A Noir' at the 1998 Milan Triennale. 183

Ola Rune see Claesson Koivisto Rune

Rolf Sachs was born in Lausanne in 1955. He lived in Munich for twelve years where he began designing furniture, then moved to London in 1994. He has shown his work both nationally and internationally in group and solo exhibitions, most recently at the Monika Sprüth Gallery in Cologne. 111, 206

Taisuke Saeki, Harumi Sakamoto, Hiroyuki Mitsui and **Iida Kouichi** are industrial designers currently working for the Corporate Design Centre of Sharp, Japan. 189

Masatoshi Sakaegi was born in Chiba-ken, Japan in 1944. In 1983 he founded his studio which specializes in ceramic and melamine tableware and ceramic sculpture. In 1997 he was selected as one of the ten world-famous designers of the 50th 'Premio Faenza', the international exhibition of contemporary ceramics in Faenza, Italy. 145

Salt was founded by Karina Holmes, who specializes in knitted textiles, and June Swindell, who works mainly with woven textiles. Based in London, they produce modular blinds, window treatments, sheers and screens. Projects include the Bankside lofts by Piers Gogh and a commission from the British Embassy in Moscow. 166

Salvatore & Marie was founded by Salvatore Pischedda and Marie Darmody and is based in Milan. Pischedda was born in Italy in 1964 and is a designer and artist. Darmody, born in Ireland in 1963, is a designer. 151

Takahide Sano holds a diploma in industrial design from the Hongo High School of Tokyo. He worked for the Toshiba Design Centre from 1976 to 1988, specializing in audio-visual equipment. He started to design on a freelance basis in 1988 and collaborates with numerous companies including WMF, Sottsass Associati, Seiko and Biesse. 144

Denis Santachiara was born in Campagnola, Italy in 1950. He began his career as a designer for a car company, while also producing analytical and conceptual art. In 1990 he founded Domodinamica with Cesare Castelli, producing experimental design. He has designed lights for FontanaArte, LucePlan and Oceano Oltreluce and furniture for Campeggi. 34, 209

Santos & Adolfsdóttir was founded by Margaret Adolfsdóttir and Leo Santos-Shaw who met whilst studying printed textile design at Middlesex Polytechnic, UK. Both worked previously as freelance fashion textile designers, and Santos-Shaw as an in-house designer for Thierry Mugler in Paris. Santos & Adolfsdóttir produces interior textiles and surface design for clients including Barneys, New York and Japan, and Whistles, London. 174

Richard Sapper was born in Munich in 1932. After studying philosophy, anatomy, graphics, engineering and economics, he worked in the styling department of Mercedes-Benz in Stuttgart. In 1956 he worked with Gio Ponti and then, until 1975, with Marco Zanuso in Italy. From 1970 to 1976 Sapper worked as a consultant to Fiat and Pirelli, and since 1980 he has been the worldwide product design consultant of the IBM Corporation. He has designed lighting for Artemide and Siemens, tableware and appliances for Alessi, furniture for Unifor, Castelli and Knoll International, stop-watches for Heuer and notebook computers for IBM. He has been resident Professor of Industrial Design at the Academy of Art in Stuttgart since 1986. 202

William Sawaya was born in Beirut in 1948 and graduated in 1973 from the National Academy of Arts. He worked in the USA and France before moving to Italy in 1978. In 1984, with Paolo Moroni, he founded Sawaya and Moroni where he is artistic director and project manager. 61

Georgia Scott is a lighting designer. She studied at Middlesex Polytechnic and at Brighton University, UK. 123

Max Shepherd was born in 1974 and holds a Bachelors degree in three-dimensional design (furniture) from Leeds Metropolitan University, UK. He worked for the Conran Shop and Michael Young before setting up his own studio in 1997. He has undertaken interior design projects in Japan and the UK in collaboration with Ou Baholyadhin Studio and the architect Juan Dols, and also designs furniture for private clients. 40

Vincent Shum was born in Hong Kong in 1966. He has worked in Hong, Kong, China and Japan, and his work has been exhibited in Asia, North America and Europe. He is currently Section Head of Industrial Design at Nanyang Polytechnic in Singapore. 194

Claudio Silvestrin was born in 1954 and trained in Milan at AG Fronzoni. He completed his studies at the Architectural Association in London where he now lives. He teaches at the Bartlett School of Architecture in London and at the Ecole Supérieure d'Art Visuel in Lausanne. His interior design projects include shops for Giorgio Armani (Paris); offices, shops and a residence for Calvin Klein (Paris, Milan and New York); and spaces for museums and art galleries internationally. 218

Iain Sinclair is a London-based product designer working on furniture and lighting, clocks and watches, tableware, hi-fidelity equipment and other electronic-based hardware. He has recently marketed a range of pocket flashlights. He has held chairs in industrial design at London's Royal College of Art and Imperial College. 113

Borek Sípek was born in Prague in 1949. He studied industrial design at Prague University, then architecture in Hamburg and Delft. In 1983 he moved to Amsterdam and set up his own studio. Projects include the Tsjeck Pavilion for the World Exhibition 2000 in Hanover, objects for Driade, Scarabas and Scaralux, limited editions for Steltman Galleries and the interior architecture of Art Factory, a computer animation company in Prague (1995). He received La Croix Chevalier dans l'Ordre des Arts et des Lettres in 1991 and the Prins Bernard Fonds Prize for Architecture and Applied Arts in 1993. He is currently working in Prague. 50, 130, 151, 153, 163

Rochelle Smith was born in 1970 and is a Senior Designer with TKO Product Design. A graduate in architecture from Carnegie Mellon University, Pittsburgh, she went on to study industrial design at Central St Martin's in London, receiving a Masters degree in 1996. Since then she has worked with TKO for clients such as Alcatel, Hasbro, Honda R&D, Mars, NEC, Procter & Gamble, Sanyo and Sony. 188

Michael Sodeau studied product design at Central St Martin's College of Art and Design, London. He was a founder partner of design group Inflate in 1995. In 1997 he left Inflate to set up a new partnership with Lisa Giuliani, and launched 'Comfortable Living', his first furniture and homeware collection. 180

Ettore Sottsass was born in 1917 in Innsbruck. He completed his architectural studies in 1939 at the University of Turin and since 1947 has worked in Milan. In 1958 he became the chief consultant for design at Olivetti and was responsible for innovative design concepts in information electronics. He became involved in experimental projects, starting with the radical architecture of the 1960s. This work was followed up with the Memphis Group. In 1980 he founded Sottsass Associati and clients include Alessi, Cassina, Mitsubishi, Olivetti, Seiko, Zanotta, Esprit and Knoll. Among his architectural projects are interior furnishings for Esprit, a bar in the Il Palazzo Hotel, Japan; the Daniel Wolf apartment block in Colorado; and a hotel and shopping mall in Kuala Lumpur. 113, 222

Rainer Spehl was born in Germany in 1971. He has a Bachelors degree in furniture design from Ravensbourne College of Design and Communication, and a Masters degree from the Royal College of Art, London. He is currently working for Moebelle Furniture Design in Düsseldorf. 91

Ayala Sperling Serfaty was born in Israel in 1962. She studied Fine Art at Middlesex Polytechnic, UK and art history and philosophy at Tel Aviv University. She was awarded a scholarship from the Sharet Fund, Israel in 1984 and presented with first prize in the Annual Furniture Design Competition in Israel in 1993. 46

Philippe Starck was born in Paris in 1949 and trained at the Ecole Camondo there. He has been responsible for major interior design schemes including François Mitterrand's apartment at the Elysée Palace; the Café Costes; the Royalton and Paramount Hotels in New York; the Delano Hotel in Miami; and the Mondrian in Los Angeles. He has also created domestic and public multi-purpose buildings such as the headquarters of Asahi Beer in Tokyo and the Ecole Nationale Supérieure des Arts Décoratifs in Paris. Recent schemes include the Saint Martin's Lane hotel and the Sanderson Hotel, both in London, as well as an incineration plant in Paris/Vitry due to be completed in 2004. As a product designer he collaborates with Alessi, Baleri, Baum, Disform, Driade, Flos, Kartell, Rapsel, Up & Up, Vitra, Vuitton and Xo. From 1993 to 1996 he was worldwide artistic director for the Thomson Consumer Electronics Group. 30, 48, 50, 225

Jasper Startup was born in 1961 and graduated from Middlesex Polytechnic, UK with a degree in furniture design in 1983. He received a Masters degree in 1994 following an industrial design course at Central St Martin's College of Art and Design, London. Since 1983 he has worked freelance, designing for companies including Tangerine and Paul Priestman Associates. He has been a design tutor at Kingston University, at Central St Martin's College of Art and Design, and since 1995 at Chelsea College of Art and Design. 221

Studio Harry & Camila was founded by Harry and Camila Vega, born in The Netherlands in 1966 and Chile in 1972, respectively. They met at the Domus Academy in 1994 and have since developed a range of textiles. 180

Silvia Suardi graduated in architecture from Milan Polytechnic. She worked on a family residence on Lake Garda and on a project to restyle railway stations in Lombardy before joining Michele de Lucchi's studio in 1996. She has recently produced designs for Rosenthal Studio Line. 83

Reiko Sudo was born in Ibaraki Prefecture, Japan, and educated at the Musashino University of Art. Before co-founding Nuno Corporation in 1984, she worked as a freelance textile designer and has since designed for the International Wool Secretariat, Paris and for the clothing company Threads, Tokyo. She has received many prizes for her work, including the Roscoe Award in 1993 and 1994. 175

Sauli Suomela see Arni Aromaa

Hiroko Suwa was born in Kiryu, Gunma Prefecture, Japan. He worked as a textile engineer for various companies before joining Nuno Corporation where he is now Production Manager. In 1998 his work formed part of the 'Structure and Surface: Contemporary Japanese Textiles' exhibition at the Museum of Modern Art in New York. 173

Svitalia Design was founded in 1986 by Susan Guempel and Urs Kamber who have studios in Agra, Switzerland and Milan. Guempel was born in 1956 in Germany and studied textile design in Basle. Kamber was born in 1948 in Switzerland and studied architecture in Zurich, interior design in Basle and industrial design in Milan. The practice is involved in product design, interior decoration and architecture. Since 1989 Svitalia has manufactured under its own name, moving its head office to Ticino in Switzerland. 205

Carlo Tamborini studied industrial design at the Istituto Europeo di Disegno in Milan. Since graduating he has worked as a freelance designer collaborating with Lissoni Associati, Fontana Arte and Palluccoitalia. He is also a founder member of the group Codice 31. 98

Chifuyu Tanaka was born in Tokyo in 1957. He joined Canon in 1979. 186

Tangerine is a London-based product design company. Over the last ten years it has worked on telecom products, electronic consumer goods, housewares, transport and healthcare with clients such as British Airways, Apple Computers, Hitachi, Waterford Wedgwood and Procter & Gamble. 192

Sarah Taylor studied textile design at Heriot-Watt University in Galashiels, Scotland, where she is now a lecturer in visual studies. She has exhibited her work in the UK, Germany and Israel and took part in the 5th International Textile Competition in Kyoto in 1997. In 1998 she was part of a touring group show, 'Lux', which focused on contemporary designer-makers working with light. 167

Ilkka Terho see Valvomo

Renaud Thiry was born in Paris in 1968. He studied design and applied arts at De Montfort University in Leicester, UK, then graduated in industrial design from the ENSCI/Les Ateliers. Since 1995 he has been a freelance designer working for companies such as Ligne Roset, Habitat and Cinna, as well as producing two designs himself under the name 'flandesign'. 88, 132

Olafur Thordarson was born in Reykjavik in 1963. He trained as a carpenter and cabinet-maker and took a Masters degree in architecture at Columbia University in New York in 1990. He has worked as a project architect and designer with Gaetano Pesce with whom he collaborated on the Organic Buildings in Osaka, the Chiat/Day offices and the Umbrella Chair. Together with partner Donna Fumoso, Thordarson runs Dingaling Studio Inc. 213

Kurt Thut was born in Switzerland in 1932. He works in his family business, manufacturing products. 77

Hugo Timmermans was born in 1967. He studied at the Academy of Industrial Design, Eindhoven, then started his own business combining traditional woodwork with design. Several early designs were taken up by Droog Design. He founded OVAL Research and Development with Job Smeets in 1995, then set up Optic Product Development in 1997. 143

Nina Tolstrup worked as a design manager, photo-journalist, editor and marketing coordinator before founding Tolstrup and Co. She teaches at the Danish Design School in Copenhagen and was a board member of the Design Foundation under the Ministry of Cultural Affairs from 1996 to 1999. In 1998 she participated in the development of the Danish government's new Design Policy. 162, 206

Tadeo Toulis is a senior industrial designer at Lunar Design. In 1996 and 1997 he conducted independent research as a Fulbright Scholar in Italy, affiliating with the Milan Polytechnic and the American Academy in Rome. He received his Masters degree in industrial design from the Pratt Institute in New York. 210

Jorg Tragatschnig was born in Gmünd, Austria in 1955. Since 1980 he has been a designer for Porsche Design. 114

Javier Ruiz-Tapiador Trallero was born in Zaragoza, Spain in 1955. He graduated from the University of Barcelona and in 1986 set up B.D. Zaragoza SA, specializing in product design. His work also includes public building, housing and interior design. In 1998 his Albeus ceramic washbasin was selected for the Compasso d'Oro, and the following year received the Top Ten Award from the iF Design Forum in Hanover. 220

Sherife Ünal was born in Turkey in 1972 and has lived in Germany since 1976. She studied textile design at the Fachhochschule für Design and Medien, Hanover and exhibited at the spring 1999 Premier Vision in collaboration with Masters of Linen. 172

Valvomo is a Helsinki-based company founded in 1993 by Ilkka Terho, Teppo Asikainen, Vesa Hinkola, Markus Nevelainen, Kari Sivonen, Jan Tromp, Rane Vaskivuori and Timo Vierros. The company produces objects for major European manufacturers, and its projects include furniture for the Stockholm Comic Library; the interior and furniture for a restaurant, Soup, in Helsinki; and office and exhibition spaces. 47, 81

Ben van Berkel was born in Utrecht in 1957. He studied architecture at the Rietveld Academy in Amsterdam and the Architectural Association in London, graduating in 1987. He set up the architectural practice Van Berkel & Bos with Caroline Bos in 1988. Realized projects include the Karbouw and ACOM office buildings; the REMU electricity station; the Aedes East Gallery for Kristin Feireiss in Berlin; the Erasmus bridge in Rotterdam; the renovation and extension of the Rijksmuseum Twenthe in Enschede; and the De Kolk project in Amsterdam. 136

Erick Van Egeraat studied architecture at the Technical University in Delft, The Netherlands. He worked for various architectural practices before co-founding Mecanoo in 1983. He left to form Erick Van Egeraat twelve years later. In 1995 he designed the glass roof and Andrassy boardroom for the Ing Bank in Prague. The following year he was awarded first prize in the competition for the Ichtius Hogeschool in Rotterdam. 136

Dick van Hoff was born in Amsterdam in 1971. He trained as a building worker and window dresser before studying three-dimensional design at the Hogeschool voor de Kunsten in Arnhem. In 1995 his tap Stop Kraan was taken up by Droog Design and he has since had several other pieces developed Droog and DMD, as well as Rosenthal and United Colors of Benetton. 217

Frans Van Nieuwenborg was born in Venlo, The Netherlands in 1941. He studied at the Academy of Industrial Design in Eindhoven, graduating in 1963, then worked for various design offices and architects. In 1986 he opened his own industrial design studio. He has lectured at the Rietveld Academy and is currently special lecturer at the School for Visual Arts in Ghent. 112

Fabiaan Van Severen was born in Antwerp, Belgium. He studied Fine Art at the Sint-Lucas Institute in Ghent before becoming a furniture designer. He has been producing furniture pieces since 1986 and today works on a freelance basis for companies such as Gelderland in The Netherlands and Forms and Surfaces in the USA. 50, 66

Maarten Van Severen is an interior and furniture designer. He recently completed the Maison à Floirac with the architect Rem Koolhaas, and the interior entrance hall of the City Hall in Ghent. He works for clients such as Vitra, U-line Lighting and Target Lighting. He is a visiting professor at the Academy of Fine Arts in Maastricht, The Netherlands. 18, 33, 66

Rane Vaskivuori see Valvomo

Pernille Vea graduated from the Institute of Industrial Design at the Danish Design School in Copenhagen in 1996. He is a member of the design group Kropsholder. He taught at the Danish School from 1996 to 1998, and since 1998 has been an in-house designer for the company Danish Steel House. 36

Priit Verlin was born in Estonia in 1971. He has worked at the Tartu Art College for four years and designs for Class X Furniture. 49

Arnout Visser was born in 1962 and studied at the Art School in Arnhem, The Netherlands from 1984 to 1989, then at the Domus Academy, Milan in 1990. Since then he has been working as a freelance designer in Arnhem, specializing in glass and ceramics. He has been a member of Droog Design since its foundation in 1992. 135

Henk Vos was born in The Netherlands in 1939 and studied at the Academy of Design in Rotterdam from 1956 to 1960. In 1963 he opened his own interior design office and furniture shop, designing mainly for Gelderland Meubelindustrie. In 1996 he founded a design store, Maupertuus, in Groningen, combined with a studio for industrial design and architecture run by his two sons. 61

Maarten Vrolijk (born 1966) collaborates with several prominent companies in The Netherlands and abroad. His work can be seen in various museums such as the Museum of Modern Art, New York and the Stedelijk Museum in Amsterdam. He held a retrospective exhibition at the Groninger Museum in 1997. 132

Marcel Wanders graduated in product design from the Art Academy in Arnhem, The Netherlands, in 1988. He was one of the founder members of WAAC Design and Consultancy, working with companies such as KLM, Swatch and Apple. In 1995 he opened his own studio, Wanders Wonders, and his clients now include Cappellini, Rosenthal and British Airways. He was given a double nomination for the Rotterdam Design Prize in 1999. 158, 159, 220

Mikael Warnhammar is a carpenter, builder and architect. He graduated from and now teaches in the furniture department of the Högskolan för Design och Konst in Gothenburg, Sweden. He works for IKEA and recently received the Excellent Swedish Design Prize. 216

Weyers & Borms are self-taught designers. They began their collaboration in the 1980s and today are active in all areas of applied art from product design, logos and graphics to theatre, film-set and costume design. They often work with other artists to create one-off items, although some of their lights and textiles have been produced in limited batch production. 120

Peter Wheeler see Mary Little

Lorenz Wiegand was born in 1964. He holds a Masters degree in industrial design from the Domus Academy and in 1997 founded POOL Products, a loose cooperation of designers, architects and artists for product development. 25

Theo Williams was born in Oxford, UK in 1967. He studied in Bristol and Manchester and graduated in industrial design in 1990. He works as a freelance designer and has also worked in-house for Technogym Italia, designing cardio-fitness equipment. He has a continuing collaboration with Nava Design and recently became a design consultant for Pyrex Europe. He has developed products for Prada and has been commissioned to design desk accessories for Armani and packaging for Calvin Klein Jeans. 205

Gerd Wilsdorf was born in 1947 and studied product design in Pforzheim, Germany. He worked as design-coordinator at Optische Werke G. Rodenstock, Munich, and since 1986 has been head designer at Siemens Elektrogeräte. 217

Ken Wood is a principal and director of industrial design at Lunar Design. He holds a Bachelors degree in industrial design from Ohio State University and previously worked as an independent industrial designer in the Bay Area of northern California. 193

Dirk Wynants was born in Turnhout, Belgium in 1964. He graduated in 1987 as an interior and furniture designer from the Sint-Lucas Institute in Ghent. He started his career by distributing foreign furniture imports and later founded Extremis in order to design and market a line of outdoor furniture. 79

Simon Yan received a Bachelors degree from the Pratt Institute, School of Art and Design, New York. He works for Herbst LaZar Bell where he is responsible for consumer, industrial and medical products. 212

Yellow Circle/Yellow Design was formerly known as Team Industrieform, founded by Günter Horntrich in 1973 and active in the fields of product planning, design development, industrial design, graphics and packaging. In 1992 the practice expanded to include Yellow Circle. 201

Michael Young was born in Sunderland, UK in 1966. He graduated from Kingston University in 1992 and established MY022 four years later. He has held one-man shows throughout Europe as well as in Japan. 57

ACQUISITIONS BY DESIGN COLLECTIONS IN 1999

Dates given in parentheses refer to the dates of the designs (from 1960 to the present day).

AUSTRALIA

POWERHOUSE MUSEUM, SYDNEY, NEW SOUTH WALES
FURNITURE
Caroline Casey, elliptical folding screen (1994)
Stefan Lie, table, Ribs (1996)
TABLEWARE
Giles Bettison, vase, Magenta Vessel (1995)
Giles Bettison, vase, Yellow Vessel (1995)
Claude Champy, sculptural vase, Grande Urne (1996)
Dante Marioni, goblet, Ivory Pair (1996)
Dante Marioni, jug, Ivory Pair (1996)
TEXTILES
Karen Binns, textile, Mundoes (1998), manufactured by Yurundiali
Aboriginal Corporation
Paula Duncan, textile, Gomilaroi Gathering (1998), manufactured by
Yurundiali Aboriginal Corporation
Ann Johnson, textile, Tribes Gathering (1998), manufactured by
Yurundiali Aboriginal Corporation
Alf Newman, textile, Snakes Nesting (1998), manufactured by
Yurundiali Aboriginal Corporation
Val Priestly, textile, Garden of Eden (1998), manufactured by
Yurundiali Aboriginal Corporation
Aubrey Swan, textile, Snakes and Goannas (1998), manufactured by
Yurundiali Aboriginal Corporation

CANADA

MUSÉE DES ARTS DÉCORATIFS DE MONTRÉAL
FURNITURE
Cini Boeri, armchair, Ghost (1987), manufactured by Fiam Italia SpA
Shiro Kuramata, armchair, Miss Blanche (1988), manufactured by
Ishimaru Co. Ltd
Shiro Kuramata, stool, Acrylic Stool (1990), manufactured by
Ishimaru Co. Ltd
Gaetano Pesce, armchair, I Feltri (1986), manufactured by Cassina
SpA
Gaetano Pesce, chair, 543 Broadway (1992–5), manufactured by
Bernini SpA
Gaetano Pesce, table, Kiss (1997)
Karim Rashid, table, Aura (1990), manufactured by Zeritalia®
Ali Tayar, screen (1997–8), manufactured by Warner Co.
Ali Tayar, table, NEA (1998)
LIGHTING
Gaetano Pesce, lamp, Verbal Abuse (1994–8)
Studio Tetrarch, lamp, Pistillo (1969), manufactured by Valenti
Marcel Wanders, floor lamp, Extra Big Shadow (1998),
manufactured by Cappellini
TABLEWARE
Sergio Asti, flower/fruit container, Vitruvio (1966–9), manufactured
by Anthologie Quartett
Laura Handler, Dennis Decker, Amanda Honig Magalhaes, goblet,
Gallery Glass (1992), manufactured by Metrokane Inc.
Hans Maier-Aichen, bowl, Buco (1995), manufactured by Authentics
Eduardo Paolozzi, plate, The Kalkulium Suite (1987), manufactured
by Wedgwood
Studio Alchimia, coffeepot and sugar bowl prototypes (1980–5),
manufactured by Alessi SpA
TEXTILES
Alessandro Mendini, rug, Christina (1984)
PRODUCTS
Constantin Boym, kitchen container, Use It (1995), manufactured by
Authentics
Constantin Boym, laddle, spatula and tongs (1996), manufactured
by Authentics
Morison S. Cousins, peeler, T.2 (1998), manufactured by
Tupperware
Michele de Lucchi, fan, hairdryer and heater prototypes (1979),
manufactured by Girmi
Karim Rashid, wastepaper basket, Garbo (1996), manufactured by
Umbra
Karim Rashid, handbag, Bow (1997), manufactured by Issey Miyake
Inc.

DENMARK

THE DANISH MUSEUM OF DECORATIVE ART, COPENHAGEN
FURNITURE
Arne Jacobsen, 2 chairs (1971), manufactured by ASKO
Verner Panton, chair, Phantom (1990s)
Torben Skov, chair, VIO (1983–4)
LIGHTING
Xavier Mariscal, table lamp, Valencia (1985–6)
TABLEWARE
Inger Louise Bach, ceramic cutlery (1997)
Ole Jensen, dinner service (1997–8)
Tora Urup, dinner service glass and porcelain prototypes (1997–8)

FRANCE

MUSÉE DES ARTS DÉCORATIFS, PARIS
FURNITURE
Joe Colombo, Combi-Center (1963–4)
Shiro Kuramata, stool (1990)
Marc Newson, Pod of Drawers (1987)
Francis Ullmann, desk (1972)
LIGHTING
Carlotta de Bevilacqua, floor lamp, Yin (1997)
Andrea Branzi, lamp, Ellisse (1998)
Ernesto Gismondi, table lamp, Espèria (1997)
TABLEWARE
Gaetano Pesce, vase, Fish Design (1996)
PRODUCTS
Shiro Kuramata, clock, Clock with Five Hands (1986)
Shiro Kuramata, clock, Just in Time (1986)

GERMANY

KUNSTMUSEUM DÜSSELDORF IM EHRENHOF
FURNITURE
Hans Ehrich, folding chair (1997)
PRODUCTS
electric shavers, Remington deluxe, manufactured by Philips
electric shavers, Philishave, manufactured by Philips
hairdryer, Moulinex
mini radio, International
portable radio, Grundig

VITRA DESIGN MUSEUM, WEIL AM RHEIN
FURNITURE
M. Calka, desk, Boomerang
M.A. Ciganda, armchair, Eva
Jakob Gebert, table, Spanoto, prototype
Frank O. Gehry, cardboard chair
Michele de Lucchi, chair, Riviera
Javier Mariscal, stools, Duplex
Alessandro Mendini, redesign Panton chair
Richard Schultz, dining chair, Topiary
M. Umeda, cabinet, Ginza
Christian Wassmann, foldable stool, Constantin
LIGHTING
Verner Panton, ceiling lamp, VP-Globe
PRODUCTS
Braun products of the 1970s and 1980s
Burdick, office furnishings
G. Drocco, F. Mello, coat stand, Cactus

THE NETHERLANDS

MUSEUM BOYMANS-VAN BEUNINGEN, ROTTERDAM
FURNITURE
Ineke Hans, chair, Eat Your Heart Out – 16 Ways to Make One Chair
(1997)
Ineke Hans, undercover chair, chaise longue (1997)
LIGHTING
Dick van Hoff, hanging lamp (1997)
Bruno van Hooijdonk, standing lamp (1998)

STEDELIJK MUSEUM, AMSTERDAM
FURNITURE
A&E Design, folding stool, Stockholm (1995)
Ron Arad, chair, Fantastic Plastic Elastic (1997)
Shin & Tomoko Azumu, chair and stool, Wire Frame (1998)
Erik Balavoine, meditation stools, Yme and Mir (1990)
Bar & Knell Design, chair, Confetti (1998)
Bar & Knell Design, children's chair, Pampers Boy (1998)
Bar & Knell Design, children's chair, Pampers Girl (1998)
Bar & Knell Design, children's chair, Pampers grün (1998)
Riccardo Blumer, chair, Laleggera (1996), manufactured by Alias
Wolf Brinkman, cupboard, Slappe Kast (1996)
Bob Copray, Stefan Scholten, chair, No. 2 (1997), prototype
Bob Copray, Stefan Scholten, chair, No. 3 (1997), prototype
Creadesign, chair, Trice (1985)
Björn Dahlström, chair, BD 1 (1994)
Björn Dahlström, chair, BD 6 (1996)
Frans de la Haye, chair, Centennial (1996), manufactured by Ahrend
Dum Office, church seats (1998)
Terje Ekstrøm, chair, Ekstrem (1987)
Giorgio Gurioli, chair, Joy (1997), manufactured by Acerbis
International SpA
Sigurdur Gústafsson, chair, Faxe (1998)
Sigurdur Gústafsson, chair, Tango (1997)
Ineke Hans, 2 chairs, Eat Your Heart Out (1997)
Richard Hutten, baby chairs, Bronto (1999)
Niels Hvas, chair (1997)
Jouko Järvisalo, chair, Kova (1998)
Yrjo Kukkapuro, easy chair, Karuselli 412 (1964–5), manufactured
by Haimi
Yrjo Kukkapuro, footstool (1964–5), manufactured by Haimi
Stefan Lindfors, Lindfors 01 (1999)
Antti Nurmesniemi, garden bench (1983)
Antti Nurmesniemi, sauna stool (1980s)
Peter Opsvik, children's chair, Sitti (1993)
Panic, chair, Line 1 (1998)
Verner Panton, chair, Phantom (1998)
Anna von Schewen, low chair with ottoman, Latta (1998)
Erla Solveig Oskarsdóttir, chair, Jaki (1999)
Torsteinsen Design, chair, B-dimension (1997)
Torsteinsen Design, chair, Rav (1995–6)
LIGHTING
A. Castiglioni, lamp, Lampadina (1972)
Menno Dieperink, wall light (1998)
Dum Office, lamp, Trak (1998)
Harri Koskinen, lantern, Relations (1999)
Kho Liang Te, floor lamp (1960s)
Ingo Maurer, lamp, Bibibibi (1982), manufactured by Ingo Maurer
GmbH
Ingo Maurer, lamp, Don Quixote (1989), manufactured by Ingo
Maurer GmbH
Ingo Maurer, lamp, Eclipselipse (1989), manufactured by Ingo
Maurer GmbH
Ingo Maurer, lamp, Fukushu (1984), manufactured by Ingo Maurer
GmbH
Ingo Maurer, lamp, Hot Achille (1994), manufactured by Ingo
Maurer GmbH
Ingo Maurer, lamp, Lucellino (1992), manufactured by Ingo Maurer
GmbH
Ingo Maurer, lamp, Wo bist du Edison?, manufactured by Ingo
Maurer GmbH
Ingo Maurer, lamp, Zero One (1990), manufactured by Ingo Maurer
GmbH
Ettore Sottsass, lamp, Asa 100 (1997)
Superstudio, lamp, Gherpe (1967)

Frans van Nieuwenborg, lamp, The Saint, 1998
Frans van Nieuwenborg, outdoor lamp, Logic (1989)
TABLEWARE
Tias Eckhoff, cutlery, Chaco (1990)
Tias Eckhoff, cutlery, Maya (1960)
Tias Eckhoff, cutlery, Tiki (1974)
Tias Eckhoff, cutlery, Una (1973)
Kaj Franck, glass service, Luna (1971)
Annaleena Hakatie, pitchers, Relations (1999)
Pekka Harni, dishes, ABC (1998)
Ole Jensen, kitchen utensils, Ole (1997)
Harri Koskinen, glass service, Klubi (1998)
Stefan Lindfors, salad bowl and cutlery, Lindfors 98 (1998)
Erik Magnussen, coffee services, 900, 1000, 1100 and 2000 (1976
and 1999)
Ursula Munch-Petersen, service, Ursula (1993)
Saar Oosterhof, Tablecarpetdish (1998)
Laura Partanen & Arto Kankkunen, cutlery, Artik (1997)
Markku Salo, glass service, Marius (1985)
Markku Salo, vases, Aava (1998)
Carina Seth-Andersson, dishes, Relations (1999)
Carina Seth-Andersson, glass cylinders, CSA 1 and CSA 2 (1996)
Carina Seth-Andersson, salad bowl and cutlery, Seth-Andersson
98 (1998)
Arnout Visser, glasses, Optic (1998)
Tapio Wirkkala, glass service, Gaissa (1972)
Tapio Wirkkala, glass service, Ultima Thule (1968)
PRODUCTS
Raymond Loewy, sewing machine, Elna Lotus (1964)
Onbekend, radio, Panasonic (1970)
Kees Winkelman, candleholder, Partylight (1998)
Marco Zanuso, Richard Sapper, radio, TS 502 (1964)
Marco Zanuso, Richard Sapper, television, Black Box (1970)

NORWAY

NATIONAL MUSEUM OF DECORATIVE ARTS, TRONDHEIM
TABLEWARE
Oiva Toikka, glass bottle, Mansikkapaikka series (1984),
manufactured by Nuutajärvi
TEXTILES
Per Bjørnsen, upholstery, Bobrin (1984), manufactured by AS
Gudbrandsdalen Uldvarefabrik
Pia Bjørnstad, upholstery, Bluebird (1984), manufactured by AS
Gudbrandsdalen Uldvarefabrik
Kari Skogstad, Upholstery 1 and 2 (1984), manufactured by AS
Gudbrandsdalen Uldvarefabrik
PRODUCTS
Bang & Olufsen, radio, Beocenter 2600
Disk box 3M (1980s)

THE OSLO MUSEUM OF APPLIED ART
FURNITURE
Gunilla Allard, chair, Cinema (1993), manufactured by Lammhults
Möbel AB
Tias Eckhoff, chair, Ana (1980), manufactured by Smithco Line
Tias Eckhoff, chair, Bella (1995), manufactured by Smithco Line
TABLEWARE
Tias Eckhoff, steel cutlery, Chaco (1990), manufactured by Norsk
Stålpress AS
Tias Eckhoff, steel cutlery, Tiki (1974), manufactured by Norsk
Stålpress AS
Tias Eckhoff, steel cutlery, Una (1973), manufactured by Norsk
Stålpress AS
PRODUCTS
Michael Graves, thermoflask (1994), manufactured by Alessi SpA
F. Minuti, thermoflask (1998), manufactured by Guzzini
Philippe Starck, cheese grater, Mister Meumeu (1992),
manufactured by Alessi SpA
Philippe Starck, colander, Max Le Chinois (1987), manufactured by
Alessi SpA
Philippe Starck, lemon squeezer, Juicy Salif (1990), manufactured
by Alessi SpA
Philippe Starck, radio, Poe (1997), manufactured by Alessi SpA
Philippe Starck, tray, Les ministres (1996), manufactured by Alessi
SpA

THE WEST NORWAY MUSEUM OF DECORATIVE ART, BERGEN

TABLEWARE

Maud Gjeruldsen Bugge, glasses, Olympia (1994), manufactured by Hadeland Glassverk

Hande Heuch, teacups

Arne Jon Jutrem, underplate, Olympia (1994), manufactured by Hadeland Glassverk

Tove Lise Rokke Olsen, Anne Vinæs, beakers, Slipp

Grete Rønning, Sarah Rosenbaum, service, Saturn (1994), manufactured by Porsgrund Porcelain

PRODUCTS

Christian Sunde, clock radio, one-off

SWEDEN

NATIONALMUSEUM, STOCKHOLM

FURNITURE

Gunilla Allard, armchair, Cinema (1994), manufactured by Lammhults Möbel AB

Ron Arad, rocking chair (1981), manufactured by One Off

Björn Dahlström, chair, BD: 6 (1998), manufactured by CBI/Klara AB

Jan Dranger, armchair, Rolig (1997), manufactured by IKEA

Sigurdur Gustafsson, chair, Tango, manufactured by Källemo AB

Jonas Lindvall, sideboard, manufactured by Angra AB

Mattias Ljunggren, chair, Gute (1998), manufactured by Källemo AB

TABLEWARE

Paula Barton, vase (1996)

Lena Bergström, dish (1997), manufactured by Orrefors Glasbruk

Lena Bergström, vase (1998), manufactured by Orrefors Glasbruk

Jonas Bohlin, vase, Liv (1997), manufactured by Reijmyre Glasbruk

Brita Flander, vases, Nice and Cannes, manufactured by Reijmyre Glasbruk

Maria Kariis, champagne glasses (1999), manufactured by Reijmyre Glasbruk

Anders Ljungberg, vase (1998)

Anne Nilsson, bottle, Saffron (1992), manufactured by Orrefors Glasbruk

Jane Reumert, jug (1990s)

Martti Ryttkönen, bowl (1997), manufactured by Orrefors Glasbruk

Carina Seth-Andersson, vase (1999)

TEXTILES

Carl Johan Hane and Inez Svensson, printed textiles, Pampas and Tegelbacken from Stockholms Rum, manufactured by Kinnasand AB

PRODUCTS

A&E Design, bathingboard, Fresh (1997), manufactured by RFSU Rehab AB

Eva Åbinger, mirror, Veritas (1998), manufactured by Simplicitas AB

Björn Dahlström, Carina Seth-Andersson, Stefan Lindfors, Glen Oliver Löw, Antonio Citterio, cooking utensils, Hackman Tools (1998), manufactured by Hackman Designor Oy AB

Designaktiebolaget Propeller, air cleaner, Blue Air (1998), manufactured by Blue Air AB

Ergonomi Design Gruppen, body-care program, Beauty (1998), manufactured by RFSU Rehab AB

Futurniture, computer, Working Snob (1997), manufactured by Toshiba

Jonathan Ive, computer, I-Mac (1998), manufactured by Apple Computer Inc.

RÖHSSKA MUSEET, GOTHENBURG

FURNITURE

Erik Chambert, sofa, Helena (1968), manufactured by Källermo AB

Sigurdur Gustavsson, chair, Tango (1998), manufactured by Källermo AB

Niels Hvass, chair, Pilestolen (1998), manufactured by Källermo AB

Mats Theselius, chair, Sven (1998), manufactured by Källermo AB

TABLEWARE

Lena Bergström, wine glass, Skål (1998), manufactured by Orrefors Kosta Boda AB

Lars Hellsten, wine glass, Skål (1998), manufactured by Orrefors Kosta Boda AB

Jan Johansson, wine glass, Skål (1998), manufactured by Orrefors Kosta Boda AB

Helen Krantz, wine glass, Skål (1998), manufactured by Orrefors Kosta Boda AB

Erika Lagerbielke, wine glass, Skål (1998), manufactured by Orrefors Kosta Boda AB

Anne Nilsson, wine glass, Skål (1998), manufactured by Orrefors Kosta Boda AB

Signe Persson-Melin, coffee cup, Signum (1991), manufactured by Höganäs keramikfabrik AB

Martti Rytkönen, wine glass, Skål (1998), manufactured by Orrefors Kosta Boda AB

Leif Stangebye-Nielsen, knife

Per B. Sundberg, wine glass, Skål (1998), manufactured by Orrefors Kosta Boda AB

Per B. Sundberg, vase (1998), manufactured by Orrefors Kosta Boda AB

Torun Vivianna Bülow-Hübe, butter knife (1984), manufactured by Dansk International Design Ltd

Torun Vivianna Bülow-Hübe, carving set (1986), manufactured by Dansk International Design Ltd

Torun Vivianna Bülow-Hübe, coffee spoon (1984), manufactured by Dansk International Design Ltd

Torun Vivianna Bülow-Hübe, serving fork (1986), manufactured by Dansk International Design Ltd

Torun Vivianna Bülow-Hübe, serving spoon (1986), manufactured by Dansk International Design Ltd

TEXTILES

Hiroshi Awatsuji, cloth (c. 1985)

Lena Bergström, cloth, Lule (1993), manufactured by Ljungbergs textiltryck AB

Lena Bergström, cloth, Ume (1993), manufactured by Ljungbergs textiltryck AB

Hans Krondahl, cloth, Ingmar (1974), manufactured by Argos Design

Louise Sass, cloth, Shinjuku (1995), manufactured by Kvadrat AS

Louise Sass, fabric, Undervejs (1997)

SWITZERLAND

MUSEUM FÜR GESTALTUNG ZÜRICH

FURNITURE

Susi and Ueli Berger, chair, Stuhl-Stuhl (1981), manufactured by Röthlisberger Kollektion

Susi and Ueli Berger, chest of drawers, Robot (1980–82), manufactured by Röthlisberger Kollektion

Susi and Ueli Berger, shelf, Kung Fu (1981), manufactured by Röthlisberger Kollektion

Lukas Buol and Marco Zünd, shelves, Zoll D (1993), manufactured by Nils Holger Moormann

Christoph Dietlicher, chair, Faltstuhl (1998)

Neue Werkstatt, stool, Platz (1995), manufactured by Neue Werkstatt

Felix Zoller, modular boxes, Dado (1991), manufactured by Horni Metallbearbeitung

LIGHTING

Ingo Maurer, lamp, Bulb Clear (1966), manufactured by Domani AG

Reto Schöpfer, lamp, Updown 01/02 (1994), manufactured by Belux AG

Neue Werkstatt, pendulum lamp, Billard (1988), manufactured by Neue Werkstatt

TEXTILES

Caroline Flueler, fabrics and handprints (1994–5), manufactured by Fabric Frontline

Sonnhild Kestler, handprinted scarfs (1997–8)

Karin Wälchli and Guido Treichlin, handprinted scarfs, Chalet 5 (1998)

PRODUCTS

Jürg Brühlmann, trolley (1983), manufactured by Frech-Hoch AG and Georg Utz AG

Jürg Brühlmann, trolley (1986), manufactured by Frech-Hoch AG and Roland Stauble AG

Les Ateliers du Nord, set of pocket torches (1997), manufactured by Leclanché

Walter Schüppach, loudspeaker (1994), manufactured by Stereolith SES SA

UK

THE DESIGN MUSEUM, LONDON

PRODUCTS

back and cushion for Barracuda wheelchair, Jay 2, manufactured by Jay Medical Ltd

camera, 600B SLR, manufactured by Rolleiflex

camera, c-1400L TTI SLR, manufactured by Olympus

camera, LT Zoom, manufactured by Olympus

camera mount, Monoball, manufactured by Arca Swiss

car seat, n-Joy, manufactured by Recaro

computer, Macintosh, manufactured by Apple Computer Inc.

electric wheelchair, Saracen 4WD, manufactured by GBL Wheelchairs

mobile phone, Ericsson 688/888 mobile phone, manufactured by Ericsson

personal organizer, Psion 5, manufactured by Psion

surfboard, Tri-fin, manufactured by Blacker Surfboards

suspension wheelchair, Barracuda, manufactured by Everest & Jennings

tricycle attachment, manufactured by Chevron Wheelchairs

wine bottle, Braille, manufactured by Chapoutier

VICTORIA AND ALBERT MUSEUM, LONDON

LIGHTING

Freeplay Energy Group, lantern, Freeplay Self-Powered Lantern (1998)

TABLEWARE

Hella Jongerius for Droog Design, vase, Soft Vase (1994), manufactured by DMD

Walter Keeler, teapot and toast rack, Toast Machine (1998–9)

Robin Levien, teapot, cup and saucer and milk jug, Trend (1982), manufactured by Thomas (Rosenthal)

TEXTILES

Ellen and Robert Ashley, marbled silk (1990s)

Brintons of Kidderminster, carpet samples (1970s)

Dawn Dupree, wall-hanging, Flood (1997)

Maria Schade, batik silk, Lanzettformen I (1996–7)

Lori Weitzner, upholstery fabrics (1993-5), manufactured by Larson Inc.

Lori Weitzner, upholstery fabrics (1997), manufactured by Pallas Textiles

woven textiles (1993–5), Nuno Corporation

PRODUCTS

Ron Arad, CD rack, The Soundtrack (1998), manufactured by Alessi SpA

USA

MUSEUM OF FINE ARTS, BOSTON, MASSACHUSETTS

FURNITURE

Aldo Cibic, console, Belvedere (1982), manufactured by Memphis

dressing table, Plaza, manufactured by Memphis

Michael Graves, bed, Stanhope (1982), manufactured by Memphis

Michele de Lucchi, chair, First (1983), manufactured by Memphis

Michele de Lucchi, end-table, Kristall (1981), manufactured by Memphis

Peter Shire, armchair, Bel Air (1982), manufactured by Memphis

Peter Shire, side-table, Brazil (1981), manufactured by Memphis

Peter Shire, table, Hollywood (1983), manufactured by Memphis

Ettore Sottsass, bookcase, Cargo (1979), manufactured by Studio Alchimia

Ettore Sottsass, bookcase, Factotum (1980), manufactured by Studio Alchimia

Ettore Sottsass, room divider, Carlton (1981), manufactured by Memphis

Ettore Sottsass, table, Le Strutture Tremano (1979), manufactured by Studio Alchimia

George James Sowden, armchair, Palace (1983), manufactured by Memphis

Gerard Taylor, bookcase, Le Palme (1983), manufactured by Memphis

LIGHTING

Martine Bedin, lamp, Super (1981), manufactured by Memphis

Michele de Lucchi, floor lamp, Grand (1983), manufactured by Memphis

Michele de Lucchi, lamp, Oceanic (1981), manufactured by Memphis

Michele de Lucchi, lamp, Sinerpica (1979), manufactured by Studio Alchimia

Ettore Sottsass, floor lamp, Treetops (1981), manufactured by Memphis

Ettore Sottsass, lamp, Callimaca (1980), manufactured by Artemis

TABLEWARE

Michele de Lucchi, vase, Antares (1983), manufactured by Memphis

Peter Shire, teapot, Anchorage (1983), manufactured by Memphis

Ettore Sottsass, fruit bowl, Murmansk (1982), manufactured by Memphis

Ettore Sottsass, fruit dish, Sol (1982), manufactured by Memphis

Ettore Sottsass, vase, Alcor (1983), manufactured by Memphis

Ettore Sottsass, vase, Alioth (1983), manufactured by Memphis

Ettore Sottsass, vase, Altair (1982), manufactured by Memphis

Ettore Sottsass, vase, Euphrates (1983), manufactured by Memphis

Ettore Sottsass, vase (1983), manufactured by Memphis

Ettore Sottsass, vase, prototype of Altair (1982), manufactured by Memphis

Ettore Sottsass, Marco Zanini, stem glass (1983), manufactured by Memphis

Matteo Thun, cocktail glass, Ladoga (1982), manufactured by Memphis

Matteo Thun, teapot, Chad (1983), manufactured by Memphis

Matteo Thun, teapot (1982–3), manufactured by Alessi Quartett

Matteo Thun, vase, Danubio, manufactured by Memphis

Matteo Thun, vase, Titicaca (1982), manufactured by Memphis

Matteo Thun, vase, Volga (1983), manufactured by Memphis

Marco Zanini, bowl, Rigel (1982), manufactured by Memphis

Marco Zanini, fruit bowl, Regolus (1983), manufactured by Memphis

Marco Zanini, glass, Cassiopea (1982), manufactured by Memphis

Marco Zanini, teapot, Colorado (1983), manufactured by Memphis

Marco Zanini, vase, Alpha Centauri (1982), manufactured by Memphis

TEXTILES

Alessandro Mendini, carpet, Oriented (1980), manufactured by Studio Alchimia

Alessandro Mendini, tapestry, Kandissone (1980), manufactured by Studio Alchimia

Natalie du Pasquier, carpet, California (1983), manufactured by Memphis

Daniela Puppa, fabric panel, Explosante-Fixe (1980), manufactured by Studio Alchimia

PRODUCTS

George James Sowden, clock, Oppenheimer (1983)

George James Sowden, clock, Metropole (1982), manufactured by Memphis
Ettore Sottsass, telephone, Enorme (1986), manufactured by Brondi Telefonia SpA

BROOKLYN MUSEUM OF ART, NEW YORK

FURNITURE

Mark Brazier-Jones, console table, Lyre (1992)
Wendell Castle, table (1977–83)
Karim Rashid, kid chair (1997), manufactured by Fasem International
Karim Rashid, planar couch (1997), manufactured by Idée Co. Ltd
Karim Rashid, table, Aura (1997), manufactured by Zeritalia

TABLEWARE

Carlo Alessi Anghini, coffeepot, Bombe (1945), manufactured by Alessi SpA
Carlo Alessi Anghini, creamer, Bombe (1945), manufactured by Alessi SpA
Carlo Alessi Anghini, sugar bowl and lid, Bombe (1945), manufactured by Alessi SpA
Carlo Alessi Anghini, teapot, Bombe (1945), manufactured by Alessi SpA
Carlo Alessi Anghini, tray, Bombe (1945), manufactured by Alessi SpA
Pierangelo Caramia, teapot, Penguin (1993), manufactured by Alessi SpA
Achille Castiglioni, assorted cutlery and serving ware, Dry (1982–5), manufactured by Alessi SpA
Achille Castiglioni, oil bottle, Dry (1984), manufactured by Alessi SpA
Achille Castiglioni, vinegar bottle, Dry (1984), manufactured by Alessi SpA
Stefano Giovannoni, fruit holder, Fruit Mama (1993), manufactured by Alessi SpA
Stefano Giovannoni, round tray, Girotondo (1989–90), manufactured by Alessi SpA
Gerald Gulotta, assorted dishware, Chromatics (1970), manufactured by Porzellanfabrik Arzberg AG
Gerald Gulotta, assorted flatware, Chromatics (1970)
Gerald Gulotta, assorted tableware, Optics (1984), manufactured by Yamaka Shoten
Gerald Gulotta, casserole dish, Classic Elegance (1983) manufactured by Corning Glass Works
Gerald Gulotta, cordial glass (1994), manufactured by Crisal
Gerald Gulotta, flatware, Axis (1989–90), manufactured by Dansk International Designs, Ltd
Gerald Gulotta, flatware, Rondure (1996), manufactured by Dansk International Designs, Ltd
Gerald Gulotta, glass, Chromatics (1970), manufactured by Crisal
Gerald Gulotta, place mats, Chromatics (1970)
Gerald Gulotta, pyrex covered container (1985), manufactured by Corning Glass Works
Gerald Gulotta, teapot and lid, Yixing (1989–90)
Gerald Gulotta, vase, Flat (1988), manufactured by Sao Bernardo
Kent Ipsen, vase (1976)
Dominick Labino, vases (1968–75)
Enzo Mari, fruit bowl, Adal (1968), manufactured by Alessi SpA
Enzo Mari, vase/carafe, Trinidad (1969), manufactured by Alessi SpA
Enzo Mari, vase, Pago-Pago (1969), manufactured by Alessi SpA
Alessandro Mendini, pepper mill, Anna Pepper (1998), manufactured by Alessi SpA
Karim Rashid, pepper mill, Juneau (1996), manufactured by Nambe Studio
Karim Rashid, pepper mill, Tuscany (1996), manufactured by Nambe Studio
Ettore Sottsass, decanter, Ginevra (1996), manufactured by Alessi SpA
Ettore Sottsass, glasses, Ginevra (1996), manufactured by Alessi SpA
Ettore Sottsass, oil bottle (1978), manufactured by Alessi SpA
Ettore Sottsass, pepper shaker (1978), manufactured by Alessi SpA
Ettore Sottsass, salt shaker (1978), manufactured by Alessi SpA
Ettore Sottsass, vase, Sirio (1982), manufactured by Toso Vetri D'Arte
Ettore Sottsass, vinegar bottle (1978), manufactured by Alessi SpA
Philippe Starck, teapot, Ti-Tang (1991–2), manufactured by Alessi SpA
Philippe Starck, creamer/sugar bowl, Su-Mi Tang (1991–2), manufactured by Alessi SpA

PRODUCTS

Marianne Brandt, cocktail shaker (1925), manufactured by Alessi SpA
Andrea Branzi, kettle, Mama-O (1988), manufactured by Alessi SpA
Achille Castiglioni, stand, Dry (1984), manufactured by Alessi SpA
Joe Colombo, clock, Optic (1970), manufactured by Alessi SpA
Frank Gehry, kettle, Pito (1988), manufactured by Alessi SpA
Michael Graves, kettle with bird-shaped whistle (1985), manufactured by Alessi SpA
Alessandro Mendini, corkscrew, Anna G (1998), manufactured by Alessi SpA
Karim Rashid, bow and tummy bags (1997), manufactured by Issey Miyake Inc.
Karim Rashid, multi-purpose container, Garbino (1996), manufactured by Umbra
Karim Rashid, multi-purpose container, Garbo (1996), manufactured by Umbra
Karim Rashid, torso bag (1997), manufactured by Issey Miyake Inc.
Karim Rashid, tower clock (1996), manufactured by Nambe Studio
Karim Rashid, two abaxial clocks (1992), manufactured by Abaxial Studio
Aldo Rossi, espresso coffee maker, La Conica (1982), manufactured by Alessi SpA
Richard Sapper, automatic teapot, Bandung (1987), manufactured by Alessi SpA
Richard Sapper, espresso coffee maker (1979), manufactured by Alessi SpA
Richard Sapper, kettle with melodic whistle (1983), manufactured by Alessi SpA
Ettore Sottsass, stand (1978), manufactured by Alessi SpA
George Sowden for Sowden Design, calculator, Dauphine (1997), manufactured by Alessi SpA
Philippe Starck, fly-swatter, Dr Skud (1998), manufactured by Alessi SpA
Shigeru Uchida, clock, Dear Vera 1 (1991), manufactured by Alessi SpA
Guido Venturini, garlic press, Nonno di Antonio (1996), manufactured by Alessi SpA

THE CHICAGO ATHENAEUM, MUSEUM OF ARCHITECTURE AND DESIGN, CHICAGO, ILLINOIS

FURNITURE

Mario Bellini, chair, Bellini (1998), manufactured by Heller Inc.
Smith Celentano, desk collection, Nambé Design (1997), manufactured by Nambé Mills
Bulo Design Team, workstation, M2 (1997), manufactured by Bulo Office Furniture
Miguel Angel Ciganda, sofa, Duna (1997), manufactured by CASAS
Maurizio Duranti, home office, Gitano (1997), manufactured by Gallotti & Radice
ITO Design, table series, Carré (1998), manufactured by Davis Furniture Industries Inc.
Daniel Korb, office furniture, P.O.S. (1997), manufactured by DLW Büroeinrichtungen GmbH
Maya Lin, The Maya Lin Collection (1998), manufactured by Knoll Inc.
Mark Muller, shelving system, Tangent (1997), manufactured by Nienklimper
Pasi Pänkaläinen, chair and table, Aerna 022/220 (1996–7), manufactured by Arvo Piiroinen Oy
Jorge Pensi, stacking chair, Gorka (1998), manufactured by AGI
David Ryan and Associates, seating series, Rover (1997), manufactured by Metro Furniture Corporation
Juerg Sporri, side-table and chair, Zic and Zic-Zac (1998), manufactured by ZOOM
Philippe Starck, wash table (1998), manufactured by Duravit AG
Wiege, basic swivel chair, Modus (1998), manufactured by Wilkhahn

LIGHTING

Jean François Crochet, floor lamp, Chtador (1998), manufactured by Terzani Sergio & Co. Srl
Roberto Fiorato, in-ground luminaires, Cyclo Series (1997), manufactured by Prisma SpA
Tobias Grau, wall/ceiling lamp, OVAL (1998), manufactured by Tobias Grau KG GmbH & Co.
Jean-Pierre Généraux Design, desk lamp, Spot On (1998), manufactured by Jean-Pierre Généraux Design
Sally Sirkin Lewis, task lamp, Libra (1996), manufactured by J. Robert Scott
Paolo Targetti and Piero Landini, ceiling lights, Mondial F-1 (1998), manufactured by Targetti USA LLC
Valvomo Design, floor lamp, Globlow (1997), manufactured by Valvomo Design
Noel Zeller, booklight, Itty Bitty Volume 2 (1997), manufactured by Zelco Industries Inc.

TABLEWARE

Peter Aldridge, bowl, Harmony (1997), manufactured by Steuben
Gerald Gulotta, flatware, Rondure (1997), manufactured by Dansk International Designs Ltd
Ralph Krämer, carving set, Trancho (1996), manufactured by C. Hugo Pott GmbH
Michael Schneider Product Design, cheese knives, Twin Collection (1998), manufactured by Zwilling J.A. Henekels AG
Jasper Morrison, tableware, Moon: Cipango Blue (1998), manufactured by Rosenthal AG
Sieger Design, cutlery, Materia I (1997), manufactured by WMF AG
Ann Wählström for Kosta Boda, glass series, Cosmos (1996–8), manufactured by Kosta Boda

TEXTILES

Ruth Adler Schnee, woven upholstery textile, Cadenza (1998), manufactured by Anzea
Jhane Barnes, textiles (1998), manufactured by Jhane Barnes Textiles
Barbara Brenner, decorating fabric, Chicago (1998), manufactured by nya nordiska
Knoll Textiles Design Team, panel fabric, Freehand, Frequency and Foundation (1998), manufactured by Knoll Textiles
Kurt Meinecke, area rugs, Meinecke Collection (1998), manufactured by Herman Miller
Suzanne Tick, drapery fabric, Veil (1998), manufactured by Knoll Textiles
Lori Weitzner, poetry textiles (1997), manufactured by Arkitex Fabrics Ltd

PRODUCTS

500 Group, rolling workshop, ZAG (1998), manufactured by ZAG Industries Ltd
Carlos Agular, single lever tap, Panda (1997), manufactured by CIFIAL
Ancona 2, bar tools, Ekco (1998), manufactured by Ekco Housewares Inc.
Big Design, bath accessory line, Livello and Gelee (1998), manufactured by Interdesign Inc.
Ayse Birsel for Olive Design Inc., dish drainer, Abtropfgestell (1997), manufactured by Authentics Artipresent GmbH
Bresslergroup Inc. and CFM Technologies, CFM full-flow wafer washer (1997), manufactured by CFM Technologies
Julian Brown, tape dispenser, Hannibal (1998), manufactured by Rexit SpA
Cesaroni Design Associates and Zenith, colour television, Z27X31D 27" (1997), manufactured by Zenith Electronics Corporation
Dell Design staff and Design Edge, net PC, Dell OptiPex (1997), manufactured by Dell Computer Corporation
Erik Demmer, Christian Schäffler, washbasin unit, Pollux 1 (1997), manufactured by High Tech Vertriebs GmbH
Design Continuum Italia srl, mountaineering boot, Y-Tech (1997), manufactured by Koflach Sport GmbH
Jewel Durbin for Core Design Ltd, bakeware, Wilton (1998), manufactured by Wilton Industries
Ecco Design Inc., portable pencil sharpeners, Boston (1998), manufactured by Hunt Corporation
Eleven LLC, SI binding (1998), Burton Snowboards
Fitch Inc., JBL harmony radio (1997), manufactured by JBL Consumer Products
Flex Development BV, children's cutlery, Smile (1998), manufactured by Van Kempen & Begeer
Mark Gajewski, ceiling fan, San Francisco (1998), manufactured by Minka Group
Lutz Gebhardt, professional knife system (1998), manufactured by AMC International AG
Michael Graves, cook's tools (1998), manufactured by Marco Home Products for Target Stores
Michael Graves, electric can opener (1998), manufactured by Black & Decker for Target Stores
Michael Graves, toaster (1998), manufactured by Black & Decker for Target Stores
Konstantin Greie, laundry basket, 2-Hands-2 (1997), manufactured by Authentics Artipresent GmbH
György Gyimóthy, wastepaper basket (1998), manufactured by Mobilia-Artica GmbH
Paul Haney, stereo VCR, ProScan PSVR74 (1998), manufactured by Thomson Consumer Electronics
Hauser Inc., printer, Office Jet 500 Series (1997), manufactured by Hewlett-Packard
Peter Haythornthwaite Design, garage door opener, Merlin (1997), manufactured by Merlin Garage Door Openers Ltd
Herbst LaZar Bell Inc., camera, Kodak Advantix Switchable (1997), manufactured by Eastman Kodak Company
Herbst LaZar Bell Inc., shredder, Shredmaster Shark 200 (1998), manufactured by General Binding Corporation
Human Factors Industrial Design, salad spinner, OXO Good Grips (1998), manufactured by OXO International
Industrielle Produkt, built-in kitchen stove, Dessauer Geratewerke (1998), manufactured by Dessauer Gerätewerke
Industrielle Produkt, washbasin, Thomas Reverse (1998), manufactured by R&L Thomas GmbH & Co.
Takeshi Ishiguro for IDEO, keyboard, Yamaha PSS-7 (1997), manufactured by Yamaha Corporation
Carsten Jørgensen, espresso cup, Doppio (1998), manufactured by Bodum
Carsten Jørgensen, espresso maker, Verona (1998), manufactured by Bodum
Ed Kilduff for Pollen Design, pocket corkscrew (1998), manufactured by Metrokane Inc.
Kodak Design and Engineering Team, digital video camera, Kodak Digital Science DVC 323 (1997), manufactured by Eastman Kodak Company
John Kolwaite, two-way radio, FSR (1998), manufactured by Thomson Consumer Electronics
Ralph Krämer, orange peeler, Pomelo (1997), manufactured by C. Hugo Pott GmbH
Ralph Krämer, oyster opener, Marisco (1997), manufactured by C. Hugo Pott GmbH
Ron C. LaGro, ice cream scoop (1997), manufactured by Rowoco Division of Wilton Industries
Les Ateliers du Nord, flashlights, Leclanché (1997), manufactured by Leclanché SA
Les Ateliers du Nord, wrist-watch, ADN (1996), manufactured by AN System SA
Bruno Leverrier, electric ice cream maker, Krups La Glaciere (1997), manufactured by Krups North America Inc.
Lexmark Design Center, colour jetprinter, Lexmark 3200 (1998), manufactured by Lexmark International Inc.
Olavi Lindén, universal cutter (1998), manufactured by Fiskars Inc.
Christopher Loew for IDEO, flat panel display, Samsung TFT400 (1997), manufactured by Samsung Electronics Corp.
Lunar Design, Xerox Home Centre (1997), manufactured by Xerox Corporation
Hans Maier-Aichen, shopping bag, Rondo (1997), manufactured by Authentics Artipresent GmbH
Maytag Appliances, washer and dryer, Maytag Neptune (1997), manufactured by Maytag Appliances
Motorola Design Team, word message pager, Motorola Jazz (1997), manufactured by Motorola Inc.
Wolfgang Münscher, Lutz Rabold, digital telephones, Gigaset Product Family (1997–8), manufactured by Siemens Design & Messe GmbH
Paul Ocepek, LCD television, RCA 4" (1998), manufactured by Thomson Consumer Electronics
Thomas Overthun for IDEO, audible player (1997), manufactured by Audible Inc.
Philippe Piret, toaster oven, Krups ProChef Premium (1998),

manufactured by Krups North America Inc.

Phoenix Product Design, shower column, Pharo (1998), manufactured by Hansgrohe GmbH & Co.

Podd Morrow Design Inc., smoke alarm and heat alarm, Firex 5000 (1998), manufactured by Maple Chase Company

Luigi Prandelli, colander, 883 (1998), manufactured by Meptra SpA

Karim Rashid, frames, Wave, Shimmer, Moon (1997), manufactured by Nambè Mills

Tom Renk, backlit remote control, CRK76 (1998), manufactured by Thomson Consumer Electronics

RKS Design Inc., Dash-Lite (1997), manufactured by LHI Inc.

Roche Harkins Design, protector razor (1997), manufactured by Schick/Wilkinson Sword

Carsten Schmidt, coat hook, Toro (1998), manufactured by unique interieur

Dieter Sieger, kitchen/bath tap, Tara Bridge (1998), manufactured by Dornbracht

Smart Design Inc., bar set – cork pull and bottle opener (1998), manufactured by OXO International

Smart Design Inc., bread knife, Natural Grip (1998), manufactured by OXO International

Smart Design Inc., humidifier, Kaz 4200 CoolMist (1997), manufactured by Kaz Inc.

Smart Design Inc., table top line, Good Grips (1998), manufactured by OXO International

Smart Design Inc., travel hairdryer (1997), manufactured by Brookstone

Staubitz Design Associates, mini paper shredder, Jaws (1998), manufactured by Royal Consumer Business Products/Olivetti Office

Strong Design Ltd, flower pot, Yaozers (1998), manufactured by Alem

Studio Red, WAN maker (1998), manufactured by Larscom

Tesign, rope winch, Wire (1998), manufactured by Haacon

TODA, tea kettle, Uplift (1998), manufactured by OXO International

Tupperware Design Team, ovenworks (1998), manufactured by Tupperware Company

Matthew Wright, Myna Page (1998), manufactured by Philips Consumer Communications

Yamaha Product Design Laboratory, Wind MIDI controller WX5 (1998), manufactured by Yamaha Corporation

Yellow Circle, children's paint box, Rondini (1998), manufactured by Pelikan Vertriebsgesellschaft mbH & Co.

Nicole Zeller, LumiLock (1998), manufactured by Zelco Industries Inc.

THE COOPER-HEWITT NATIONAL DESIGN MUSEUM, NEW YORK

TABLEWARE

Vivianna Torun Bülow-Hube, flatware, Vivianna (1997), manufactured by Georg Jensen Solvsmedie

Laura Diaz de Santillana, vase (1998)

Gerald Gulotta, flatware, Axis (1989–90), manufactured by Dansk International Designs Inc.

Gerald Gulotta, flatware, Rondure (1998), manufactured by Dansk International Designs Inc.

Laura Handler, Dennis Decker and Amanda Hong Magalhaes, glasses, Gallery (1993), manufactured by Metrokane Inc.

Arne Jacobsen, flatware (1957), manufactured by Georg Jensen in 1998

Yoichi Ohira, vase, Bambu from Pasta Vitrea series (1998)

Henk Stallinga, vase, Slab (1995), manufactured by Stallinga BV

PRODUCTS

camera, Kodak Pocket Instamatic 10 (1974), manufactured by Eastman Kodak

Bob Daenen for Tupperware USA, Stig Lillelund, Jakob Heibert, Hanne Dalsgaard Jeppesen for Erik Herlow Design Firm, container set, Impressions (1995), manufactured by Tupperware Corporation

Henry Dreyfuss, camera, Big Shot (1971), manufactured by Polaroid Corporation

Henry Dreyfuss, camera, Swinger (1965), manufactured by Polaroid Corporation

Henry Dreyfuss, camera, SX-70 (1972), manufactured by Polaroid Corporation

Laura Handler, perfume bottle, Flirt (1998), manufactured by Prescriptives

Laura Handler, solid perfume container, Calyx (1990s), manufactured by Prescriptives

Karim Rashid, wastepaper basket, Garbo (1996), manufactured by Umbra

THE DENVER ART MUSEUM, DENVER, COLORADO

FURNITURE

Gae Aulenti, side-chair (1968), manufactured by Kartell SpA

Mario Bellini, tables, Gli Scacchi (1971), manufactured by B & B Italia

Rodolfo Bonetto, table, Quattro Quarti (1969), manufactured by Bernini SpA

Charles and Ray Eames, stool, Time Life (1960), manufactured by Herman Miller Inc.

Arata Isozaki, side-chair, Marilyn (1988), manufactured by Tendo Company Ltd

Shiro Kuramata, armchair, Sing Sing (1985), manufactured by XO

Masayuki Kurokawa, armchair, Aluminum (1975), manufactured by Ingot-Batta

Vico Magistretti, armchair, Gaudi (1970), manufactured by Artemide SpA

Jasper Morrison, lounge chair, Thinking Man's (1987), manufactured by Cappellini International Interiors

Pierre Paulin, lounge chair and ottoman, F598 (1973), manufactured by Artifort

Gaetamo Pesce, lounge chair, Feltri (1987), manufactured by Cassini SpA

Ettore Sottsass, Jr, bookcase, ES-4 (1993), manufactred by Giotto Green Design Ltd

Shigeru Uchida, armchair, September (1977), manufactured by Studio 80/Toptome

Shigeru Uchida, chair, Okazaki (1996), manufactured by Studio 80/Toptome

Shigero Uchida, chair, Rattan (1974) prototype, manufactured by Studio 80/Toptome

Masanori Umeda, chair, Getsuen (1998), manufactured by Edra SpA

Robert Venturi, side-chair, Deco 665 (1979–84), manufactured by Knoll International

Robert Venturi, side-chair, Sheraton 664, manufactured by Knoll International

Marco Zanuso, Jr, chest of drawers, MZ-4 (1993), manufactured by Giotto Green Design Ltd

Marco Zanuso, Jr, chest of drawers, MZ-7 (1993), manufactured by Giotto Green Design Ltd

Marco Zanuso, Jr, side-chair, Lambda (1963), manufactured by Gavina

LIGHTING

Mario Botta, table lamp, Shogun (1986), manufactured by Artemide SpA

Masayuki Kurokawa, lamp, Domani (1976), manufactured by Yamagiwa

Masanori Umeda, light, Umeda Stand (1986), manufactured by Yamagiwa H&F Inc.

TABLEWARE

anonymous, dinnerware (1960s), manufactured by Block

Michele de Lucchi, candlestick, Chandeliere (1990), manufactured by Produzione Privata

Michele de Lucchi, vase, MDL-8 (1993), manufactured by Giotto Green Design Ltd

Michele de Lucchi, vase, Vaso Bianco (1990), manufactured by Produzione Privata

Ludovico de Santillana, bowl, Pierre Cardin (1969), manufactured by Venini SpA

Marco Ferreri, centrepiece, Antipodi (1996), manufactured by Danese

Johanna Grawunder, vase, JG-4 (1993), manufactured by Giotto Green Design Ltd

Masayuki Kurokawa, cutlery, Ascent (1996), manufactured by Accent

Masayuki Kurokawa, glasses, Blue Tumblers (1996), manufactured by Takenaka Works Co. Ltd

Ettore Sottsass, Jr, vase, Mirto 111 (1997), manufactured by Maru Tomi Co. Ltd

Ettore Sottsass, Jr, vase, Mirto 112 (1997), manufactured by Maru Tomi Co. Ltd

Giotto Stoppino, vase (1960), manufactured by Heller Inc.

Masanori Umeda, Startray (1985), manufactured by Nichinan Co. Ltd

Masanori Umeda, tea set, Mutsuguro (1985), manufactured by Yamaka Shouten Co. Ltd

Masanori Umeda, vase, Yantra (1997), manufactured by Maru Tomi Co. Ltd

Masanori Umeda, vase, Yantra C (1997), manufactured by Maru Tomi Co. Ltd

Massimo Vignelli, dinnerware, Max (1964), manufactured by Heller Inc.

PRODUCTS

Joe Colombo, desk clock, Optic (1970), manufactured by Ritz-Italora

Masayuki Kurokawa, wall clock, CFB (1983), manufactured by Fuso Gomu Industry Company

Masayuki Kurokawa, watch, Rabat (1987), manufactured by Citizen Watch

Erik Magnussen, tea kettle (1988), manufactured by Stelton, Gentofte

Ettore Sottsass, Jr, mirror, ES-3 (1993), manufactured by Giotto Green Design Ltd

Ettore Sottsass, Jr, calculator, Summa 19 (1970), manufactured by Olivetti SpA

Shigeru Uchida, clock, Dear Morris (1989), manufactured by Acerbis International SpA

Lawrence von Bamford, knife, Outdoorsman (1972), manufactured by Design Research X

Lawrence von Bamford, knife, Backpacker (1972), manufactured by Design Research X

Marco Zanuso, bottle openers, MZ-1, MZ-2 and MZ-3 (1993), manufactured by Giotto Green Design Ltd

MUSEUM OF ART, LOS ANGELES

FURNITURE

Janice Feldman, rocker, Windsong (designed 1993, manufactured 1997)

Frank Gehry, armchair, Cross Check (designed 1992, manufactured 1997)

Sam Maloof, rocking chair (designed 1959, manufactured 1997)

Paul Tuttle, chaise longue, Skate (designed 1993, manufactured 1997)

MUSEUM OF MODERN ART, NEW YORK

FURNITURE

Constantin Boym, containers, USE IT (1995), manufactured by Authentics GmbH

Antonio Citterio and Glen Oliver Löw, folding extension table, Battista (1991), manufactured by Kartell SpA

Christopher Connell, chair, Pepe (1992), manufacutred by MAP

Hans Coray, chair, Landi (manufactured 1950–62), manufactured by P & W Blattmann Metallwaren-Fabrik

Shiro Kuramata, drawers, 49 Drawers (1970), manufactured by Aoshima Shoten Co. Ltd

Shiro Kuramata, Side 2 (1970), manufactured by Aoshima Shoten Co. Ltd

Shiro Kuramata, chair, Miss Blanche (1989), manufactured by Ishimaru Co.

Enzo Mari, chair, Sof-sof (1971), manufactured by Driade SpA

Marc Newson, chair, Wood (1988), manufactured by Cappellini SpA

Marc Newson, chaise lounge, Orgone (1989), manufactured by Cappellini SpA

Enzo Mari, box, Flores (1991), manufactured by Danese Srl

Alberto Meda, chaise lounge, Long Frame (1994), manufactured by Alias Srl

Jasper Morrison, storage module, Bottle (1993), manufactured by Magis Srl

Renzo Piano and Noriaki Okabe, airport lobby seating (1993), manufactured by Okamura Corporation

LIGHTING

Harry Allen, lighting fixtures (1994), manufactured by Harry Allen and Associates

Sebastian Bergne, lighting fixture, Lamp Shade 1 (1991), manufactured by Radius GmbH

Joseph Forakis, hanging lighting fixture, Havana (1993),

manufactured by Foscarini Murano SpA

Lyn Godley and Lloyd Schwan, lamp, Crinkle (1996), manufactured by Godley Schwan

PRODUCTS

automobile taillights, MX5 Miata (1983), manufactured by Mazda Motor Corporation

Santina Bonini and Ernesto Spicciolato, bathroom accessories, Arctic Series (1994), manufactured by Gedy SpA

Paul Bradley and Lawrence Lam, computer pointing device, 3-D Mouse (1991), manufactured by Logitech Inc.Antonio Citterio and Glen Oliver Löw, container system, Mobil (1993), manufactured by Kartell SpA

Bob Evans, diving fin, Tan Delta Force Fin (1994), manufactured by Bob Evans Designs Inc.

Howatt Archery, longbow, ML-14 Mountaineer (1994), manufactured by Martin Archery

Takeshi Ishiguro, salt and pepper shakers, Rice (1994), prototype

Per Jari and Jan Orn, pacemaker, Multilog 2040 (1988), manufactured by Pacesetter AB

Kirk Jones and Doug Olson, bicycle wheel, SPIN (1989), manufactured by Innovations in Composites Inc.

Masayuki Kurokawa, pen, Gom (1992), manufactured by Fuso Gum Industry Co. Ltd

Masayuki Kurokawa, push pins and magnets, Gom (1984), manufactured by Fuso Gum Industry Co. Ltd

Masayuki Kurokawa, scuba gear, Fieno (1993), manufactured by Grand Bleu Inc.

Hans Maier-Aichen, wastepaper baskets, LIP (1993), manufactured by Authentics GmbH

Gordon Randall Perry, hand-held magnifiers, ClearVision II (1994), manufactured by Designs for Vision Inc.

Sanford Redmond, packaging, dispenSRpak (1986), manufactured by Sanford Redmond

Jhoon Rhee, mask, Jhoon Rhee Safety Face (1976), manufactured by Rheemax Inc.

Riedell Skating Shoes, Inc. and Scott Riegelman, skate boot inner shell, In-line (1994), manufactured by BioMechanical Composites

Marc Sadler, motorcyclist's back protector, Bap (1992), manufactured by Dainese SpA

Richard Sapper and Samuel Lucente, computer, Leapfrog (1989), manufactured by IBM Corporation

Paul Schudel, clock, DK (1980), manufactured by Designum

Vent Design and Stephen Peart and Bradford Bissell, wet suit, Animal (1988), manufactured by O'Neill Inc.

PHILADELPHIA MUSEUM OF ART, PENNSYLVANIA

FURNITURE

Rodney Kinsman, bench, Seville (1992), manufactured by OMK Design Ltd

TABLEWARE

Walter Keeler, cylindrical lidded teapot on stand (1998)

PRODUCTS

Trevor Baylis, radio, Freeplay (1993), manufactured by BayGen

James Dyson, vacuum cleaner, Dual Cyclone DC02 (1995), manufactured by Dyson Appliances

Anthony Evans, football boots, SpinGrip Outsole (1997), manufactured by Umbro International

Paul Priestman, radiators, Hot Springs (1996), manufactured by Bisque Radiators

SUPPLIERS

Helle Abild. E. Helle@abild.com
Adele C., Via Barzaghi 9, Milan I-20050, Italy. T. (0)362 99 28 52. F. (0)362 99 26 35
Werner Aisslinger, 33 Leibnizstrasse, Berlin, Germany. T. (0)30 31505400. F. (0)30 31505401. E. aisslinger@berlin.snafu.de
Ajeto, Czech Glass Craft srl, 167 Lindava, 47158 CZ, Czech Republic. T. (0)424 75 16 13/14. F. (0)424 75 16 12
Aktiva, 10B Spring Place, London NW5 3BH, UK. T. (0)207 428 9325. F. (0)207 428 9882
Alessi SpA, Via Privata Alessi 6, Crusinallo, Verbania VB, Italy. T. (0)323 86 86 11. F. (0)323 86 61 32. E. pub@alessi.it
Harry Allen & Associates, 207 Avenue A, New York, NY 10009, USA. T. (0)212 529 7239. F. (0)212 529 7982. E. hasallen@earthlink.net
Allglass Snc, Via Le Roma 59, S. Dono di Masanzago, Padova 35010, Italy. T. (0)49 93 60 168. F. (0)49 93 64 049
Gabriele Allendorf, Dall'Armistrasse 15, Munich 80638, Germany. T. (0)89 15 97 02 02. F. (0)89 15 97 02 04
Simon Andrews, c/o Kingston University, Knights Park, Kingston KT1 2QJ, Surrey, UK. T. (0)208 547 2000. F. (0)208 547 7365
Antares Iluminacion SA, 42 Pol.Ind.La Mina, Paiporta E-46200, Spain. T. (0)96 397 60 31
Anthologie Quartett, Schloss Hunnefeld, Bad Essen D-49152, Germany. T/F. (0)5472 94090
Apple Computer Inc., 20730 Valley Green Drive, Cupertino 95014, California, USA. T. (0)650 728 0530. F. (0)415 495 0251
Aqua Creations Ltd, 69 Maze Street, Tel Aviv, Israel 65789. T. (0)972 3 5602197. F. (0)972 3 5607756. E. albi@aquagallery.com
Ron Arad Associates Ltd, 62 Chalk Farm Road, London NW1 8AN, UK. T. (0)207 284 4963/5. F. (0)207 279 0499. E. ronarad@mail.pro-net.co.uk
Arclinea Arredamenti SpA, Viale Pasubio 50, Caldogno (Vi) 36030, Italy. T. (0)444 39 41 11. F. (0)444 39 42 60. E. arclinea@arclinea.it
Arnolfo di Cambio, Compagnia Italiana del Cristallo srl, 53034 Colle di Val d'Elsa, Siena Loc. Pian dell'Olmino, Italy. T. (0)577 92 82 79. F. (0)577 92 96 47. E. dicambio@cyber.dada.it
Artemide SpA, Via Canova 34, Milan 20145, Italy. T. (0)2 34 96 11.1. F. (0)2 34 53 82 11. E. pr@artemide.com
Asplund, 31 Sibyllegatan, Stockholm 11442, Sweden. T. (0)8 662 52 84. F. (0)8 662 38 85
Authentics, Max Eyth Strasse 30, Holzgerlingen D-71088, Germany. T. (0)7031 68050. F. (0)7031 6805 99
Azumi, 953 Finchley Road, London NW11 7PE, UK. T. (0)208 731 9057. F. (0)208 731 7496
Emmanuel Babled, Via Segantini 71, Milan 20143, Italy. T. (0)2 58 11 11 19
Georg Baldele Design, 5 Old Street, 3rd Floor/rear, London EC1V 9HL, UK. T. (0)207 490 3889
Baleri Italia, Via F. Cavallotti 8, Milan 20122, Italy. T. (0)2 76 01 46 72. F. (0)2 76 01 44 19. E. info@baleri-italia.com
Ralph Ball, 177 Waller Road, London SE14 5LX, UK.
Belux AG, Bremgarterstrasse 109, CH-5610 Wohlen, Switzerland. T. (0)56 618 73 73. F. (0)56 618 73 27. E. belux@belux.ch
Mathias Bengtsson, 11 Wendover Court, Chiltern Street, London W1M 1HD, UK.
Benza Inc., 413 West 14th Street No. 301, New York, NY 10014, USA. T. (0)212 243 4047. F. (0)212 243 4689. E. benzainc@aol.com
Marc Berthier, Design Plan Studio, 141 Bd St-Michel, 75005 Paris, France. T. (0)1 43 26 49 97. F. (0)1 43 26 54 62. E. dpstudio@wanadoo.fr
Jurgen Bey, Passerelstraat 44A, 3023 ZD Rotterdam, The Netherlands. T. (0)10 425 8792. F. (0)10 425 9437. E. bey@luna.nl
Bisazza Mosaico SpA, Viale Milano 56, Alte, Vicenza 36041, Italy. T/F. (0)444 70 75 11
Bius – Mary Little and Peter Wheeler, 120 Battersea Business Centre, 103 Lavender Hill, London SW11 5AL, UK. T. (0)207 924 7724. F. (0)207 924 6524
Blue Project, Via Guariento 5, Bassano del Grappa, Vicenza 36061, Italy. T. (0)424 50 52 05. F. (0)424 50 82 17
Boffi SpA, Via Oberdan 70, Lentate sul Seveso 20030, Milan, Italy. T. (0)362 5341. F. (0)362 56 50 77. E. boffimarket@boffi.it
Bond Projects UK Ltd, 38 Grosvenor Gardens, London SW1W 0EB, UK. T/F. (0)171 730 3011. E. bond.puk@btinternet.com
Bonzon Design, 358 Estrada do Jipao, Ubatuba 11680-000, São Paulo, Brazil. T. (0)124 32 3250
Boum Design, 527 East 6th Street 5w, New York, NY 10009, USA. T. (0)212 254 1070. F. (0)212 431 6121
Ronan Bouroullec, 15 Rue des Ursulines, Saint Denis 93200, France. T. (0)1 48 20 36 60
Böwer GmbH, 1 Mettinger Strasse, Neuenkirchen D-49586, Germany. T. (0)5465 9292 0. F. (0)5465 9292 15
BRF srl, Loc. S. Marziale 21, Colle val d'Elsa, Siena 53034, Italy. T. (0)577 92 94 18. F. (0)577 92 96 48. E. biancucci@brfcolors.com
Brueton Studio, 145-68 228th Street, Springfield Gardens, New York, NY 11413, USA. T. (0)718 527 3000. F. (0)718 712 6783. E. start@brueton.com
Brunati Italia, Via Catalani 5, Lissone 20035, Milan, Italy. T. (0)39 24 56 33 1. F. (0)39 24 56 26 7
Debbie Jane Buchan, 3 Hutchinson Avenue, Edinburgh EH14 1QE, Scotland.
Bulo Office Furniture, Industriezone Noord B6, Mechelem 2800, Belgium. T. (0)15 28 28 28. F. (0)15 28 28 29. E. info@bulo.be
Sigi Bussinger, Hellabrunnerstr 30, Munich 81543, Germany.
Bute, c/o Caro Communications, First Floor, 49-59 Old Street, London EC1V 9HX, UK. T. (0)207 251 9112. Fax: (0)171 490 5757. E. pr@carocom.demon.co.uk
Julia Büttelmann, Crellestr 19-20, Berlin 10827, Germany. T. (0)30 788 3119
La Cambre (ENSAV), Fabienne Collet, 21 Abbaya de La Cambre, Brussels 1000, Belgium. T. (0)2 64 89 619. F. (0)2 64 09 693
Campana Objetos Ltda, Rua Barão de Tatui 219, São Paulo 01226030, Brazil. T. (0)11 8253408/(0)11 36674317. F. (0)11 8253408
Campeggi srl, Via Cavolto 8, Anzano del Parco (Como) 22040, Italy. T. (0)31 63 04 95. F. (0)31 63 22 05
Canon Inc., 30-2 Shimaruko 3-chome, 146-8501, Ohta-ku, Japan. T. (0)3 3758 2111. F. (0)3 5482 9711. E. richard@cpur.canon.co.jp
Chiara Cantono, Via Malpighi 3, 20129 Milan, Italy. T. (0)2 29518792. F. (0)2 29518189
Cappellini SpA/Units srl, Via Marconi 35, Arosio (Como) 22060, Italy. T. (0)31 75 91 11. F. (0)31 76 33 22
Cassina SpA, Via L Bisnelli 1, Meda/Milan I-20036, Italy. T. (0)362 372.1. F. (0)362 34 22 46/ 34 09 59. E. info@cassina.it
Chaplet Systems Inc., Taipei Office, 13 WU-Chung Fifth Road, WU-ku Industrial Park, Taipai County, Taiwan R.O.C. T. (0) 886 2298 8989. F. (0) 886 2298 8422
ClassiCon GmbH, Perchtinger Strasse 8, Munich 81379, Germany. T. (0)89 74 81 33 0. F. (0)89 7 80 99 96
Class X Furniture, Tartu Kunstikool, Tahe 38b Tartu, Estonia. T. (0)3727366056. E. Priit.Verlin@neti.ee *or* unt@uninet.ee
Carl Clerkin, Unit 205, Oxo Tower Wharf, 205 Barge House Street, London SE1 9PH, UK. T. (0)207 928 0143
Nigel Coates, Branson Coates Architecture, 23 Old Street, London EC1V 9HL, UK. T. (0)207 490 0343. F. (0)207 490 0320
Codice 31, Via le Regina Giovanna 26, Milan 20129, Italy. T. (0)2 29 51 77 22. F. (0)2 66 98 33 87
Colombo Design SpA, Via Baccanello 22, Terno d'Isola (BG) 24030, Italy. T. (0)35 49 49 001. F. (0)35 90 54 44. E. info@colombodesign.it
Gianfranco Coltella/Le Meduse, Corso Piemonte 69, Saluzzo (CN) 12037, Italy. T/F. (0)175 24 92 36
Comune di Milano, c/o MAP, Via Guercino 2, Milan 20154, Italy. T. (0)2 34 53 21 63. E. mapdesig@iol.it
Comma Inc., 9 West 19th Street, New York, NY 10011, USA. T. (0)212 929 4866. F. (0)212 924 3667. E-mail comma19@aol.com
Copetti Design, Zona Art Campagnola 1, Gemona (UD) 33013, Italy. T. (0)432 98 12 50. F. (0)432 97 09 17. E. info@copettidesign.com
Copray & Scholten, Vestdijk 141a, 5611 CB Eindhoven, The Netherlands. T. (0)40 213 00 60. F. (0)40 212 61 54
Cor Unum, 9 Gruttostraat, Den Bosch, 52 NL-5212 VM, The Netherlands. T. (0)73 691 1499. F. (0)73 614 2706
Costantino By Ardes srl, Viale Unita D'Italia 123, Taranto 74100, Italy. T. (0)99 77 61 538. F. (0)99 77 24 070. E. costantino@dear.com
Cotelletto, Oppemer Strasse 50, Wurselen 52146, Germany. T. (0)2405 42 14 48. F. (0)2405 42 14 49. E. cotelletto@aol.com
Création Baumann London, Baumann Fabrics Ltd, 41-2 Berners Street, London W1P 3AA, UK. T. (0)207 637 0253. F. (0)207 631 4972
Dd David Design, Stortorget 25, Malmö 21134, Sweden. T. (0)40 30 00 00. F. (0)40 30 00 50. E. info@david.se
De Lucchi srl (Produzione Privata), Via Pallavicino 31, Milan 20145, Italy. T. (0)2 43 00 81. F. (0)2 43 11 82 22. E. amdl@architectures.it
De Padova srl, Corso Venezia 14, Milan 20121, Italy. T. (0)2 77 720.1. F. (0)2 77 72 02 80
Design Gallery Milano 99, 46 Manzoni, Milan 20121, Italy. T. (0)2 79 89 55. F. (0) 02 78 40 82
Bernhard Dessecker, c/o Ingo Maurer, Kaiserstrasse 47, Munich 80801, Germany. T. (0)89 381 606-0. F. (0)89 381 606 20
Dinersan Inc. (Nick Dine Design), 270 Lafayette Street, Site 402, New York, NY 10012, USA. T. (0)212 925 0004. F. (0)212 965 9009
Dingaling Studio Inc., 71 Broadway No. 13D, New York, NY 10006, USA. T. (0)212 979 2325. F. (0)212 863 9741
DMD, Parkweg 14, Voorburg, The Netherlands. T. (0)70 386 4038. F. (0)70 387 3075
Driade SpA, Via Padana Inferiore 12A, Fossadello di Caorso 29012, PC, Italy. T. (0)523 81 86 60. F. (0)523 82 23 60
Droog Design, Keizersgracht 518, 1017 EK Amsterdam, The Netherlands. T. (0)20 62 69 809. F. (0)20 63 88 828. E. gbakker@xs4all.nl
Emily Du Bois, 583 East H Street, Benicia 94510, California, USA. T. (0)707 745 0829
François Duris, 13 Rue Emile Desvaux, Paris 75019, France. T. (0)1 42 49 06 72. F. (0)1 42 78 33 29
Edizioni Galleria Colombari, Via Solferino 37, Milan 20121, Italy. T. (0)2 29 00 15 51. F. (0)2 29 00 13 75
Edra SpA, Via Livornese Est 106, Perignano 56030, Italy. T. (0)587 61 66 60. F. (0)587 61 75 00
El Ultimo Grito, 26 Northfield House, Frensham Street, London SE15 6TL, UK. T. (0)207 732 6614. F. (0)207 277 6761. E. grito@BTInternet.com
EOOS, Hernalser Hauptstrasse 17/31, Vienna A-1170, Austria. T. (0)1 40 53 987. F. (0)1 40 53 9877
ERCO Leuchten GmbH, Postfach 2460, Lüdenscheid D-58505, Germany. T. (0)2351 551 345. F. (0)2351 551 340. E. m.krautter@erco.com
Erie Ceramic Arts Company, 3120 West 22nd Street, PA 16506, USA. T. (0)814 833 7758. F. (0)814 838 7584
Everyday Design, 38 Kulosaaren Puistotie, Helsinki 00570, Finland. T. (0)9 621 6636. F. (0)9 621 1636
Extremis, Weegschede 39b, Gijverinkhove 8691, Belgium. T. (0)58 299725. F. (0)58 298118. E. info@extremis.be
Christopher Farr, 212 Westbourne Grove, London W11, UK. T. (0)207 792 5761. F. (0)207 792 5763
Feldmann & Schultchen, 7 Timmermannstrasse, Hamburg, Germany. T. (0)40 51 00 00. F. (0)40 51 70 00
Ferro e Fogo, Rua Antonio Chagas 966, São Paulo, 04714-001, Brazil. T. (0)11 5182 3268
Fiam Italia SpA, Via Ancona 1/B, Tavullia 61010, Pesaro, Italy. T. (0)721 20051. F. (0)721 202432
Fink – Robert Foster, GPO Box 1806, Canberra City, ACT 2601, Australia. T. (0)6 241 9529. F. (0)6 247 2221
Jacopo Foggini, Via Sannio 24, Milan 20137, Italy. T. (0)2 54 10 14 09
Fontana Arte, Alzaia Trieste 49, Corsico 20094, Milan, Italy. T. (0)2 45 12 330
Frandsen Lyskilde AS, 8-10 Industrivej, Braedstrup 8740, Denmark. T. (0)76 58 18 18. F. (0)76 58 18 19
Fredericia Furniture AS, Treldevej 183, Fredericia 7000, Denmark. T. (0) 7592 3344. F. (0)7592 3876. E. sales@frederician.com
Fujitsu, 1015 Kami Kotanaka, Nakahara Kawasaki 211, Kanagawa, Japan. T. (0)44 754 3492. F. (0)44 754 3582
John Gabbertas, Obuque Workshops, Stamford Works, Gillett Street, London N16 8JH, UK. T. (0)207 503 2112. F. (0) 207 275 7495
F. Th. Gärtner Industrial Design, Steckelsgasse 18, Heidelberg D-69121, Germany. T. (0)6221 484744. F. (0)6221 484526. E. Gaertner-Design@t-online.de
Garcia Garay Iluminación Diseño, San Antonio 13, Sta. Coloma de Gramenet 08923, Barcelona, Spain. T. (0)93 466 10 16. F. (0)93 386 23 72
GelderLand, 7 Stationsweg, Culemborg 4101 N6, The Netherlands. T. (0)50 5244244. F. (0)50 5244255
Christian Ghion, 156 Rue Oberkampf, Paris 75011, France. T. (0)1 49 29 06 90. F. (0)1 49 29 06 89
Glaskoch, Postfach 1354, Bad Driburg D-33003, Germany. T. (0)5253 862 60. F. (0)5253 862 94
Gloria srl, Via Provinciale 44, Lallio/Bergamo 240040, Italy. T. (0)35 69 33 77. F. (0)35 20 33 17. E. info@baleri-italia.com
Natanel Gluska, Renggerstrasse 85, CH-8038 Zurich, Switzerland. T. (0)1 48 30 366
Davide Groppi, Via Taverna 138, Piacenza 29100, Italy. T. (0)523 49 80 57. E. davidegroppi@alcon.com
Pawel Grunert, c/o Alicja Trusiewicz, Via Bramante 22/L, Perugia 06100, Italy. T/F. (0)75 572 6470. E. alicjet@tin.it
Gitta Gschwendtner, Unit 2.05 Oxo Tower, Barge House Street, London SE1 9PH, UK. T. (0)207 928 0143
Dögg Gudmundsdóttir, Lundtoftegade 26 1 th, 2200 Copenhagen, Denmark. T. (0)35 85 36 35. E. daggadogg@hotmail.com
Habitat 2000 Collection, 196 Tottenham Court Road, Heal's Building, London W1B 9LD, UK. T. (0)207 255 3636. F. (0)207 255 6002
Hackman Designor Oy Ab, Hämeentie 135, Helsinki FIN-00560, Finland. T. (0)358 204 39 11. F. (0)358 204 39 51 60
Halifax by Tisettanta, Unitec SpA, Via Tofane 37, Giussano (Mi) 20034, Italy. T. (0)3 62 35 61. F. (0)3 62 35 64 00. E. info@tisettanta.it
Ashley Hall Design, 33A Englefield Road, London N1 4EU, UK. T. (0)207 249 8055
Doug Halley, c/o Product Design Department, Glasgow School of Art, Foulis Building, 158 Renfrew Street, Glasgow G3 6RF, Scotland. T. (0)141 353 4614. F. (0)141 353 4655
Isabel Hamm, 29 Gocherstrasse, Cologne, Germany. T. (0)221 73 91 492. F. (0)221 73 91 493
Noa Hanyu, 24-26 Saiwai-cho, Koga 306-0024, Ibaraki, Japan.
Masako Hayashibe, 2-13-5 Shimouma, Setagaya, Tokyo 154-0002, Japan. T/F. (0)3 3412 8216
Heller Inc. USA., 41 Madison Avenue, New York, NY 10010, USA. T. (0)212 685 4200. F. (0)212 685 4204
Herbst LaZar Bell Inc., 355 North Canal, Chicago 60606, Illinois, USA. T. (0)312 454 1116. F. (0)312 454 9019
Hishinuma Associates, 4-10-4 Jingumae, Shibuya-ku, Tokyo 150-0001, Japan. T. (0)3 5770 8333. F. (0)3 5770 8334
Horm, Via Crocera di Corva 25, Azzano Decimo (Pordenone) 33082 , Italy. T. (0)434 64 07 33. F. (0)434 64 07 35. E. horm@horm.it
Wayne Hudson, 51 Warwick Street, Hobart 7000, Tasmania, Australia.
Richard Hutten, 52 Marconistraat, Rotterdam 3029, The Netherlands.
Julius Hyde Furniture, 23/28 Penn Street, London N1 5DL, UK. T. (0)207 729 4805
I + I/Paolo Giordano, Via Salento 5, Milan 20141, Italy. T. (0)2 34 53 81 52. F. (0)2 33 10 41 87
Idee Co. Ltd., 6-1-16 Minami-Aoyama, Minato-ku, Tokyo 107, Japan. T. (0)3 3409 7080. F. (0)3 3486 1580
Iform AB, PO Box 5055, Malmö, SE-200 71, Sweden. T. (0)40 303610. F. (0)40 302288
IKEA of Sweden, Box 702, Almhult 34381, Smaland, Sweden. T. (0)47 68 10 00. F. (0)47 61 51 23
Immersion Corporation. E. FEELit@immerse.com
Inflate Ltd, Third Floor Rear, 5 Old Street, London, EC1V 9HL, UK. T. (0)207 251 5453. F. (0)207 251 2602. E. info@inflate.co.uk
Inter Bodum AG, 100 Kantonsstrasse, Triengen 6243, Switzerland. T. (0)41 935 45 00. F. (0)41 935 45 80
Iris Licht, 169 Erzh.Karl.Str, Vienna A-1220, Austria. T. (0)1 280 67 77. F. (0)1 282 33 73
Iwasaki Design Studio, 201 2-25-7 Kamazawa Setagaya-ku, Tokyo 154-0012, Japan. T. (0)3 3487 5388. F. (0)3 3487 5348
JKN Arnhem – Jan Broekstra, Julianalaan 5, 6824 KG Arnhem, The Netherlands. T. (0)26 44 34 180. E. jkn.arnhem@wxs.nl
Hella Jongerius, Schietbaaniaan 75b, 3021 LE Rotterdam, The Netherlands. T. (0)10 4770253. F. (0)10 4778300
W.F. Kaiser, 28 W.-von-Siemens-Strasse, Diez/Lahn D-65582, Germany. T. (0)6432 91 51 22. F. (0)6432 91 51 29

Kam Sun Wohnbedarf GmbH, Zeppelin Strasse 9, Laupheim 88471 , Germany. T. (0)7392 15 04 33.

Kartell SpA, Via della Industrie 1, Noviglio (MI) 20082, Italy. T. (0)2 90 01 21. F. (0)2 90 53 316

Yehudit Katz, 11 Natan Hechachan, Tel Aviv 63413, Israel.

Knoll International Ltd, 1 Lindsey Street, East Market, Smithfield, London EC1A 9PQ, UK. T. (0)207 236 6655. F. (0)207 248 1744

Kockums/David Design, Stortorget 25, Malmö 21134, Sweden. T. (0)40 300000. F. (0)40 300050. E. info@david.se

Aki Kotkas, Hameentie 130E, Helsinki 00560, Finland.

Roman Kovár, 1126 Oskara Nedbala, Hradec Kralove 500 02, Czech Republic.

Kraut Royal, Vogelsangerstrasse 193, Cologne D-50825, Germany. T. (0)221 170 42 33

Kuma's (Kyoko Kumai), Sumiyoshi-cho, Oita-City 870-0032, Japan. T. (0)97 534 9178. F. (0)97 536 0634

Kundalini srl, Via Plutarco 6, Milan 20145, Italy. T. (0)2 498 95 87. F. (0)2 481 94 560. E. kundalini@tin.it

Lammhults Möbel AB, PO Box 26, Lammhult 360 30, Sweden. T. (0)472 2695 00. F. (0)472 2605 70. E. info@lammhults.se

Danny Lane, 19 Hythe Road, London NW10 6RT, UK. T. (0)208 968 3399. F. (0)208 968 6289

Sophie Larger, 70 Boulevard de L'Hôpital, Paris 75013, France.

Eric LaRoye, 37/1 Koningsstraat, Oostende B-8400, Belgium. T/F. (0)32 59 50 18 80

Chunghie Lee, 29 40 Hwagok-dong, Kangsu-ku, Seoul 157-019, Korea. T. (0)2 602 6959. F. (0)2 606 9300. E. artfiber@chollian.net

Mark Lee, 200 Bowery Street, Suite 8D, New York, NY 10012, USA. T. (0)212 925 6253. F. (0)212 219 9968. E. mark@marklee.wet

Ligne Roset, Serrières de Briord, Briord 01470, France. T. (0)4 74 36 17 00. F. (0)4 74 36 16 95

Jeremy Lord, The Colour Light Co. Ltd, 12 Craycombe Farm, Faldbury, Pershore, Worcestershire WR10 2QS, UK. T. (0)1346 861086. F. (0)1386 861056. E. jeremylord@colourlight.com

Lucefer-Licht, 2 Strlitzer Strasse, Berlin D-10115, Germany. T. (0)30 44 31 93 30. F. (0)30 44 31 93 333

Lucitalia, Via Pelizza da Volpedo 50, Cinisello B-20092, Milan, Italy. T. (0)2 61 26 651. F. (0)2 66 00 707. E. lucital@tin.it

Lunar Design, 537 Hamilton Avenue, Palo Alto, CA 94301, USA. T. (0)650 326 7788. F. (0)650 326 2420

Luxlab, 6 Rue Gobert, Paris 75011, France. T. (0)1 43 73 59 45. F. (0)1 43 74 59 16. E. tgaugain@club-internet.fr

Magenta Design, Wildbader Strasse 11, Mannheim 60239, Germany. T. (0)621 18304 0. E. e-mail@magenta.de

Magis srl, Via Magnadola 15, Motta di Livenza (Treviso) 31045, Italy. T. (0)422 76 87 42/3. F. (0)422 76 63 95

Cecilie Manz, 27 Dampfaergevej, Copenhagen, DK 2100K, Denmark.

Sharon Marston, Studio 54, 1 Clink Street, Soho Wharf, London SE1 9DG, UK. T. (0)207 234 0832. F. (0)207 407 7459

Mauser Office GmbH, Waldeck D-34513, Germany. T. (0)5623 581 0. F. (0)5623 581208

Memphis, Via Olivetti 9, Milan 20010, Italy. T. (0)2 93 29 06 83. F. (0)2 93 59 12 02

Ross Menuez, 186 Powers Street, Brooklyn, New York, NY 11211, USA. T. (0)718 218 7443. F. (0)718 218 8147

Mesh Co., Studio 2F1, 2 Michael Road, London SW6 2AD, UK. T. (0)7020 963742. F. (0)7775 785 121. E. mesh@dial.pipex.com

Metalarte SA, Avenida de Barcelona 4, Sant Joan Despi (Barcelona) 08970, Spain. T. (0)34 934 770 069. F. (0)34 934 770 086

Microsoft Corporation, One Microsoft Way MS 19, Redmond, WA 98052-6399, USA. T. (0)206 703 3432

Miscellaneous Design, 19 Ostbanegade, Copenhagen K-2100, Denmark. T/F.(0)35 55 49 33

Anthony Mixides, c/o Kingston University, Knights Park, Kingston KY1 2QJ, Surrey, UK. T. (0)208 547 2000

Marre Moerel, 182 Hester Street No. 13, New York, NY 10013, USA. T. (0)212 219 8985. F. (0)212 925 2371. E. marremoerel@rcn.com

Moonlight Aussenleuchten GmbH, Gerwerbegebiet Hemmet, Wehr D-79664, Germany. T. (0)7762 1018. F. (0)7762 2203

Moormann Möbel GmbH, 2 An der Festhalle, Aschau i.ch., D-83229, Germany. T. (0)8052 4001. F. (0)8052 4393. E. info@moormann.de

Carlo Moretti srl, 3 Fondamenta Manin, Murano-Venezia 30141, Italy. T. (0)41 73 92 17/73 65 88. F. (0)41 73 62 82

Moroso SpA, Via Nazionale 60, Cavalicco di Tavagnacco 1–33010, Udine, Italy. T. (0)432 577 111. F. (0)432 570 761. E. info@moroso.it

Mosquito Tribologies Corporation, PO Box 164, Aurora, Ontario, L4G 3H3, Canada. T. (0)888 666 8480. F. (0)905 238 1815

N2, Breisacherstrasse 64, Basel 4057, Switzerland. T. (0)61 693 40 15. E. n2@n2design.ch

NAC Sound srl, Via Boncompagni, Rome 7900187, Italy. T. (0)6 44 55 730

Nava Design SpA, Martin Lutero 5, Milan 20126, Italy. T. (0)2 25 70 251. F. (0)2 26 30 05 18

Maxine Naylor, 177 Waller Road, London SE14 5LX, UK.

NEC Design Ltd, Takanawa Kowa Building, 20-36, 2-chome, Takanawa, Minato-ku, Tokyo 108 0074, Japan. T. (0)3 5449 3288. F. (0)3 5449 2974

Julie Nelson, PO Box 17357, London SW9 0WB, UK. T. (0)208 519 8694. E. jfnelson1@aol.com

Néotù, 25 Rue du Renard, Paris 78004, France. T. (0)1 42 78 96 97. F. (0)1 42 78 26 27. E. NeotuParis@neotu.com

News Design DFE AB, 11 Stora Skuggans Väg, Stockholm 11542, Sweden. T. (0)468 612 4900. F. (0)468 458 0020

Nikon Corporation Japan, Fuji Building, 3-2-3 Marunouchi, Chiyoda-ku 100-833, Tokyo, Japan. T. (0)3 3214 5311. F. (0)3 3216 1454 or T. (0)3 3773 8113. F. (0)3 3773 8102

Nuno Corporation, Axis B1F 5-17-1 Roppongi, Minato-ku, Tokyo 106-0032, Japan. T. (0)3 3582 7997. F. (3)3 3589 3439

Obrira, 7 Paracel Susstrasse, Rathenow 14712, Germany. T. (0)3385 50 32 58. F. (0)3385 51 69 06

Olivari B. SpA, Via Matteotti 140, Borgomanero 28021, Novara 28100, Italy. T. (0)322 83 50 80. F. (0)322 84 64 84. E. olivari@olivari.it

Optic Product Development, Van 'T Hofflaan 6 HS, 1097 EP Amsterdam, The Netherlands. T. (0)20 668 6564. F. (0)20 463 4549

Oras, 2 Isometsantie, Rauma 26101, PO Box 40, Finland. T. (0)2 831 6324. F. (0)2 831 6400

Orrefors Kosta Boda AB, Box 8, Orrefors 38040, Sweden. T. (0)481 34000. F. (0)481 30350

Paschen & Companie GmbH, Stromberger Strasse 27, Wadersloh 59329, Germany. T. (0)2523 28-0. F. (0)2523 92 06 43

Pesce Ltd, 543 Broadway, New York, NY 10012. T. (0)212 941 0280. F. (0)212 941 0106. E. PesceLtd@aol.com

Gallery Gilles Peyroulet & Cie, 80 Rue Quincampix, Paris 75003, France. T. (0)1 42 78 85 11. F. (0)1 42 78 85 12

Philips Electronics BV, 24 Emmasingel, Eindhoven 5611 AZ, The Netherlands. T. (0)40 27 59 066. F. (0)40 27 59 091

Poltrona Frau, Strada Statale 77 km, Tolentino 62029, Italy. T. (0)733 9091. F. (0)733 97 16 00

Post Design, c/o Memphis srl, Via Olivetti 9, Pregnana Milanese 20010, Italy. T. (0)2 93 29 06 63. F. (0)2 93 59 12 02

Gregory Prade, 30 Gellabrunner Strasse, Munich, Germany. T. (0)89 62 42 07 77. F. (0)89 62 50 06 72

Pressalit AS, Pressalitvej 1, Ry DK-8680, Denmark. T. (0)8788 8788. F. (0)8788 8769. E. pressalit@pressalit.com

Prima Ricerca and Sviluppo SpA, Via Campagna 58, 22020 Faloppio fraz, Gaggino (CO), Italy. T. (0)31 99 10 09. F. (0)31 99 13 09. Or Via della Anatrelle 2, Albate (CO) 22100, Italy. T. (0)31 52 66 23. F. (0)31 58 95 18

Radi Designers, 89 Rue de Turenne, Paris 75003, France. T. (0)1 4271 2957. F. (0)1 4271 2962

Rapsel SpA, Via Volta 13, Settimo Milanese (Mi) 20019, Italy. T. (0)2 33 50 14 31. F. (0)2 33 50 13 06

Ravarini Castoldi & C. srl, Via Gardone 20, Milan 20139, Italy. T. (0)2 55 21 06 08. F. (0)2 56 94 503. E. ravarini@pn.itnet.it

Readymade, 147 West 26th Street, 5th floor, New York, NY 10001, USA. T. 212 989 9473

REEEL, 52 Marconistraat, Rotterdam 3029 AK, The Netherlands. T. (0)10 925 4612. F. (0)10 925 7603

Matthias Rexforth, 44 Goethe Strasse, Kassel 43119, Germany. F. (0)2151 70 10 10

Rosenberg Ring Design, Rua Morato Coelho, 299 Conj. 3, São Paulo 05417-010, São Paulo, Brazil. T. (0)11 3061 3809

Rosenthal AG, Wittelsbacherstrasse 43, Selb D-95100, Germany. T. (0)9287 72566. F. (0)9287 72271

Röthlisberger Kollektion, Dorfstrasse 73, Gumligen, Switzerland. T. (0)31 951 41 17. F. (0)31 951 75 64

Royal Leerdam Collection 'Arum' Cristal, 8 Lindedijk, Leerdam 4140AA, The Netherlands. T. (0)345 67 16 50. F. (0)345 67 16 64

Rolf Sachs, Unit 3A, 101 Farm Lane, London SW6 1QJ, UK. T. (0)207 610 0777. F. (0)207 386 9344

Sahco Hesslein GmbH & Co., Kreuzburger Strasse 17-19, Nurnberg D-90471, Germany. T. (0)911 99 87 0. F. (0)911 99 87 480. E. mail@sahco-hesslein.com

Sakaegi Design Studio, 1-74 Nakamizuno-chou, Seto-City No. 489-0005, Aichi-Prefecture, Japan. T. (0)561 48 3991

Salt, 117 Oxo Tower, Barge House Street, London SE1 9PH, UK. T. (0)207 593 0007

Salvatore & Marie, Via Vigevano 33, Milan 20144, Italy. T. (0)2 89 53 04 70

Santos & Adolfsdottir, 4 Middle Ground, Favant, Salisbury, Wiltshire SP3 51P, UK. T. (0)1722 714669

Sawaya & Moroni SpA, Via Andegari 18, Milan 20121, Italy. T. (0)2 86 39 5 1 F. (0)2 86 46 48 31

Schiffini Cucine Design, PO Box 321, La Spezia 19100, Italy. T. (0)187 93 37 34. F. (0)187 93 23 99. Or c/o Badalotti & Morelli, Via Tommaso Grossi 3, Cantu (Como) 22063, Italy. T. (0)31 71 57 45. F. (0)31 71 05 66

Schmidinger Modul Wohn & Objektbedarf GmbH, 146 Stangenach, Schwarzenberg A-6867, Vorarlberg, Austria. T. (0)5512 2782 14. F. (0)5512 2782 12. E. w.schmidinger@schmidinger.modul.vol.at

Georgia Scott, Cockpit Studios, 8 Northington Street, London WC1N 2N, UK. T. (0)207 916 2368. F. (0)207 916 2455

SCP Ltd, Kelly Compten Springate, 135–139 Curtain Road, London EC2A 3BX, UK. T. (0)207 739 1869. F. (0)207 729 4224. E. scp@scp.co.uk

sdr+ GmbH, Mauritiussteinweg 60, D-50676 Cologne, Germany. T. (0)221 923 0919. F. (0)221 923 0939. E. info@sdr-plus.com

Seiko Communications BV, 9F S11 Building, 8 Nakase 1-chome, Mihama-ku, Chiba-shi, Chiba 261, Japan. IDEO UK. T. (0)207 485 1170. F. (0)207 813 0585. E. shecht@ideo.com

Serien Raumleuchten GmbH, 3-7 Hainhauser Strasse, Rodgau 63110, Germany. T. (0)6106 13480. F. (0)6106 18804. E. serien@t-online.de

Sharp Corporation, Corporate Design Centre, 22-22 Nagaike-cho, Abeno-ku, Osaka 545 8522, Japan. T. (0)6 6621 3637. F. (0)6 6629 1162

Sharp Electronics (Europe) GmbH, Sonninstrasse 3, Hamburg 20097, Germany. T. (0)40 23 76 2512. F. (0)40 23 76 2300

Max Shepherd Design, Unit 8A, 20-30 Wilds Rents, London SE1 4DG, UK. T. (0)207 378 9399. E. max@maxshepherd.net

Vincent Shum, c/o Nanyang Polytechnic GSI Industrial Design Section, 180 Ang Mo Kio, ave 8, Singapore 569830. T. (0)65 550 0671 F. (0)65 454 9871. E. vincent_SHUM@nyp.gov.sg

Siemens Electrogeräte GmbH, Hichstrasse 17, D-81669 Munich, Germany. T. (0)89 45 90 29 29/29 37 F. (0)89 45 90 20 31. E. christoph.pott-sudholt@bshg.com

SIG Workshop, 3-4 Asahigaoka, Matsuto 924 0004, Ishikawa, Japan. T. (0)762 75 6157. F. (0)762 74 9090

Slamp, Via Bolivia 16, Pomezia 00040, Rome, Italy. T/F. (0)6 91 08 545

Snowcrash, Linnegatan 23, Box 483, S-351 06 Vaxjo, Sweden. T/F. (0)470 74 24 00. E. info@snowcrash.se

Soehnle Waagen GmbH & Co., 24 Fornsbacher Strasse, Murrhardt 71540, Germany. T. (0)7192 2810. F. (0)7192 1544

Sony Corporation, 6-7-35 Kitashinagawa, Shinagawa-ku, Tokyo 141-0001, Japan. T. (0)3 5445 6780. F. (0)3 5448 7823

Spatial Interference Ltd, 190 Royal College Street, London NW1 9NN, UK. T. (0)207 284 0248. F. (0)207 916 1517. E. cprocter@dircon.co.uk

Starfish, 4 Ella Mews, Cressy Road, London NW3 2NH, UK. T. (0)207 482 4331. F. (0)207 267 5705. E. alva@isssisdes.demon.co.uk

Startup Design (Jasper Startup). E. startup@inddesign.netkonect.co.uk

Steltman Galleries, 330 Spuistraat, Amsterdam 1012VX, The Netherlands. T. (0)20 622 8683. F. (0)20 620 7588

Stiletto Designvertreib, Petersburger Platz 2, D-10249 Berlin, Germany. T. (0)30 427 38 27. F. (0)30 422 57 50. E. hallo@stiletto.de

Studio Harry & Camila, Creators of Signs, Via G. Meda 43, Milan 20141, Italy. T. (0)2 84 64 141

Studio Sípek, 7 Jeleni, Prague 1 11800, Czech Republic. T. (0)424 24373647. F. (0)424 24372331

Sunways GmbH, Macairestrasse 5, D-78467 Konstanz, Germany. T. (0)7531 99677 0. F. (0)7531 99677 10

Svitalia, Piazzetta, Agra 6927, Ticino, Switzerland. T. (0)91 994 3345. F. (0)91 994 6561

Tangerine Product Design, 8 Baden Place, Crosby Row, London SE1 1YW, UK. T. (0)207 357 0966. F. (0)207 357 0784

Sarah Taylor, 2 The Wynd, Melrose TD6 9LD, Scotland. T. (0)1896 822133

3 Designers, 5 Impasse Chartiere, Paris 75005, France. T. (0)1 43 54 97 01

Walter Thut AG, 38 Bruneggerstrasse, Moriken 5103, Switzerland. T. (0)62 893 12 84. F. (0)62 893 11 10

Nina Tolstrup, 47 Warwick Mount, Brighton BN2 1JY, UK. T. (0)1273 570 179

Tonelli srl, Via della Produzione 49, Montelabbate (PS) 61025, Italy. T. (0)721 48 11 72. F. (0)721 48 12 91. E. tonelli@tonellidesign.it

Torchco Ltd, PO Box 807, Hildersham CB1 6BX, Cambs., UK. T. (0)1223 893363. F. (0)1223 892611

Tunnel srl, Kommunardu 32, 170 00 Prague 7, Czech Republic. T. (2) 6671 2753. E. rovarna@tunnel.cz

Umbra, 2358 Midland Avenue, Scarborough MIS IP8, Ontario, Canada. T. (0)800 387 5122. F. (0)416 299 1706

Units srl, Via Marconi 35, Arosio (Como) 22060, Italy. T. (0)31 75 91 11. F. (0)31 76 33 22

Valvomo Design, Uudenmaankatu 33E, Helsinki, Finland, FIN 00120. T. (0)9 6122 3124. F. (0)9 6122 3150. E. antikainen@netsurfer.fi

Van Nieuwenborg Industrial Design Consultancy Group, 99c Plantsoen, Leiden 2311 KL, The Netherlands. T. (0)71 5123230. F. (0)71 5131587

Fabiaan Van Severen, 5 Brandstraat, Sint Martens Latem B 9830, Belgium. T. (0)9 282 27 66

Vayu snc, 4a Via Roma, Molvena 36060, Venice, Italy. T/F. (0)424 70 83 99

Pernille Vea, 19 Ostbandgade, Copenhagen K-2100, Denmark. T/F. (0)35 55 49 33

Verrerie de Nonfoux, Nonfoux 1417, Switzerland. T. (0)24 435 1692. F. (0)24 435 1694

Vieler International, 34 Breslauer Strasse, Iserlohn D-58642, Germany. T. (0)2374 52220. F. (0)2374 52226. E. info@vieler.com

Vitra (International) AG, Klunenfeldstrasse 22, CH-4127 Birsfelden, Switzerland. T. (0)61 377 15 09. F. (0)61 377 15 10. E. info@vitra.com

Weyers & Borms, Antwerpse Steenweg 48, 9140 Tielrode, Belgium. T. (0)3 7110517. F. (0)3 7111947

Lorenz Wiegand, Pool Products, Metzerstrasse 19, D-10405 Berlin, Germany. T. (0)30 440 555 16. E. POOL-products@t-online.de

Wilsonart, c/o Inside Design – Jim Huff, 214 Riverside Drive No. 301, New York, NY 10025, USA. T. (0)212 678 2413. F. (0)212 678 4247

Wireworks, 131A Broadley Street, London NW8 8BA, UK. T. (0)207 724 8856. F. (0)207 258 1528

XO, RN 19, Servon 77170, Paris, France. T. (0)1 60 62 60 60. F. (0)1 60 62 60 62

Yamaha Corporation, 10-1 Nakazawa-cho, Hamamatsu, Shizuoka Prefecture 4308650, Japan. T. (0)53 460 2883. F. (0)53 463 4922

Ycami, Via Provinciale 31/33, Como, 22060 Novedrate, Italy. T. (0)31 78 97 311. F. (0)31 78 97 350. E. info@ycami.com

Zanotta SpA, Via Vittorio Veneto 57, Nova Milanese (Mi) 20054, Italy. T. (0)362 36 83 30. F. (0)362 45 10 38. E. zanottaspa@zanotta.it

Zeus, c/o Noto srl, C. so San Gottardo 21/9, Milan 21036, Italy. T. (0)2 89 40 11 98. F. (0)2 89 40 11 42. E. zeusnoto@tini.it

Zumtobel Staff GmbH, Schwiezer Strasse 30, Postfach 72, A-6851 Dornbirn, Austria. T. (0)5572 390 0. F. (0)5572 20 721. E. info@zumtobelstaff.co.at

PHOTOGRAPHIC CREDITS

The publisher and editors would like to thank the designers and manufacturers who submitted work for inclusion, and the following photographers and copyright holders for the use of their material (page numbers are given in parentheses):

240

Gabriele Allendorf (123 below right)
Anna and Petra (90, 149 right)
A. Beretta (109 left)
Adolf Bereuter (221 centre, above – Fatty Containers)
Boris Braakhuis (151 right)
Hilde Braet (155 below left)
Erik Brahl/Ole Akhøj (70 below right) © Brahl Fotografie (69 above and below left, 105 above)
Bruno Bruchi (132 left – both Conversazione images)
Santi Caleca (131 centre, below, 200)
Gillian Cargill (122 right)
Tina Chambers/National Maritime Museum, London (167 left)
Bitetto Chimenti
   (32, 56 above and below right, 78 below left, 86, 98 below)
Gianfranco Coltella (117 left)
Richard Davies (162)
Margherita Del Piano and Claudio Navone (209)
Donato Di Bello (25)
Liz Dichane (23 below left)
Graeme Duddridge (94)
Du Ribeiro (88 above, centre – Piramidal)
Rick English Photography (193 below left)
Everyday Design (224)
John Farrow (49 centre, below)
Andrea Ferrari (222 left)
M. Fijalkowski (63 above and below left)
C. Fillioux (153 below left)
Fotostudio M. Zechany, Vienna (107 centre, above)
Luca Fregoso (216 above left and right)
Julio Garcia Garate (123 left)
Gino Gareza (19 above right)
Bob Goedewaagen (61 above and below left, 99)
Carlos Guerreiro (154)
Alfred Hablützel, Basel (76 above and below right)
Ashley Hall (52)
Lubomir Häna (130 centre)
Hans Hansen/Vitra (34, 35 left)
Julian Hawkins (40 below right)
Avraham Hay (171 above left and right)
Sofie Helsted (120 above right)
Thomas Henning (72 below left and right)
Vesa Hinkola (47 below right)
Véronique Huygues (88 below left)
Herman Huys (120 below right)
Hiroshi Ikeba (196 below right)
Kowa Ikeuchi (62)
Inflate Design Studio (208 above right)
Takeo Ishimatsu (167 above and below right)
Kinta Kimura (144)
Ralph Klein (89 below, 117 right, 134 left)
Ralph Klein and Georg Valerius (134 right)
Rene Koster (96 left, 135 above left, 217 centre, below)
Jacob Kristensen (36 centre)
Edo Kuiper (151 below left, 153 below right, 163 below left)
Per Larsson (135 right)
Richard Learoyd (181)
Manhong Lee (170 above, far left)

© Morgane Le Gall (88 centre, below, 138, 139)
Andrea Lhotáková (133, 196 above and below left)
Brian Lim and Joy (194 below right)
Christoph Lison, Ingmar Kurth and Martin Url (97)
Marsel Loermans (64, 65, 158, 159, 220 below right)
Blanche Mackey (213 centre, above)
Malcolm and Gus (196 above right)
Marzia Maroni (53 below left and right)
Daniele Martin (151 top left)
Tuomas Marttila (81 below)
Mr Marzioni/Poltrona Frau (83 above)
Bernard Matussière (132 below left)
Sue McNab (175)
Philip Metz (100 right)
Timothy Miller (56 left, 205 centre, above)
Koji Miura (107 below left)
Moggy (192 below right)
NEC Design Ltd (188)
Holger Neu (196 centre, above)
Brigitte Niedermair
   (21, 88 above left, 91 bottom right, 203 left and below centre)
Bart Nieuwenhuijs (170 above right – Origami)
Olgoj Chorchoj (152)
Eduardo Ortega (96 centre)
Andrès Otero (45 left, 47 above right, 148 left, 182)
Alessandro Paderni (45 right)
Robert Pelletier (38 above right)
Maarten Pieterse (132 above right)
Lucy Pope (121)
Gregory Prade (89 above)
Paul Prader (143 below)
Marino Ramazzotti (131 above right, 148 above right)
Ramazzotti & Stucchi (39 right)
Ed Reeve (40 below left)
Markus Richter (31)
Sheila Rock (111, 206 right)
Romano Fotografie/Giussano (83 below)
Tiziano Rossi (132 below right)
M. Salmi (109 above and below right)
Hidetoyo Sasaki, Japan (211 – all Seiko watches)
B. Schaub (70 above and below left)
Gerrit Schreurs (112)
Jan-Chr. Schultchen (201 centre, left, 22 below left and centre)
Nils Schumm/Markus Richter (80 right)
David Simmonds (38 centre, below)
P. Slapal (50 above left)
Luciano Soave (79 right)
Steve Speller (50 below left)
David Spero (87 above left and right)
Henrik Spohler, Hamburg (114 right)
Starfish (87 below left)
Christian Stoll (217 below left)
Studio Azzurro (130 right, 131 centre, above)
Studio Diametro (82, 91 bottom left, 96 right)
Studio Ito Design (222 right)
Kenshow Sugimoto (145)
Solve Sundsbo (51)

Sergio Sutto (132 centre, above)
Peter Tahl (61 above right)
Kozo Takayama (110 left, 192 below left)
Kozo Takayama and Shinichi Sato (110 left)
Luca Tamburlini
   (78 above left and right, 91 centre, bottom, 128, 129)
Tandem, Lissone (114 above left)
Bruce Tanner (123 above right)
Tollhoff/Schwertle (69 right)
Nina Tolstrup (206 above left)
Emilio Tremolada (149 left and centre)
Chris Tubbs (57 bottom right)
Tom Vack (77 right)
Verme (66 below left and right)
Philip Vile (54, 55, 66 above left, 107 above left)
Uwe Walter (91 centre, left)
© Falko Wenzel (57 centre, right)
Richard Williams (208 above left, below left, centre and right)
Christian Winsel (117 right)
Peter Wood (116 right)
Miro Zagnoli (91 top left, centre and right)
Marco Zanardi (113 below left).